T0331510

The important achievement of John Morris' *Securing Finance and Mobilizing Risk* is to bring the insights of the cultural economy literature to bear on the problematics of international political economy. The result is a conceptually and empirically sophisticated account that offers fresh insight into the contemporary operation of central banking and the way financial risk is governed.

Martijn Konings, *University of Sydney, Australia*

Securing Finance, Mobilizing Risk

Drawing on the history of modern finance, as well as the sociology of money and risk, this book examines how cultural understandings of finance have contributed to the increased capitalization of the UK financial system following the Global Financial Crisis. Providing both a geographically-inflected analysis and re-appraisal of the concept of performativity, it demonstrates that financial risk management has a spatiality that helps to inform understandings and imaginaries of the risks associated with money and finance.

The book traces the development of understandings of risk at the Bank of England, with an analysis that spans some 1,000 reports, documents and speeches alongside elite interviews with past and present employees at the central bank. The author argues that the Bank has moved from a relatively broad-brush approach to the risks being managed in the financial sector, to a greater preoccupation with the understanding and mapping of the mobilization of financial risk.

The study of financial practices from a critical social sciences and humanities perspective has grown rapidly since the Global Financial Crisis and this book will be of interest to multiple subject areas including IPE, economic geography, sociology of finance and critical security studies.

John Hogan Morris is Research Assistant in Responsible Finance in the Centre for Business in Society at Coventry University. He completed his PhD in 2015 in the Geography Department at Durham University (UK), and earlier that year his work won 'Best Graduate Student Paper' at the New Directions in International Political Economy Conference at University of Warwick. John has published in the *Journal of Cultural Economy* and is currently co-editing a special issue on 'Security and Finance' in the journal *Finance & Society*. He also has a section on 'Financial Security' in the International Political Economy of Everyday Life project. He has taught Economic Geography and International Political Economy at Durham University and University College London. John was an invited judge at the London Area Final of the Bank of England's Two Point Zero challenge and has provided informal advice on public communications to the European Central Bank.

RIPE Series in Global Political Economy

Series Editors: James Brassett
University of Warwick, UK
Eleni Tsingou
Copenhagen Business School, Denmark
and
Susanne Soederberg
Queen's University, Canada

The RIPE Series published by Routledge is an essential forum for cutting-edge scholarship in International Political Economy. The series brings together new and established scholars working in critical, cultural and constructivist political economy. Books in the RIPE Series typically combine an innovative contribution to theoretical debates with rigorous empirical analysis.

The RIPE Series seeks to cultivate:

- Field-defining theoretical advances in International Political Economy
- Novel treatments of key issue areas, both historical and contemporary, such as global finance, trade and production
- Analyses that explore the political economic dimensions of relatively neglected topics, such as the environment, gender relations and migration
- Accessible work that will inspire advanced undergraduates and graduate students in International Political Economy.

The *RIPE Series in Global Political Economy* aims to address the needs of students and teachers.

Polanyi in Times of Populism
Vision and Contradiction in the History of Economic Ideas
Christopher Holmes

A Global Political Economy of Democratisation
Beyond the Internal–External Divide
Alison J. Ayers

Securing Finance, Mobilizing Risk
Money Cultures at the Bank of England
John Hogan Morris

For more information about this series, please visit: www.routledge.com/RIPE-Series-in-Global-Political-Economy/book-series/RIPE.

Securing Finance, Mobilizing Risk

Money Cultures at the Bank of England

John Hogan Morris

Routledge
Taylor & Francis Group

LONDON AND NEW YORK

First published 2018 by Routledge

2 Park Square, Milton Park, Abingdon, Oxfordshire OX14 4RN
52 Vanderbilt Avenue, New York, NY 10017

Routledge is an imprint of the Taylor & Francis Group, an informa business

First issued in paperback 2019

British Library Cataloguing-in-Publication Data
A catalogue record for this book is available from the British Library

Library of Congress Cataloging-in-Publication Data
A catalog record has been requested for this book

ISBN: 978-1-138-08067-6 (hbk)
ISBN: 978-0-367-90416-6 (pbk)

Typeset in Times New Roman
by Wearset Ltd, Boldon, Tyne and Wear

For my parents and brothers

Contents

Figures

Preface

Undertaking this book project on central banking, risk management and financial stability has foregrounded Viviana Zelizer's point that money is neither 'socially anonymous' nor does it 'flatten' valued personal ties. Instead, I am indebted to a wide community of financial and economic scholars for their gifts of collegiality. The development of this book is closely tied to a number of people I have had the fortune to meet since the Global Financial Crisis.

The project that eventually became this book started in 2012. A preoccupation with economic governance that emerged during my 2009 Master's dissertation developed into a PhD proposal. What was an initial interest in the economic discourses and ideas being forwarded in the aftermath of the Global Financial Crisis, eventually became a full-blown fixation on the financial stability thinking at the Bank of England since the early 1990s. It was David Hudson who convinced me that I could do a PhD and, on David's advice, I asked Paul Langley and Ben Anderson to supervise my PhD on the Bank of England and Financial Stability. Moving to the Geography Department at Durham University turned out to be the best decision I have ever made. Ben's enthusiasm and willingness to engage with an area that he does not specialize in were unbelievable and I was lucky to have someone of his analytical strength to interrogate my arguments. I cannot overstate how much of a positive influence Paul has been on my work and career to date. He is extremely generous and it was stimulating to work with him while he was writing his own book on financial governance, namely *Liquidity Lost*. I feel both lucky and proud to have been mentored by him. I would like to thank my PhD examiners Michael Pryke and Gavin Bridge for pushing me constantly during a two-hour viva. Michael and Gavin prompted and stretched me on the geographical contribution of the project, and thinking about this for a year afterwards prompted my interest in functional mobility and the mobilization of risk. In many ways, the book project was born out of an extremely rigorous and productive examination process.

In 2013, I attended my first Critical Finance Studies Conference in Stockholm and I discovered a truly remarkable collective. As something of an academic nomad who has moved through philosophy, political science, geography, science and technology studies and business studies, I am so grateful to have found such a wonderful group of people. At three Critical Finance conferences since, in

Amsterdam, Southampton and Leicester, I have presented ideas and arguments on central banking, press conferences, stress testing, derivatives and Value-at-Risk that have morphed and evolved into those presented in this manuscript. In particular I would like to express my gratitude to the generosity and curiosity of Joyce Goggin, Marieke de Goede, Claes Ohlsson, Natalie Roxburgh, Simon Lilley, Geoff Lightfoot, Ann-Christine Frandsen, Ivan Ascher, Randy Martin, Bob Meister, Keith Hoskin, Peter Pelzer, Clea Bourne, Emily Rosamund, Skip McGoun, Thomas Bay, Benjamin Lozano and Philip Goodchild. Alongside these colleagues, I would like to thank Louise Amoore and Brett Scott for their kindness and engaging conversations.

Since completing my PhD in 2015, I have secured a series of temporary posts at University College London and Coventry University. These positions have given me some measure of financial stability while working on the book project. I would like to thank Tiago Mata, Jason Dittmer, Sally Dibb, Lyndon Simkin and Lindsey Appleyard for taking a chance on me after various job interviews. The posts in Science and Technology Studies and Geography at University College proved to be an essential base for conducting research interviews in London and for developing a wide network of former and current financial professionals and activists. During my teaching fellowship in UCL Geography, I was given considerable freedom to teach a third-year undergraduate module in the Geographies of Money and Finance. I would like to thank that excellent cohort of 25 students for providing a sounding-board on many of the key themes of this book, and for challenging me in every seminar and lecture with perceptive comments and questions. I would like to thank my colleagues in the Centre for Business in Society at Coventry, and in particular Nick Henry and Hussan Aslam, for allowing me time and space to finalize the manuscript.

From 2015, I have benefitted immensely from an ongoing dialogue with the International Political Economy cluster of the Politics and International Studies Department at the University of Warwick and this book is largely a product of their generosity. I would like to thank Andre Broome and Matt Kranke for inviting me to attend the Warwick Manuscript Development workshop in 2015. Chris Clarke proved to be a thoughtful and challenging discussant and helped improve my sample chapters and book proposal to a point where I was able to secure a contract with Routledge. I would also like to thank Matt Watson for his support throughout the project. James Brassett has been a driving force behind this book project and I don't think I could have executed it without his enthusiasm and guidance. As part of this process the focus, thrust and ideas expressed in this book have been greatly influenced by the helpful suggestions of two anonymous reviewers and the editorial board of the RIPE Series in Global Political Economy.

Warm thanks must go to Carola Westermeier, Sian Lewin, Lauren Tooker, Lorenzo Genito and Andrew Telford, who have helped immeasurably by agreeing to read large sections, if not the whole manuscript, as this book progressed into its final form. These reviewers tightened the philosophical arguments and interrogated the empirical material in relation to their own excellent PhD projects. I thank Lauren for a series of challenging and stimulating cross continental discussions on performativity and the implications of lively practices. I am indebted to Sian's input into tightening the arguments of Chapter 5 and the way she generously shared her unpublished work on the wider regulatory contexts behind cultural change in finance, which was invaluable. My ongoing collaboration with Nathan Coombs on stress testing and regulatory technologies is essential for my work. It would not have been possible for me to generate the interview materials without Nathan's drive, direction and encouragement. I would like to thank both the Bank of England Press Office and the Bank interviewees for generously allowing me to use these interview materials in Part III of the book. I am grateful for Amy Greer-Murphy's help in juggling proofreading duties with the arrival of her beautiful daughter Anna.

Some of the material contained in this book has also been published previously in 'The performativity, performance and lively practices in financial stability press conferences', *Journal of Cultural Economy* 9, no. 3 (2016): 245–260. http://dx.doi.org/10.1080/17530350.2015.1136831. I would like to extend my thanks to Taylor and Francis for granting permission to reproduce the material here in Chapters 3 and 7. I would like to acknowledge the Bank of England Content and Strategy Division for granting non-exclusive permission for the reproduction of content from Bank of England publications.

Writing the final half of the book – alongside other work commitments and life events – has been difficult and here I want to use this space to highlight the enormous pressures faced by early career researchers in UK institutions and foreground the link to mental health problems. The academy is in danger of losing some of its brightest young talents. I would like to thank Jack, Naomi, Jess, Ingrid, Esther, Philip, Mariana, Hung-Ying, Vanessa, Josh, Gillian, Sophie, Sarah, Alice, Hannah, Rox, James, Kabir, Gabor, Pip, Will, Shera and Beth. Their friendship made a huge difference to me and I drew great strength from them and their kindness. Finally, I would not be where I am without the unconditional love and support of my family, David, Hilda, Sam and Peter. I could not have done this without you all.

Abbreviations

ABS	Asset-Backed Securities
ACS	Annual Cyclical Scenario
AIG	American International Group
BBA	British Banking Association
BES	Biennial Exploratory Scenario
BIS	Bank for International Settlements
CBEST	An intelligence led testing framework which assesses firms' cyber resilience.
CCP	Central Counterparties
CDO	Collateralized Debt Obligations
CDS	Credit Default Swaps
CRD	Capital Requirements Directive
CRE	Commercial Real Estate
DJ	Disc Jockey
DNA	Deoxyribonucleic acid
EBA	European Banking Authority
ECB	European Central Bank
EMEs	Emerging Market Economies
ES	Expected Shortfall
EU	The European Union
EURCHF	The Euro and Swiss Franc pair
FCA	Financial Conduct Authority
FPC	Financial Policy Committee
FMI	Financial Market Infrastructures
FpML	Financial Product Mark-up Language
FSA	Financial Services Authority
FSR	Financial Stability Review/Report
(G)FSB	(Global) Financial Stability Board
ICB	International Committee on Banking
IMF	International Monetary Fund
LCFI	Large and Complex Financial Institutions
LIBOR	London Interbank Offered Rate
LOLR	Lender of Last Resort

LTCM	Long Term Capital Management
MLF	Modeling Language for Finance
MPC	Monetary Policy Committee
MPR	Monetary Policy Report
OTC	Over the Counter (derivatives)
PRA	Prudential Regulation Authority
RAMSI	Risk Assessment Model of Systemic Institutions
RMBS	Residential Mortgage-Backed Securities
SARS	Severe Acute Respiratory Syndrome
SBR	Services Banking Reform act
SCAP	Supervisory Capital Assessment Programme
SRB	Systemic Risk Buffer
SSF	Social Studies of Finance
SVaR	Stressed Value-at-Risk
TARP	Troubled Assets Relief Programme
UK	United Kingdom
US	United States
VaR	Value-at-Risk

Introduction

Financial stability as speculative security

Introduction: a background of stability

> Our job is to create a background of stability which enables other people to do interesting things. They will be interesting: we will not be and we will be faceless ... but that outcome is really very important, that we will not be interesting or new or newsworthy and that will be a sign of our success.
>
> (Mervyn King, 27 January 2004)

In the above 2004 statement, the then Governor of the Bank of England, Sir Mervyn King, described the central bank of the United Kingdom as being 'faceless', uninteresting and working in the shadows towards the vital aim of financial stability. Given such self-proclaimed anonymity, should it then come as a surprise that Bowman *et al.* (2012) have argued that the increasingly prominent and crucial financial stability interventions of central banks have been both under investigated and undertheorized? This apparent lacuna on financial stability can be starkly contrasted with an expansive interdisciplinary literature which provides a much fuller account of the monetary policy objectives of the contemporary central bank (Guthrie and Wright, 2000; Smart, 2006; Krippner, 2007; Hall, 2008; Holmes, 2009, 2014; Mann, 2010; McCormack, 2012, 2015; Braun, 2015, 2016; Siklos, 2017). This book aims to make a prescient empirical contribution, then, by bringing the financial stability functions of a central bank into the forefront of critical attention.

Furthermore, the image of the central banker set out by King in the above quotation is one of the dour, boring, grey suited technocrat working behind the scenes to ensure financial stability – at once 'faceless ... not ... interesting or newsworthy'. And yet, just four years after this statement by King, central banks embarked on a series of unprecedented interventions in, and interactions with, markets in order to mobilize an atmosphere of confidence following the widespread evaporation of liquidity in the global financial system (Langley, 2015). As Martijn Konings (2009, pp. 3–4) opined while the dust was only just beginning to settle on the Subprime Crisis, 'the time might well be ripe for public authority to push back against the hegemony of the market ... this is seen as opening up a space for re-regulation'. Amid such high hopes, some authors did argue that the collapse of Lehman Brothers had changed everything. Stuart Mackintosh (2014, p. 406) argues that the crisis led to a fundamental rethinking of financial governance culminating in a 'paradigm[1] shift' in the 'worldview' of policy makers and regulators. Against this view, other authors, perhaps disillusioned with what they picture as piecemeal change, have labelled the Global Financial Crisis as 'the status quo crisis' (Helleiner, 2014; Mugge, 2014). It is the central assertion of this book that neither of these accounts tell the full story. There has been change, but it has not been revolutionary or paradigmatic change. Under the supervision of the Bank of England, the UK's financial system has increased its capitalization.[2] This, in part, is about capital accumulation, but more than this, it is also about cultural processes of capitalization within the Bank of England.

The Bank of England may have gained new regulatory responsibilities and policy tools following the Global Financial Crisis but, even so, this was not the point where the Bank suddenly discovered security through risk management. This book therefore conceptualizes the Bank of England's financial stability governance over the past 21 years as constituting governance through what Marieke de Goede (2012) has called 'speculative security'. By this term, de Goede refers to security practices that are 'speculative in both means and ends'. Such security is imperfect as it is precisely a matter of both embracing and mitigating the future, neither pre-emptively ruling it out nor simply and fatalistically accepting what will be. Focusing on what will be referred to here as performed *money cultures*, this book argues that for much of the past 21-year period the Bank reported potential risks with a somewhat broad-brush approach. For example, the positives and negatives of credit derivatives were often treated as two sides of the same coin. This book develops the argument, then, that the Bank was taking a gamble of sorts on the ability of financial risk management to disperse risk through investment techniques and was less certain about the relative likelihood of risks materializing. I label this culture *speculating on risk*.

I characterize the subtle shift in speculative security practices as a move from speculating *on* risk to speculating *for* risk. This argument hinges on Marieke de Goede's (2012: p. *xx*) point that speculation 'historically denotes *both* a practice of sighting, surmising, and anticipating', and a practice of investing on chance, involving 'considerable financial risk on the chance of unusual profit'. Therein, taking a gamble on the ability of financial risk management to disperse risk throughout the system eventually became supplanted with a conception of speculation in which the Bank sought to sight, map, code and visualize the mobilization of risk better. This change in money cultures pivots on 'misfires' or counter-performativity that emerged both before and throughout the financial crisis. Critically, the crisis did not herald 'the end of (financial) alchemy', as Mervyn King (2016) put it. Rather, the Bank has undergone a cultural shift whereby efforts have been made to better see risk, better code and understand the mobilization of risk, and to widen the risk imagination. While seeing risk better and understanding the mobilization of risk are concerned with making risk visible, the practices of coding risk and widening the risk imagination are more squarely concerned with what Orit Halpern (2014) calls making 'new relationships appear and producing new objects for action and speculation'. These cultural developments have contributed to the increased capital levels in the UK financial system.

In making this argument, the analysis serves to make a two-fold conceptual contribution. First, the book contributes to a growing interdisciplinary literature concerned with the interconnections between finance and security (Martin, 2007; Dillon, 2008; Lobo-Guerrero, 2010; de Goede, 2010, 2012, 2017; Aitken, 2011; Amicelle, 2011; Amoore, 2011, 2013; Boy *et al.*, 2011; Langley, 2013, 2015; Zarate, 2013; Boy, 2015; Gilbert, 2015a, 2015b; Amicelle and Jacobson, 2016; Best, 2017; Lightfoot and Lilley, 2017). And while 'security' is a malleable and ambiguous term, such analyses cluster around the place of financial risk management in the securing of life through contemporary securitization techniques (Langley, 2008b; French and Kneale, 2012). This is in alignment with Frederic Gros' (2012) conception of security in which it is the 'continuity of vital processes' for life, through the 'tracing and monitoring of auto-regulated flows' and circulations by means of 'protection, control, and regulation' (Toynbee Lagoutte, 2017, pp. 82–83). As such, volatility plays a key role. Fundamentally and as Benjamin Lee (2015, p. 133) puts it in a poignant tribute to Randy Martin and his work:

> It is volatility that holds all these forms of 'risking together' together. They are all social ways of accessing volatility for the upside that it can produce, because volatility captures the dynamic side of change, confronting it produces the tension out of which innovation is born. But the secret to accessing volatility is not simply to chase the upside risk and avoid its downside, but instead to create a zone or spread, the movement through which creates enough volatility to keep you going.

Financial security, then, is a matter of both and at once embracing and mitigating the future as risk and uncertainty. This 'Finance/Security' literature *is critical*, primarily because it is largely inflected with readings of Michel Foucault's (2007) *Security, Territory, Population* lectures – on calculative rationalities, liberal governance and operations of power (Lobo-Guerrero, 2010; de Goede, 2010; Amoore, 2013; Langley, 2013, 2015; Best, 2017). Such Foucauldian scholarship reveals that a straightforward embracing of unbridled security logics that, in Foucault's (2007, p. 68) parlance, 'allow things to happen', misses the point that the security brought by finance is imperfect. Laissez-faire, then, is potentially destructive because, as Foucault himself pointed out, risky elements can only be minimized rather than totally eliminated (Foucault, 2007, p. 34). Illustrating this point, Gordon Clark (2005, pp. 104–105) has memorably pointed out that one of the ways money can metaphorically be seen as being akin to 'mercury' is through the 'poisonous' propensity of both substances if 'poorly managed'. Finance/Security, then, not only highlights the intensification of governmental apparatuses and assemblages, but also attends to their contradictions, violence and insecurities (de Goede, 2012; Amoore, 2013).

In particular, this book enters a debate between a small section of authors for whom the categories of speculation and security are themselves conceptually and practically fused together (de Goede, 2010). Randy Martin (2007) brings together American foreign policy with financial risk management, such that security objectives in the Middle East are pursued through a speculative derivative logic of 'indifference' (see also Lightfoot and Lilley, 2017). In a similar vein, Louise Amoore (2013) both elucidates and traces the uncertain financial and derivative logics that underpin homeland security practices. Emergent possible futures are abstracted, if not eviscerated, from the underlying probabilities of such events happening (Amoore, 2013, p. 61). For Paul Langley (2008b), the 'everyday investor' subject with a defined contributions pension is an uncertain subject seeking to secure her future lifestyle through the performance of the portfolio the pension is invested in. Alternatively, and in a seminal contribution, Marieke de Goede (2012, pp. *xx–xxi, xxv*) argues that the pursuit of terrorist monies is a security practice that is speculative in both 'means and ends', as forms of association are mapped and visualized by looking 'sideways and forwards', while, the target of such governmental intervention is uncertain futures.

Nina Boy (2015, p. 541) discusses finance/security in relation to sovereign debt. While Boy argues that one cannot decentre the symbolic value of the sovereign state when thinking about debt, I would argue that this does not rule out a Foucauldian reading. For Boy (2015), the 'sovereign safety' reflected in the credit risk of the sovereign bond allows the risky to circulate alongside the safe. Speculation, then, is enabled by the 'effective fiction' of the sovereign political community. Following this reasoning, then, bio-political security of circulations is still tightly bound with sovereign forms of government and social organization and the safe is circulated alongside the risky (Foucault, 2007, p. 34). In his later writings, Langley (2015) gives us an account of financialized security such that financial crisis interventions were promulgated in order to modulate uncertain circulations that supported advanced liberal life. Apparatuses of security then, were employed to support speculative circulations of differing velocities.

Finance/Security in its present Foucauldian form does have a tendency to view Anglo-American and neoliberal security culture as being somewhat homogenous. Against this totalizing impulse, Lagna (2015, p. 284) argues that a Foucauldian IPE 'replicates similar institutions everywhere', so that it then becomes 'difficult to appreciate how individuals relate to such discursive structures through different perceptions, objectives and capabilities'. The thesis offered in this book is that different perceptions of risk have developed over time at the Bank of England. Financial risk management is about movement and culture – the mobilization of risk and the money cultures this begets. These can be processes of mobilizing risks by abstracting out and making some attribute indifferent to an underlying you don't own – such as oil from sovereign Iraqi territory (Martin, 2007). At other times, this mobilization of risk involves gathering together some attributes and recombining others, such as in open heart surgery to fit a pacemaker or the shocking and macabre collage of Jean-Michel Basquait's *Slave Auction*.

As Randy Martin recently argued, finance is just one example of a wider and often benign principle of recombination. For example, we can find a derivative logic in the everyday musical practices of 'sampling' because the 'composer was displaced by the DJ or producer who assembled cuts or smaller sound loops out of a vast range of stylistic possibilities' (Martin, 2015, p. 188). Dance, 'hip-hop', 'skate-boarding' and 'derivatives' are all forms of what Martin referred to as 'risking together'. Following Martin, the mobilization and recombination of virtual risks is a productive social logic. But, it may be rightly asked, how does this relate to money cultures? This leads me to the second conceptual contribution of the book and relates Martin's work on mobility and movement to Georg Simmel's (1897, 1900) writings on distance, motion and culture. Mobility and movement, then, are the pivots for the dialogue between these two critical readers of finance.

As such, the book draws much intellectual sustenance from the way that geographers have gleaned insights from Simmel's (1900) seminal philosophical and sociological contribution, *The Philosophy of Money*. While Simmel attempted to provide a philosophy of modern life, by drawing attention to the way that perception varies over spatio-temporal context through the concrete case of money, financial geographers have noted the role that geographical concepts such as distance and motion play in Simmel's work on subjective understandings of the world and cultural forms (Allen and Pryke, 1999; Langley, 2017). In doing so, the book engages with debates around performativity at the intersection of political economy and cultural economy. While political economy is typically interested in material global and structural processes and the distribution and exercise of power, cultural economy has tended to emphasize socio-technical financial practices, financial knowledge and the way that discourses constitute the economic world. And even though each perspective may have historically been 'too frequently … tempted to look past what the other has in view', recent work in 'cultural political economy'[3] has gone some way to muddy the waters between two seemingly antagonistic positions (Martin, 2009; Best and Paterson, 2010; Christophers, 2014, 2017; Lee, 2016).

In line with this, the book develops a re-appraisal of performativity in finance. This book engages with theoretical work on financial performativity and develops an innovative account of performativity in which the concept is understood to be layered and lively. Three positions in the debate about financial performativity are identified and outlined – namely, 'Austinian', 'generic' and 'layered' performativities. Analysis of the transcripts and video footage of the Bank's press conferences shows that both Austinian and Generic performativity are at work in the 'layered performances' of financial stability by the Bank; the manner in which technical devices affect the economy intersects with the way reiterative discursive practices bring about the effect they name. Moreover, drawing on the writings of Derrida and Deleuze on iterability and difference, the book analyses the disruption, improvisation and force that is also present in the central bank's money cultures. The ostensible production of money cultures by the Bank is thus shown to draw attention to an additional layer of financial performativity that has been largely neglected in cultural economy research

– that which I group together under the umbrella term of 'lively practices'. Fundamentally, this discussion also introduces two related concepts which return across Chapters 4, 5, 6, 7 and 8, namely counter-performativity/'misfire' and improvisation. Both of these phenomena exceed their previous and seemingly derogatory labelling as performative breakdown, and instead combine to give a sense of the dynamism and evolving nature of discourse. Both misfire and improvisation, then, are lively practices and have a role to play (Morris, 2016). In particular, this book is concerned with the misfires and improvizations of the mobilization of risk.

In other words, the two-fold rupture in the money culture of *speculating on risk* is the way in which mobilization of risk concentrated, instead of dispersing, risk and brought insecurity instead of security. The Bank's ability to respond to misfire through improvisation is critical here. In such a way, central banks do not merely perform 'an economy of words' through 'open mouth operations' but mobilize various discursive/material/technical complexes of risk and uncertainty that I refer to as 'money cultures' (Guthrie and Wright, 2000; Holmes, 2009). Misfire and improvisation have led to a money culture of *speculating for risk*.

The centrality of the City of London and the Bank of England

Founded as a private institution when it received its charter in 1694, the Bank of England is one of the oldest central banks in the world. This, however, is not the reason for the focus that this book makes on this particular institution. In the second half of the twentieth century, the Bank of England emerged as the eminent global research institute in central banking, hosting the Centre for Central Banking Studies where practitioners discuss best practice in monetary and financial governance. This feature is not lost on some of its critics who argue that the institution would do better to focus on banking as it was accustomed to under the governorship of Montagu Norman.[4] However, what this means for a study of understandings of central banking and financial stability is that the publicly available outputs of the Bank of England should be considered to be at the forefront and state of the art in thinking on financial stability. More than this, the Bank of England has emerged as a focal point for political leadership during both the aftermath of the Global Financial Crisis and the vote in Britain to leave the European Union.

The book covers the 21-year period 1996–2017, namely the period that the Bank of England has been producing financial stability reports. This means that the scope of the book encompasses ten years before and after the start of the Global Financial Crisis and should therefore be of interest to scholars of the antecedents, the crisis proper and its governance and the near aftermath. That said, due to this greater time period, the book cannot focus solely on crisis governance, as Langley (2015) does in *Liquidity Lost*, although the crisis enters the picture most squarely as a series of technical problems or 'misfires' for the techniques of financial stability. Further, because the Bank of England is preoccupied with the City of London, the account of finance is based on the study of possibly the most technologically sophisticated and structurally important financial centre in the world (Norfield, 2016). London has been a hugely significant global financial centre due to a number of factors, including imperialism and its legacy, the agglomeration of knowledge and supplementary services and critically, its role in global credit practices (Langley, 2002). Significantly for a finance/security analysis, London emerged during the period of study as the global centre for derivatives practices. This is important because for both the analysis offered here, and key authors in the finance/security literature, the security logic of the derivative underpins many of the links between finance and security (Martin, 2007; Amoore, 2011; Esposito, 2011).

A note on research methods

Having set out the core empirical and conceptual contributions of the book, this section reflects on the methodology of studying money cultures at the Bank of England. There are two overarching and related obstacles for work of this kind. On the one hand, there is an epistemological problem of being able to identify a culture when one has found it. On the other hand, researching one of the most prominent central banks in the world following a major financial crisis means that access to the institution is limited. In particular, if interpretative ethnography is the best way to make claims about culture, do limitations to access to an institution badly hinder the investigation?

Considering the first issue, of knowing when one identifies a money culture, this is notoriously difficult. There are, as Raymond Williams (2006) is quick to point out, many definitions and theorizations of culture. Culture can be theorized as identity and difference, webs of meaning, ethics and the sedimentation of routines and practices (Best and Paterson, 2010, pp. 7–12). Here I draw on Williams' (2006, p. 54) analysis of culture as description of ways of life. In particular, and, as a geographically minded political economist, my sensibilities and analysis are drawn to what Allen and Pryke (1999, p. 52) describe as identifications based on different interpretations of space-time. In other words, these are 'webs of meaning' which people attribute to mobility (Geertz, 1973). This then, is a move to ground the analysis in Georg Simmel's (1900) keen attention to the way that the subjective properties of monetary relations take on an objective status of properties of a 'thing' or commodity.

Interpretative ethnography is undoubtedly the best way to do research aimed at identifying cultural traits. This is because it aims to bring to light shared meanings that constitute reality within a particular institution or group (Smart, 2006, p. 10). In an unpublished article reflecting on the use of the term 'culture' within economic sociology, Donald MacKenzie argues that 'successfully applying the concept of "culture" requires fieldwork' (MacKenzie, 2011, p. 20). MacKenzie (2009) argues elsewhere that differing ways of making sense of, and valuing, financial instruments need to be studied by the anthropologist through talking to people about how they think and calculate. However, doing this sort of research is difficult in such a politically important institution. MacKenzie himself has found this difficult in private financial institutions where he concedes that limited access has meant that he could do very little participant observation. He has compensated for this with 'extensive interviewing'. And while this present study does fall short of being interpretative ethnography, in my own way I have compensated by parsing together a study based on an immersion in all publicly available financial stability documents and media over a 21-year period, interviews with current and former employees, and participant observation during key events where the Bank engaged with the public. And while this means that I was not as immersed in the Bank of England as Graham Smart (2006) was in the Bank of Canada where he previously worked, when a researcher can claim to be advising or working on behalf of the institution they study, they should be able to infer some understanding of the cultural norms at play in an organization.

As already noted, a researcher had to negotiate access to the Bank of England. I began this study with archival research. For the five years of a study that started in 2012, approximately 1,000 documents and videos were analysed as texts. Archives have traditionally been conceived as an 'inert depository' in which the past is stored, by means of documents and texts (Pollock, 2007, p. 12). However, as Griselda Pollock argues, archives are 'pre-selected in ways that reflect what each culture considered worth storing and remembering' (Pollock, 2007, p. 12). In Derrida's conceptualization of the archive, the process of archiving is driven by conflicting desires – between destruction and preservation – or a violent amalgamation he dubs '*archive fever*' (Derrida, 1996, p. 14). In other words, archival research is not a way discovering an 'objective reality' that exists 'out there' independently in the archive. Instead, archival research works through an active process of 'condensing particular patterns and repetitions whilst ignoring others' (Law, 2004, p. 113). I have made use of the Bank of England's online and paper archives, but, because there is no fully complete financial stability archive at the Bank of England, I have used online materials to create an archive of my own. As Chris Rogers (2017) puts it when reflecting on the use of the archive for critical research, 'the archive reveals objective facts about who said what, where they said it and when they said it, explaining these facts is a highly contingent process that yields a subjective understanding of political processes'. In other words, 'research outputs based on the archive are fundamentally contestable interpretations of facts'.

In an attempt to bring in a wider set of voices and sources, supplementary research was necessary. Arlette Farge (2013) argues that if an 'archive is to serve as an effective social observatory, it will only do so through the scattered details that have broken through, and which form, a gap riddled puzzle of events'. So, while the archive can provide an institutional memory of sorts, like all memories it is fragmented and open to interpretation. In order to develop a reading through the 'ruptures and dispersions', I have supplemented archival research through other research methodologies and sources (Farge, 2013). During the two years since completing a PhD I have become known to the Bank through research projects on economics in the public sphere and on the development of stress testing. I have been able to carry out participant observation at the Bank's Open Forum for public engagement and I have also been invited by the Bank to serve as a judge on the London area final of their Two Point Zero challenge where Sixth Form schools have to make presentations about possible monetary policy decisions. The public engagement division of the Bank of England has been very open to me as a researcher. Inevitably and understandably, the Bank has been much more circumscribed around the market sensitive stress testing exercises.

I have included anonymized quotes and the perspectives from seven research interviews with past and present employees of the Bank of England, and have also been guided to key themes by confidential research interviews with a wide range of present and former professionals in risk management who have interacted with the Bank. This is an attempt to let the voice and perspective of informants shape the account (Geertz, 1973). The project on stress testing has seen me conduct interviews with three present members of staff who work on stress testing and four former Bank staff who were involved in the governance of the financial crisis. These interviews were recorded, transcribed, encrypted and anonymized. As these interviews were not directly related to the project, I have had to ask for special permission to reproduce selected excerpts from interviews. This has highlighted the need to build up trust with one's research participants. The Bank highlighted a minor typo, as well as requesting that certain parts of the excerpts I wanted to use be redacted to preserve the 'off the record' nature of their own meetings with stakeholders. The point here was the Bank did not want to set a precedent of reneging on an 'off the record' agreement. Further, in one instance the Bank asked for one quotation to be removed to reflect the informal and 'off the record' nature of the research interview. I complied with all of these requests. At no point did the Bank attempt to query or dispute my interpretation of publicly available materials and resources.

By bringing together a series of research methodologies, namely archival research, interviews and participant observation, the present study is an example of what John Law (2004) has called 'method assemblage'. The research interviews also helped to guide me when returning to the archive as key themes emerged during the interviews. Through text, interview and experience, webs of meaning become apparent to the researcher as commonalties that resonate across these different media. In particular, the drawing out of themes across the combination of interviews and publicly available speeches, reports and videos allows one to identify the discourses, understandings and practices that *cut across*, and are *co-present in*, the public stage and behind the scene performances of a central bank (Goffman, 1959; Braun, 2015). This approach has merit because while staff speeches are prefixed with the disclaimer that the speeches do not necessarily reflect the views of the Bank, they still have to receive clearance from the Bank's media teams and press office. This, it can be argued, gives a sense of appropriateness when granted group membership of the Bank of England.

Book overview

Following this introductory chapter, the book is divided into three overarching parts. The first part of the book is designed to anchor the study into wider and popular debates about finance, and to set out the theoretical conceptual contributions of the book. Chapter 1 situates this study within existing academic work on central banking and the City of London. Chapters 2 and 3 set out the key theoretical underpinnings of this study. Chapter 2 addresses the relationship between financial stability, mobility and culture by drawing on the work of Georg Simmel (1900) and Randy Martin (2015). Chapter 3 contributes to the ever-expanding literature on financial performativity and the idea of central banking as a performed domain. By developing Derrida's engagement with John Searle, this chapter argues that misfire and improvisation are important categories for explaining change in money cultures. This theoretical framework is brought to bear on two further sections. Both the concept of mobilizing risk and the concept of the performed domain contribute to cultural political economy accounts of finance. The book employs geographical concepts, of mobilization of risk and performances of money cultures, to argue that two money cultures emerged during the 21-year period of study, cultures of *speculating on risk* and *speculating for risk*. Each of these cultures is developed in the remaining two parts of the book.

Part II details the way in which *speculating on risk* emerged fully in the 1990s with the development of new risk management techniques. In this part of the book, Chapters 4 and 5 detail regulatory thinking about risk by studying the Bank's statements on credit derivatives and Value-at-Risk. Chapter 4 attends to the security logic of 'market completion' that sustained many of the proponents of credit derivatives at the Bank. In the 1990s, credit derivatives, which had a logic of risk management, were put towards profit making (J.P. Morgan, 1999, p. 2). For example, in an early publication associated with the Bank of England, it was argued that derivatives, 'should make the global allocation of risk more efficient ... the new instruments make *credit markets complete*' (Goodhart *et al.*, 1998, p. 94). This is the idea that 'in particular, credit default products' constituted the height of a sophisticated credit market that efficiently distributes risk to those most suited to bear it. The hope here is that it would make systemic collapse less likely. This, then, was a gamble by regulators on the proficiency of private sector risk management.

However, the Bank was consistently clear that these credit risk management tools were far from perfect. The Bank conceded that 'the evaluation of credit risk is more complicated than the evaluation of market risk' and still argued that 'the lack of a scientific pricing method has never been a deterrent to trading' (Goodhart *et al.*, 1998, p. 94). In drawing together a tentative conclusion on credit derivatives, the Bank wrote that although credit derivatives 'should decrease systemic risks', it should still be noted that 'some of the risks previously confined to the banking sector might spread to other economic sectors' (Goodhart *et al.*, 1998, p. 96). Amid this ambiguity, over a ten-year period the

Bank of England was continuously aware of a number of risks associated with credit derivatives including increasing complexity and valuation difficulties. The Bank then, had the tendency to list a range of associated risks without assigning probabilities or likelihoods to them. Ultimately, the Bank identified a long list of potential concerns in a broad-brush fashion.

The focus for Chapter 5 is upon a 'fatal flaw' in thinking about risk. In 1993, investment bank J.P. Morgan put its RiskMetrics set and Value-at-Risk model for measuring market risk into the public domain and lobbied for its use in risk management. It provides a 'single number estimate of how much a firm can lose to the price volatility of the instruments it holds' during normal circumstances or conditions (Buckley, 2011, p. 96). And, as such, it was grafted onto the widespread use and trade of credit derivatives to calculate the risk taken on in various positions. Value-at-Risk was designed to encourage and facilitate hedging, but had a number of risks attached to it. Chapter 5 is an account of why Value-at-Risk was adopted as a measure of market risk. The adoption of VaR was, on this reading, a result of its purported accuracy, because it was both constantly and consistently cited as an accurate measure for market risk by the Bank of England. The remainder of the chapter is concerned with repeated critiques of Value-at-Risk that were levelled following periods of financial instability. In the aftermath of the collapse of goliath hedge fund Long Term Capital Management and the Asian Financial Crisis of the late 1990s, the Bank of England acknowledged and responded to the critique that widespread use of Value-at-Risk led to mass position cutting in markets and volatility. In such a way, a technique that was thought to contribute to stability seemingly misfired and contributed to instability. The Bank was able to improvise a response to this that legitimized continued use of VaR in finance. Chapter 6 completes its analysis of VaR by analysing how, in the context of the Global Financial Crisis, the technique was again criticized, although the critique was now being centred on the assumption of normality within the calculation. As Andrew Haldane of the Bank of England argued at this time, 'VaR suffers a fatal flaw as a risk management and regulatory measure: it is essentially silent about risks in the tail beyond the confidence interval' (Haldane, 2012b, p. 16). The extreme financial events, rather than normality assumed in VaR, were a considerable example of misfire. On this occasion, the Bank of England took the critique and limitations of VaR considerably more seriously.

Part III of the book addresses the emergent culture of *speculating for risk*, a culture which seeks to visualize and understand the mobilization of risk better. Part III begins with Chapter 6 and returns to the relationship between movement and money cultures. Chapter 6 foregrounds the category of misfire as a dynamic process and lively practice, and fully teases out the misfires of dispersal and normality. It is argued that these constituted a spectacular financial misfire which then begot a series of improvisations and another money culture during and after the Global Financial Crisis. The argument being advanced then is that we need to take seriously two instances of counter-performativity, or misfire, of the money culture of *speculating on risk*. The first significant misfire was the way that credit derivatives concentrated, rather than dispersed, risk through, around and across the financial system. The second misfire was the way that Value-at-Risk assumed normal conditions holding, rather than extreme conditions and low probability/high-impact events. Ultimately this is about a shift from speculating or gambling on the financial stability pay-offs of risk management techniques, towards a greater concern with mapping, coding and understanding the mobilization of risk with much more precision and granularity.

Importantly, this is not to argue that one money culture simply supplants another, but that in some aspects the two coalesce and, in others, there is a period of contestation, such as that between practices of computing from historical data against subjective probabilities involved in forecasting.

Chapter 6 argues that this culture has been pursued through improvised attempts to centralize, visualize and map the trade of derivatives and to standardize derivative products so that investors can better gauge how risks are being mobilized. As Andrew Haldane of the Bank of England has said, these are attempts to 're-wire the global financial web, transforming it from a dense, complex cats-cradle to a simplified hub-and spoke configuration' (Haldane, 2012a, p. 13). The chapter also introduces the technical regulatory practice of stress testing and the way that the Bank is attempting to operationalize and aggregate financial risks through the development of an Annual Cyclical Scenario (ACS).

Chapter 7 is also concerned with stress testing. The focus in this chapter is an improvisation which has led to the widening of the risk imagination towards thinking about extreme events. The chapter makes the case that stress testing involves multiple forms of possibilistic thinking, and draws a distinction between plausible scenarios and hypothetical scenarios. This practice is increasingly speculative in the sense of visualizing and understanding future risks because they appeal to post-probabilistic measures of risk to scenarios concerned with 'potentially fatter tail' (risks) (Haldane, 2012b, p. 17). In other words, risks that fall outside of historically derived 'normal' conditions. Indeed, this would involve more subjective forms of probability, such that 'stress-tests of the impact of extreme financial events on the functioning of the global financial web would play the role of weather warnings' (Haldane, 2012b, p. 17). The chapter also traces the rhetorical work that has gone into publicly establishing that the scenarios are hypothetical, rather than being based on evidence of a shock that is expected to occur. The chapter charts the development of much more hypothetical Biennial Exploratory Scenarios, before concluding that the Bank is now more publicly engaging with the financial stability implications of three contentious political issues or events, namely climate change, cyber security and the Brexit referendum.

Chapter 8 pulls together the developments of the previous two chapters; namely it attempts to better understand the mobilization of risk and the widening of the risk imagination, to argue that the Bank sees them as contributing to both a better capitalized system and individual institutions. Capitalization, then, is integral to resilience. The chapter analyses Bank of England thinking on resilience to provide evidence that the Bank is working with both a systemic understanding of resilience and a neoliberal governmental approach to the capitalization of individual institutions. The chapter then considers the performative politics of financial resilience, focusing squarely on the way that resilience seeks to close down instability by absorbing losses with good quality capital and therein stimulating confidence. Here the chapter argues that the Bank is only too well aware that this process is fragile, complex and open to misfire. This was initially responded to by increasing calls for institutions to improve their transparency, which would consequently promote greater market discipline. The chapter concludes by making the case that the Bank sees stress testing and the systemic risk buffer, and, in particular, salient features of the money culture of *speculating for risk*, as improving capitalization and the resilience of banks and the financial system.

Finally, the conclusion briefly rehearses the key arguments of the book before reflecting on a likely trajectory for financial stability governance by drawing together four key themes: (i) the multiple derivative logics through which financial security operates, (ii) the performative politics of misfire, (iii) the political emboldenment of the Bank and (iv) the relation between money cultures and processes of capitalization.

Notes

1 This draws on Thomas Kuhn's (1962) work on 'revolutionary' shifts between distinct and self-contained systems of scientific thought and practice.
2 By this I refer to regulatory capital, or the capital adequacy ratio of equity that must be held as a percentage of risk-weighted assets.
3 This is not to situate the approach in the 'cultural political economy' label adopted by Sum and Jessop (2013), for whom semiotics is still determined by material forces. Instead, here I am much closer to the scholarship showcased in Best and Paterson (2010, p. 4), which attends to 'the cultural character of contemporary political economy'.
4 Tellingly, Norman drew a distinction between the practical field of banking and the intellectual pursuit of economics (Norman, in the *Evening Standard*, 16 June 1941).

References

Aitken, R. 2011. 'Financializing Security: Political prediction markets and the Commodification of uncertainty'. *Security Dialogue* 42(2), pp. 123–141.
Allen, J., and Pryke, M. 1999. 'Money cultures after Georg Simmel: mobility, movement, and identity'. *Environment and Planning D: Society and Space*, 17(1), pp. 51–68.
Amicelle, A. 2011. 'Towards a "new" political anatomy of financial surveillance'. *Security Dialogue* 42(2), pp. 161–178.
Amicelle, A., and Jacobsen, E. 2016. 'The cross-colonization of finance and security through lists: Banking policing in the UK and India'. *Environment and Planning D: Society and Space* 34(1), pp. 89–106.
Amoore, L. 2011. 'Data derivatives on the emergence of a security risk calculus for our times'. *Theory, Culture & Society* 28(6), pp. 24–43.
Amoore, L. 2013. *The Politics of Possibility: Risk and security beyond probability*. Durham NC: Duke University Press.

Best, J. 2017. 'Security, economy, population: The political economic logic of liberal exceptionalism'. *Security Dialogue* 48(5), pp. 375–392.

Best, J., and Paterson, M. 2010. *Cultural Political Economy*. Abingdon: Routledge.

Bowman, A., Erturk, I., Froud, J., and Johal, S. 2012. 'Central bank-led capitalism'. *Seattle UL Rev.* 36, pp. 455–487.

Boy, N. 2015. 'Sovereign safety'. *Security Dialogue* 46(6), pp. 530–547.

Boy, N., Burgess, J.P., and Leander, A. 2011. 'The global governance of security and finance: Introduction to the special issue'. *Security Dialogue* 42(2), pp. 115–122.

Braun, B. 2015. 'Governing the future: the European Central Bank's expectation management during the Great Moderation'. *Economy and Society* 44(3), pp. 367–391.

Braun, B., 2016. 'Speaking to the people? Money, trust, and central bank legitimacy in the age of quantitative easing'. *Review of International Political Economy* 23(6), pp. 1064–1092.

Buckley, A. 2011. *Financial Crisis: Causes, Context and Consequences.* Harlow: Pearson.

Christophers, B. 2014. 'From Marx to market and back again: Performing the economy'. *Geoforum* 57, pp. 12–20.

Christophers, B. 2017. 'The performativity of the yield curve'. *Journal of Cultural Economy* 10(1), pp. 63–80.

Clark, G.L. 2005. 'Money flows like mercury: the geography of global finance'. *Geografiska Annaler: Series B, Human Geography* 87(2), pp. 99–112.

Derrida, J. 1996. *Archive Fever*. Chicago Il: University of Chicago Press.

Dillon, M. 2008. 'Underwriting Security'. *Security Dialogue* 39(2–3), pp. 309–332.

Esposito, E. 2011. *The Future of Futures: The Time of Money in Financing and Society.* Cheltenham: Edward Elgar.

Farge, A. 2013. *The Allure of the Archive*. London: Yale University Press.

Foucault, M. 2007. *Security, Territory, Population. Lectures at the College de France 1977–1978.* Basingstoke: Palgrave Macmillan.

French, S., and Kneale, J. 2012. 'Speculating on careless lives: Annuitising the biofinancial subject'. *Journal of Cultural Economy* 5(4), pp. 391–406.

Geertz, C. 1973. *The interpretation of cultures: selected essays*. New York: Basic books.

Gilbert, E. 2015a. 'The gift of war: Cash, counterinsurgency, and "collateral damage"'. *Security Dialogue* 46(5), pp. 403–421.

Gilbert, E. 2015b. 'Money as a "weapons system" and the entrepreneurial way of war'. *Critical Military Studies* 1(3), pp. 202–219.

de Goede, M. 2010. 'Financial Security'. In Burgess, J.P. (ed.) *The Routledge Handbook of the New Security Studies*. Abingdon: Routledge, pp. 100–109.

de Goede, M. 2012. *Speculative Security: The politics of pursuing terrorist monies.* Minneapolis: University of Minnesota Press.

de Goede, M. 2017. 'Banks in the Frontline: Assembling Space/Time in Financial Warfare'. In Christophers, B., Leyshon, A., and Mann, G (eds.) *Money and Finance After the Crisis: Critical Thinking for Uncertain Times*. New York: Wiley-Blackwell, pp. 117–144.

Goffman, E. 1959. *The presentation of self in everyday life*. Garden City, NY: Anchor.

Goodhart, C., Hartmann, P., Llewellyn, D., Rojas-Suarez, L., and Weisbrod, S. 1998. *Financial Regulation: Why, how and where now?* Abingdon: Routledge.

Gros, F. 2012. *Le Principe Sécurité*. Paris: Gallimard.

Guthrie, G., and Wright, J. 2000. 'Open mouth operations', *Journal of Monetary Economics* 46(2), pp. 489–516.

Haldane, A. 2012a. 'Towards a common financial language', presented at the Securities Industry and Financial Markets Association (SIFMA) 'Building a Global Legal Entity Identifier Framework' Symposium, New York, 14 March 2012. [pdf] Available at: www.bis.org/review/r120315g.pdf (Accessed 10 May 2014).

Haldane, A. 2012b. 'Tails of the unexpected', presentation given at 'The Credit Crisis Five Years On: Unpacking the Crisis', conference held at the University of Edinburgh Business School, 8th June 2012. [pdf] Available at: https://pdfs.semanticscholar.org/55 bd/31941afbbd1072b0b022971b3ab479db6c0d.pdf (Accessed 15 May 2014).

Hall, R.B. 2008. *Central banking as global governance: constructing financial credibility.* Cambridge: Cambridge University Press.

Halpern, O. 2014. *Beautiful Data: A History of Vision and Reason since 1945.* Durham NC: Duke University Press.

Hardy, C., and Thomas, R. 2015. 'Discourse in a material world'. *Journal of Management Studies* 52(5), pp. 680–696.

Helleiner, E. 2014. *The status quo crisis: Global financial governance after the 2008 meltdown.* Oxford: Oxford University Press.

Holmes, D. 2009. 'Economy of words'. *Cultural Anthropology* 24(3), pp. 381–419.

Holmes, D. 2014. *Economy of words: Communicative imperatives in central banks.* Chicago Il: University of Chicago Press.

J.P. Morgan. 1996. *RiskMetrics – Technical Document – Fourth Edition.* J.P. Morgan: New York.

J.P. Morgan. 1999. *The JP Morgan Guide to Credit Derivatives*, J.P. Morgan: New York.

King, M. 2004. *Evidence to Economic Affairs Committee*: 94. [e-book] Available at: https://books.google.co.uk/books?id=SsUXFX7UbKsC&pg=PA86&lpg=PA86&dq= King,+Mervyn+(2004)+Evidence+to+Economic+Affairs+Committee+27h+january& source=bl&ots=cEftuqnjQn&sig=i1U9NQGALqqoqGrC4PHFg8z3uEA&hl=en&sa= X&ved=0ahUKEwjA8rG0uLTVAhXhDsAKHUweB2oQ6AEIJDAA#v=onepage&q= King%2C%20Mervyn%20(2004)%20Evidence%20to%20Economic%20Affairs%20 Committee%2027h%20january&f=false. (Accessed 12 May 2016).

King, M. 2016. *The End of Alchemy: Money, Banking, and the Future of the Global Economy.* London: W.W. Norton & Company.

Konings, M. 2010. 'Rethinking Neoliberalism and the Crisis: Beyond the Re-regulation Agenda'. In Konings, M (ed.). *The Great Credit Crash.* London: Verso, pp. 3–30.

Krippner, G. 2007. 'The making of US monetary policy: Central bank transparency and the neoliberal dilemma'. *Theory and Society* 36(6), pp. 477–513.

Kuhn, T. 1962. *The Structure of Scientific Revolutions.* Chicago: University of Chicago Press.

Lagna, A. 2015. 'Italian municipalities and the politics of financial derivatives: Rethinking the Foucauldian perspective'. *Competition & Change* 19(4), pp. 283–300.

Langley, P. 2002. *World Financial Orders: an historical international political economy.* Abingdon: Routledge.

Langley, P. 2008a. *The Everyday Life of Global Finance: Saving and Borrowing in Anglo-America.* Oxford: Oxford University Press.

Langley, P. 2008b. 'Financialization and the consumer credit boom', *Competition & Change* 12(2), pp. 133–147.

Langley, P. 2013. 'Toxic assets, turbulence and biopolitical security: Governing the crisis of global financial circulation'. *Security Dialogue* 44(2), pp. 111–126.

Langley, P. 2015. *Liquidity Lost: The Governance of the Global Financial Crisis.* Oxford: Oxford University Press.

Langley, P. 2017. 'Financial flows: Spatial imaginaries of speculative circulations'. In Christophers, B., Leyshon, A. and Mann, G. (eds.) *Money and Finance after the Crisis: Critical Thinking for Uncertain Times*. New York: Wiley-Blackwell, pp. 69–90.

Law, J. 2004. *After method: Mess in social science research*. Abingdon: Routledge.

Lee, B. 2015. 'Remembering Randy' in May, J. (ed.) 'Movement after Randy Martin'. *Social Text* 33(3) 124, pp. 133–135.

Lightfoot, G., and Lilley, S. 2017. 'Organising destruction: A Derivative Logic?'. *Organization* 24(4), pp. 534–548.

Lobo-Guerrero, L. 2010. *Insuring security: biopolitics, security and risk*. Abingdon: Routledge.

MacKenzie, D. 2009. 'Beneath all the toxic acronyms lies a basic cultural issue'. *Financial Times* 26 November, p. 12. [pdf] Available at: www.sps.ed.ac.uk/__data/assets/pdf_file/0004/36472/11473_PDFonly.pdf (Accessed 24th May 2017).

MacKenzie, D. 2011. 'Evaluation Cultures? On Invoking "Culture" in the Analysis of Behaviour in Financial Markets'. *Unpublished manuscript, University of Edinburgh, [Online]* Available at: www.research.ed.ac.uk/portal/en/publications/on-invokingculture-in-the-analysis-of-behavior-in-financial-markets(f1105f1d-78eb-423e-a52d-72467ef9134e).html (Accessed 24 May 2016).

Mackintosh, S. 2014. 'Crises and Paradigm Shift'. *The Political Quarterly*, 85(4), pp. 406–412.

Martin, R. 2007. *An Empire of Indifference: American War and the Financial Logic of Risk Management*. Durham, NC: Duke University Press.

Martin, R. 2009. 'The twin towers of financialization: Entanglements of political and cultural economies'. *The Global South* 3(1), pp. 108–125.

Martin, R. 2015. *Knowledge LTD: Toward a Social Logic of the Derivative*. Philadelphia: Temple University Press.

McCormack, D. 2012. 'Governing economic futures through the war on inflation'. *Environment and Planning A* 44(7), pp. 1536–1553.

McCormack, D. 2015. 'Governing inflation: Price and atmospheres of emergency'. *Theory, Culture & Society* 32(2), pp. 131–154.

Morris, J.H. 2016. 'The performativity, performance and lively practices in financial stability press conferences'. *Journal of Cultural Economy* 9(3), pp. 245–260.

Mugge, D. 2014. 'Policy inertia and the persistence of systemic fragility'. *The Political Quarterly* 85(4), pp. 413–416.

Norfield, T. 2016. *The City: London and the Global Power of Finance*. London: Verso.

Norman, M. 1941. Quoted in *The Evening Standard*, 16th June 1941. Bank of England Archives.

Pollock, G. 2007. *Encounters in the virtual feminist museum: time, space and the archive*. Abingdon: Routledge.

Rogers, C. 2017. 'Reflections on the Archive as a Critical Resource'. In Montgomerie, J. (ed.) *Critical Methods in Political and Cultural Economy*. Abingdon: Routledge, pp. 121–124.

Simmel, G. 1897. 'The Significance of Money for the Tempo of Life'. Cited in Goodstein, E.S. 2017. *Georg Simmel and the Disciplinary Imaginary*. Stanford CA: Stanford University Press.

Simmel, G. 1900 [2011]. *The Philosophy of Money*. Abingdon: Routledge.

Smart, G. 2006. *Writing the economy: Activity, genre and technology in the world of banking*. London: Equinox.

Sum, N.L., and Jessop, B. 2013. *Towards a cultural political economy: Putting culture in its place in political economy*. London: Edward Elgar.

Toynbee Lagoutte, J. 2017. 'Getting Personal: How Biosecurity Gets Under Our Skin'. *Green European Journal* 15, pp. 80–86.

Williams, R. 2006. 'The analysis of culture'. *Cultural theory and popular culture*, pp. 32–40.

Zarate, J. 2013. *Treasury's war: The unleashing of a new era of financial warfare*. New York: PublicAffairs.

Part I

Performing money cultures in London

1   London and the Bank of England

Introduction: the contemporary Bank of England

During the 21-year period that this book covers, there have been three Governors of the Bank of England. Baron Eddie George had been an employee of the Bank of England since 1962 and served for two five-year terms as Governor. In the early 1990s George became known in the media for his excellent working relationship with Chancellor of the Exchequer Kenneth Clarke, to the extent that governance of the UK economy was labelled the 'Ken and Eddie Show'. In 2003, he was succeeded by Sir Mervyn King. King had been Chief Economist at the Bank of England since 1991 and Deputy Governor since 1998. King's appointment broke a trend of Bank Governors being experienced bankers because King was the first professional economist to be given the key role at the Bank (Davies and Green, 2010, p. 279). It is entirely plausible to interpret this as a result of the Bank's focus on monetary policy and targets since 1997, as King had chaired the Monetary Policy Committee (MPC) since 1998. Like Baron George, Sir King served as Governor for two terms. At the end of his second term, King was replaced by Mark Carney, former Governor at Canada's central bank, the Bank of Canada.

Carney had worked for investment banking giant Goldman Sachs before switching over to the public sector. Carney gained notoriety and popularity for his decision making during the Global Financial Crisis and his stewardship of the Canadian economy during this difficult period. In 2011 Carney also began chairing the Global Financial Stability Board (GFSB). This is an organization which aims to coordinate financial authorities and standard setting bodies so that they may develop 'strong and coherent regulatory and supervisory policies' (GFSB: n.d.). Under Carney's leadership, and reacting to significant features of the global financial system prior to the Global Financial Crisis, the GFSB made progress in consolidating four main priorities (i) constructing resilient financial institutions, (ii) ending the problem of institutions that are too big to fail when they are under distress, (iii) reducing the risks within and created by shadow banking, and (iv) making derivatives markets safer (Bank of England, n.d a). In 2013, with his reputation at a very high level, Carney became the first non-Briton to be appointed Governor of the Bank of England since it was established.

Of particular import to this research, the Bank of England was divided into two separate wings in 1994, one for monetary stability and one for financial stability (Davies and Green, 2010, p. 53). The election of the New Labour government in 1997 saw two further key institutional changes occur within the Bank of England. The first was a separation of powers, between the Bank of England, the Treasury and the newly created Financial Services Authority (FSA). Two separate Deputy Governors were appointed, which exacerbated the division between monetary and financial stabilities (Davies and Green, 2010, p. 53). Broadly speaking, financial oversight was hived off to the FSA. The second was a two-tiered change relating to the enactment of monetary policy: (a) the Bank was made formally independent from political control and (b) the Bank was legally bound to a policy of inflation targeting according to a target set by the Chancellor of the Exchequer.

While these significant changes have been associated with New Labour, they can be viewed as being symptomatic of wider trends in economic governance. In particular, central banking was thought to be best served if it were to focus on establishing price stability (Conaghan, 2012). Central bank independence had been advocated by public choice political science in order to insulate monetary policy from the exigencies of self-interested governments going into the campaign for re-election (Nordhaus, 1975). Furthermore, heavy weight, and later politically important, academic economists, such as Ben Bernanke, Frederic Mishkin and Adam Posen, had argued both cogently and persuasively that inflation had real economic costs, and that inflation targeting was an effective way of shaping inflationary expectations (See Bernanke *et al.*, 1999). Since 1997 the Bank of England has been setting interest rates to target a rate of inflation of 2 per cent. The interest rate was to be set at monthly meetings by a MPC, consisting of nine members; '5 bank people and 4 external members chosen by the Chancellor' (Conaghan, 2012, p. 29).

Created in 2000 as part of the Financial Services and Markets Act, the FSA had four statutory objectives, namely: maintaining confidence in the UK financial system, contributing to the protection and enhancement of stability of the UK financial system, securing the appropriate degree of protection for consumers, and the reduction of financial crime. However, many of the events that occurred under the umbrella term of the Global Financial Crisis indicated that the tripartite arrangement between the FSA, the Bank of England and the Treasury was unclear and ineffective (Davies and Green 2010, p. 77). Certainly confidence, stability and consumer protection had been undermined by the bank run on Northern Rock in 2007, and it is arguable that some sorts of financial crimes had been committed, such as the rigging of the inter-bank LIBOR interest rate during the mid-2000s (Stenfors, 2017).

Reflections on the crisis highlighted that the FSA had been preoccupied with risk at the level of individual institutions. This was thought to have been at the neglect of systemic risk. In the aftermath of the crisis period, the FSA was dissolved and its functions divided between the newly created Financial Conduct Authority (FCA), and the Prudential Regulation Authority (PRA) within the

Bank of England. Within this change was the creation of the Financial Policy Committee (FPC). The post-crisis architecture is such that the FCA is consumer based, while the FPC regulates both institutions and the system. In terms of the latter, the FPC is charged with identifying, monitoring and taking action to remove or reduce systemic risks with a view to protecting and enhancing the resilience of the UK financial system. The members of the FPC include the Bank Governor, three of the Deputy Governors, the Chief Executive of the FCA, the Bank's Executive Director for Financial Stability Strategy and Risk, four external members appointed by the Chancellor, and a non-voting representative of the Treasury (Bank of England, n.d.*a*). The FPC is concerned with systemic issues, while the PRA is charged with the more granular task of regulating at the level of individual financial firms and institutions.

The FPC publishes a record of its formal policy meetings, and is now responsible for the Bank's *Financial Stability Review (FSR)*. These FSRs have appeared twice a year and aim to both highlight 'developments affecting the stability of the financial system, and promote the latest thinking on risk, regulation and market institutions' (FSR, 1996a). Prior to the Global Financial Crisis, the Bank had produced the review in partnership with an external organization. Initially this was with the Securities and Investments Board and then from 2000, the FSA. Significantly the name was changed in 2006, to the *Financial Stability Report* in order 'to reflect a change in content and aims' (Bank of England, n.d.*b*). The FPC of the Bank of England has been releasing financial stability reports through press conferences since 2011. In 2014 the Bank began to carry out very public stress tests[1] on important financial institutions in the UK. Stress testing involves the creation of a hypothetical scenario of economic shocks and the simulation of the impact of such shocks on the financial system. In 2016, stress testing developed in such a way that the Bank worked with two different types of test. The Annual Cyclical Scenario (ACS) is based on the Bank of England's assessment of current risks to financial stability. The Biennial Exploratory Scenario (BES) is not anchored in the underlying risk environment and cycle and is designed to use shocks that are much more speculative and unlikely to happen. The relation between money cultures and stress testing is discussed in full in Chapters 6, 7 and 8.

One further significant development is the ongoing implementation of the systemic risk buffer (SRB) suggested in the Vickers Recommendations. The Independent Commission on Banking (ICB) recommendations on ring-fencing were implemented through the Financial Services (Banking Reform) Act in 2013. The regulations require that the FPC develop a framework for a SRB that will apply to ring-fenced banks and large building societies. The UK legislation 'implementing the SRB requires the FPC to establish a framework for an SRB that applies to ring-fenced banks and large building societies that hold more than £25 billion of household and small/medium enterprise deposits' (Bank of England 2016: 5). This is designed to improve loss absorbing capacity in the core financial institutions in the UK. This is an ongoing collaboration between the PRA and the FPC and the capital plan is supposed to be in place by 2019.

Chapter 8 will discuss the role of the SRB in the context of capitalization and resilience.

Having outlined key developments in the Bank of England over the 21-year period of study, in the remainder of this chapter I set out how this book contributes to empirical and theoretical studies of central banking. Alongside this, I explain why the Bank of England is of particular import to studies of the interconnections between finance and security. In doing so, the chapter will discuss the development of financial supervision powers and the embeddedness of the Bank in a financial centre oriented towards derivative finance. The chapter concludes by emphasizing the significance of the derivative for a central bank culture of speculative security.

Central banking

Founded as a private institution in 1694, the Bank of England's key principle at the time was to 'promote the public good and benefit of our people' by managing the public debt of the government. This role of 'national banker' was clearly and squarely financial. For example, for a widely used financial textbook, central banks are described as being 'a distinct entity to a commercial bank and providing a number of regulatory, supervisory and governmental functions' (Valdez and Molyneux, 2010, pp. 20, 55). Similarly, a former First Deputy Managing Director of the International Monetary Fund sketches out another functional explanation when he says that central banks serve as 'bankers for the government by managing the national debt' and managing both exchange rates and foreign reserves (Fischer, 2005, p. 170). The most commonly encountered and recognized function of the central bank is the setting of interest rates and in doing so it controls the supply and price of money and credit (Maxfield, 1997, p. 5). Central banks also play a major role in the economy by supervising the commercial banks, and other financial institutions, by serving as a lender of last resort to struggling banks. Such financial functions are considered to promote 'financial stability'.

In an influential article, Bowman *et al.* (2012, p. 456) have pointed out that central banks' 'pivotal role in post-crisis capitalism has not been adequately politically or theoretically addressed in any existing literature'. This alludes to the fact that although authors across a range of social science disciplines including international relations, anthropology, communication studies, international political economy, sociology and human geography have pushed and pulled at the question of what a central bank is and how it operates, such work has almost exclusively looked at the monetary, inflation targeting feature of central banks (Guthrie and Wright, 2000; Smart, 2006; Krippner, 2007; Hall, 2008; Holmes, 2009, 2014; Mann, 2010; McCormack, 2012, 2015; Braun, 2015, 2016; Siklos, 2017). Despite playing a 'pivotal role' in crisis management, and consolidating their power following the crisis, the financial stability functions of central banks and their role have garnered considerably less attention[2] (Bowman *et al.*, 2012, p. 466). This is not to deny the 'centrality of stable money to capitalism', but rather, to attend to another key feature of financialized capitalism (Mann, 2013, p. 71). The distinction between monetary and financial stability policy has analytical consequences. One salient analytic consequence of this is that most studies of central bank monetary policy – in particular those outside of the European Union – can assume the relatively self-contained nature of institutions, as monetary policy is predominantly a nationally conscribed concern. That said, authors such as Hall (2008) and Holmes (2014) do point to monetary policy having been shaped, to some extent, by an 'epistemic community' of economists and a wider intellectual context (Haas, 1992; Finnemore and Sikkink, 1998). Financial stability, alternatively, is a transnational issue, requiring international co-operation, and top central bankers, such as Mark Carney, have both national and transnational roles. The point here is that institutional financial cultures are shaped by global regulatory contexts, as well as from within those institutions. In order to highlight this, I relate Bank of England thinking to the changing approach of the Basel Committee on banking regulation, although it is not obvious which institution is driving the changes (Lewin, 2017).

Further, the existing social science literature has attempted to conceptualize the power of central banks in a way which can be characterized under three main themes – functional, structural and social constructivist. Here I first review these three strands of literature before developing a fourth account which attends to performativity. The focus of the latter approach is, I argue, able to add something to the three other overarching approaches. That is to say, on the one hand, the persuasiveness of the idea of the central bank preceded its structural and functional role in the economy. On the other hand, the impact of the central bank is due to both material and discursive factors, and these two elements are inseparable.

In terms of a functional view, a central bank is a distinct entity to a commercial bank and performs a number of common and similar, yet hardly uniform, regulatory, supervisory and governmental roles. Geoffrey Ingham (2004) provides a sketch of central bank power which is functional. Central banks are said to be integral for the liquidity of the payments system as they provide short term funds to 'enable the commercial banks to balance their books and to augment their reserves after they have met the demand for loans' (Ingham, 2004, p. 137). Furthermore, central banks are said to be critically and functionally influential because of their ability to act as 'lender of last resort' (Ingham, 2004, p. 142). On such a 'neo-Chartalist' view, central banks both create money but concurrently supervise the commercial banks and other financial institutions by serving as a back-stop to struggling banks (Dodd, 2014, p. 110). The functional view is couched in the role of the state in maintaining monetary and financial stability, which is a function of both national security and the production and reproduction of state authority.

A second approach is the structural account, which seeks to build on work by scholars working from a critical historically and geographically-inflected perspective (Harvey, 2006, 2010; Mann, 2010, 2013; Jessop, 2010; Knafo, 2013; Vogl, 2015; Jacobs and King, 2016; Conti-Brown, 2017). To this we can also add the first half of Rodney Bruce Hall's analysis of central banking power (2008). These authors write about central banks using a conception of power as being relational and part of material social structures. Power is structural due to the central bank's position within capitalism. As Conti-Brown (2017) puts it, the Federal Reserve has the incontestable 'ability to influence every individual, institution or government that interacts with the global financial system ... every foreign government in crisis has felt its influence', while 'private banks are deeply connected to the Federal Reserve system'. This structural power derives from a series of relationships underpinned by the materiality of capital held by central banks and their ability to create money, allocate credit, monetize debt and value products (Hall, 2008, pp. 84–111).

Structural accounts of central banking have several variants. In Samuel Knafo's account of liberal economic governance, the Gold Standard was a 'structure of power rather than one of regulation ... it was often fueled by the need to discipline market actors (financiers) who were generally reluctant to conform to official policies' (Knafo, 2013, pp. 176–178). What made the Gold Standard radical was that it required a state bank to issue banknotes, thus constituting the kind of state intervention that became the norm for central banks.

Taking a more Marxian analysis, Harvey (2006, 2010) and Jessop (2006, 2010) argue that central banks emerged as creatures of the capitalist state that they supported. For Harvey, the institutions 'vital to capitalist reproduction are separated from those concerned with reproducing the labourer and labour power' (Jessop, 2006); and state institutions must 'attain a certain balance if society as a whole is to be reproduced' (Harvey, 2006). Further, central banks are structurally important because they help capitalism to offset its crises by moving crises around both spatially and temporally (Harvey, 2010).

For a number of authors, this structural power of the central bank sees it insulated from the traditional checks and balances of government or democratic accountability. Geoff Mann's (2010) 'international spatial political economy' is the nearest attempt to explicitly analyse and critique central banking within the geographical literature. In Mann's account of monetary policy in central banking, power is a result of 'structural limitations'. In other words, central bank power is dependent on their 'interest rate operating procedures'. The instruments any one central bank can use to affect interest rates are historically and contextually specific, but Mann argues that they can be generalized into two categories: (a) 'lending to and accepting deposits from the financial sector at rates determined by the central bank' and (b) 'participation in the market for domestic government securities' (Mann, 2010, p. 5). For Mann (2013, p. 53), the 'logic of power and space' which 'arguably characterizes today's financial capitalism' is the control of 'flows between or across territories'.

The structural account is shot through with considerations of the power inherent in the relationship between state and finance (Mann, 2013, pp. 54, 64). Joseph Vogl (2015, p. 101) writes that 'the central banks originally emerged from the dynamic of state debt, from the convergence of political and commercial exigency, and from the entanglement of fiscal policy and finance'. In such a way, the Bank of England gained prominence through acting as 'a channel for the integration of finance capital into government' (Vogl, 2015, p. 93). On this account, the structural interdependence between state and finance *preceded* other functions, and functions such as lender of last resort were gradually assumed later in the nineteenth century. In the context of the United States of America, Jacobs and King (2016) argue that 'Fed power stands out among the three branches of government ... and among democratic, capitalist countries'. The relationship between private creditors and the state is critical here. Vogl (2015, p. 11) suggests that the financial industry acts as 'an essential relay between state form and economic process' and, rather than being opposed, state and market 'exist in relation of power formed by continuous transitions alliances ... and mutual reinforcement'. The Federal Reserve Bank, then, enjoys:

> unparalleled power on domestic policy' and, further its exercise of power 'consistently favours banks and investment firms not only in response to lobbying or the seduction of revolving doors but also because thriving finance helps the Fed itself by generating revenue and pleasing its allies.

As Vogl (2015, p. 101) puts it, central banks such as the Fed feature 'a systematic opening up to an interested financial public' and, this primarily concerns new forms and fields of intervention. Central banks, then, must be considered to be 'central capitalist institutions' because they are conceived as 'safety nets for capital markets and as welfare providers for the banking and financial sectors' (Vogl, 2015, p. 105).

For Rodney Bruce Hall (2008, p. 88), the structural power invoked by Jacobs and King involves the construction of subject positions with 'the result of hierarchical binary relationships'. Here Hall is looking at the way that certain material relationships, such as 'money issuer/money user', allow a central bank to make money available to the commercial banking sector (Hall, 2008, p. 91). For example, when the inter-bank credit system is facing difficulties, central banks intervene to inject liquidity throughout the financial system (Hall, 2008, pp. 93–94). In this role, the bank's structural power creates the binary 'lender of last resort/bail out institution' (Hall, 2008, pp. 94–95).

In its various guises, structuralism is initially persuasive because it locates power within material social relationships, in particularly the ability to create capital and credit and the lender of last resort powers. However, against this view, Marieke de Goede has long criticized the idea that material practices or relationships 'exist prior to, or independently from, ideas and beliefs about them' (de Goede, 2003, p. 81). Instead, structural categories, such as capital and capitalist relationships, are contingent, contested and unstable. In *Virtue, Fortune and Faith*, de Goede goes onto argue that knowledge and interpretation are not mere adjuncts to 'material financial structures' (de Goede, 2005, p. 7). In Butler's terms, 'agency is not purely complicit with prior operations of (financial) power' (Butler, 1997, p. 10). And while I am not arguing that the material is irrelevant, I am making the case that it is intertwined with the discursive

(Hardy and Thomas, 2015). In other words, money takes a 'variety of material forms and yet also depends on a variety of accounting systems' (Dodd, 2014, p. 171), and de Goede argues as much with her repeated observations that money is sustained by writing (2003, p. 95), and that 'money, credit and capital ... (are) systems of writing' (2005, p. 5).

As touched upon previously, Rodney Bruce Hall (2008) seeks to improve on the aforementioned structural accounts of central banking by using an explicitly social constructivist framework grounded in the philosophy of John Searle. Hall therefore forwards the notion that alongside material and structural power, central banks share in the 'deontic' power of social institutions. The central focus of Hall's account is the role of credibility and price stability to 'anchor expectations' in an era of fiat money. Hall argues that being a 'bank of issue' carries with it a collectively assigned status which consequently allows it to set the rate of interest and manage the supply of credit and money (Hall, 2008, p. 57). In attempting to offer more than a structural account, the second conception of power employed by Hall is 'productive power'. By this, central banks are able to use 'discursive practices' and 'knowledge systems' to create and alter meanings. So, while structural power is employed in 'the co-constitution of subjects', via a binary, 'productive power is more diffuse and more extensive' (Hall, 2008, pp. 90–91). In monetary policy, Hall argues that central banks have the ability to fix and change both the demand and supply for money in the banking system (Hall, 2008, p. 92). In liquidity provision, central banks have the power to change social meanings by the choice of language in the public statements by high-ranking officials. The application of productive power, in both emergency liquidity funding and working with insolvent institutions, is the power to alter social meanings of market conditions, for example by transforming the social status of 'distressed' to the social status 'recovering' (Hall, 2008, p. 95).

Likewise, while social constructivism provides a fuller account of the role of central banks than that provided by the structural account, nonetheless we might question whether it is entirely satisfactory (Hall, 2008, pp. 222–223). Hall's two poles of power appear to be a way of keeping the non-discursive and material (structural) power apart from the discursive (productive) power of language. This however, is not possible when one considers a significant feature of the cultural economy literature on monetary policy, namely the idea that what central banks do is exercise *performative force*, and it is in performative practices that the material and discursive fold into each other (Holmes, 2009; Hardy and Thomas, 2015, p. 9). Power may well be 'essentially relational' (Foucault, 2014, p. 251), but it can still be argued that the relational positions are not rigid structural binaries, being much more open-ended, dynamic and performed.

Here, then, I develop a fourth strand of literature on the power of central banks, drawing together the insights of a disparate group of authors to mobilize the category of performativity in an account of central banking. In such a way, central banks can be said to bring about the conditions that they name in speeches, statements and publications. In *Writing the Economy*, Graham Smart (2006) provides a rich ethnographic study of the working patterns and behaviours

of economists within the Bank of Canada. In this account, a technology medi-
ated discourse allows communication between central bank employees in the
Bank of Canada, as well as the subsequent creation of communications materials
which are disseminated to the general public. Although Smart does not explicitly
categorize his account of the central bank, the way that he elucidates economists'
discursive practices which engender intersubjectivity and enable individual and
organizational learning initially lends itself to a constructionist categorization.
Smart argues that 'the economy' is a 'cultural construct' and an 'intersubjective
reality established through the discourse practices of collaborating economists'
(Smart, 2006, p. 22). On the other hand, the idea that economics is both 'performed' and is a 'writing intensive activity' which creates written and spoken
discourse seems to suggest that Smart collapses into an account which is performative (Smart, 2006, pp. 12, 14).

This notion of performativity in central banking has historical precedence.
For example, and moving to the Gold Standard period of the nineteenth century,
the very idea of 'the lender of last resort' function had a performative effect
rather being a bi-product of functional value. The measures associated with the
'Gold Standard' were planned in the belief that the financial system was structured by a central bank (Knafo, 2013, p. 137). This was not the case, but because
it was thought that the central bank was needed to ensure gold convertibility,
state officials created 'the very entity that the term "lender of last resort" was
'intended to describe' (Knafo, 2013, p. 137). Consequently, we can say that the
idea of the central bank exercised power, persuasion and authority *before* it performed its function of lender of last resort. Moving forward to the twentieth
century and onwards, monetary policy has been, and is, premised on the practices of experts bringing about the circumstances they describe – in this case
price stability through inflation forecasts. The Federal Reserve generates the
expectation of interest rate policy anchoring to a target in the future. It attempts
this by releasing a series of 'persuasive narratives' knitted together by a nearly
continuous stream of statistics and analytics in a chain of both people and objects
(McCormack, 2012, p. 1549). Both Douglas Holmes' (2009, 2014) and Pierre
Siklos' (2017) work shows that central bank practitioners have long worked with
the assumption *that talking about future intentions* on interest rates is just as
important as actual rate decisions. This is because the policy discourse shapes
market expectations. Holmes (2014, p. 26) develops this idea of performativity
as the 'collaboration' between central bank and public 'across a communicative
field' in which 'experimentation' is undertaken by the 'reflexive subjects' both
inside and outside of the central bank. Langley's (2013b, 2015) work on the
imbrication of the Bank of England and the Federal Reserve within apparatuses
of security that also involve market devices and actants, provides a compelling
account of the way that central bank interventions and discourses helped to performatively provoke and affectively enrol confidence in the financial system
during the Global Financial Crisis. Similarly, for Braun (2015) the communicative apparatus of the central bank performs credibility, in Goffman's (1959)
sense of a performance in one 'front of house' venue while behaving differently

behind 'closed doors' (Braun, 2015, p. 371). As Jens Beckert (2016) puts it, the considerable public performance of 'governments, central banks, politicians, economists, and statisticians' at once begets and maintains the 'fictional expectation' of money's stability.

Performativity, then, has the potential to disrupt structural binaries and renders problematic the distinctions between material and discursive, and policymakers and public, we find in Hall's social constructivist account. This is because 'discourse and discursive imagination' becomes bound to 'materialization', material practices and multiple performances (de Goede, 2012, p. 32). Structuralism claims to be able to account for performativity in its own terms, that discourse becomes something akin to a structure. However, it can equally be said that structure can be accounted for in discursive terms, that fixity, surface and boundary are particular discursive effects of stabilization (de Goede, 2012, p. 32). The central issue about whether discourse 'structures' seems to be one of stability and material essentialism versus instability and linguistic non-essentialism, and as Foucault argues in *The Order of Things*, language and history buffer modern knowledge in ways that disrupt and escape fixed, unambiguous and uncontested meanings (Foucault, 1970 cited in Best, 2008, pp. 361–362). Here however, I maintain that this does not mean that anything goes. Power can have a role to play in a performative theory of central banking because Christophers (2014, pp. 18–19) identifies in Callon (2007) a 'weaker' version of performativity in which 'calculative capacity is unequally distributed' and that 'existing balances of power … matter to Callon's performativity'. A weaker cultural economy account therefore adopts insights from the more traditional political economy account of power, in which there are important tendencies and trends within financialized capitalism that influence both processes and outcomes.

That said, a political economy approach which treats categories such as capital, class and production as natural categories and existing independently of representation and discursive practices, finds critique in the cultural economy literature. Within this literature, Amin and Thrift (2004, p. xii) note that 'production, distribution and accumulation of resources have always been a cultural performance'. In other words, economic objects are constituted through the discourse used to describe them. 'Culture' is, according to du Gay and Pryke, not a logic or sphere, opposed to 'politics' or 'economics', but is exactly the way in which we are not 'natural, living, social, religious, economic or political beings' (du Gay and Pryke, 2002, pp. 4–5). In such a way, cultural economy is anti-essentialist and further, opposed to universal accounts of human beings. Such an approach seeks to disturb any superficial and wholly artificial separation of culture from economy and attends to the 'empirical and practical' ways in which culture has been used in particular institutional or political contexts (Aitken, 2007, p. 39). The cultural political economy account emphasizes the geographical specificity of individual central banks (Conti-Brown, 2017). For example, in muddying the waters between political and cultural economy, Benjamin Lee (2016) has recently provided a performative reading of Marx's

Capital, in which the way that value arbitrage creates capitalist profit, and the continuous drive towards the capture of relative surplus value through technical innovation, depresses the market price for labour in an 'arbitrage driven performative chiasmus'. This is not to say that the techno-cultural explanation of performativity entirely denies the surrounding context of 'other biological, industrial, and political forces'. As Christophers (2014, p. 18) puts it, 'economics alone' is demonstrably 'not enough' to make the market what it is; it is 'necessary but not sufficient'. Instead, the weaker performative claim needs to be that 'economics' or discourses 'format markets in such a way as to make' their 'representations of those markets *more true*'. In advocating a 'weak' performativity, Christophers makes the case that performative 'effects follow only when certain other kinds of conditions are in place'. Related to this is a point I take from Peter Conti-Brown's (2017) approach to the Federal Reserve, which throws into doubt the ability to generate a general conceptualization of the 'central bank' precisely because we must consider the 'space within which' individual central banks operate. In other words, an appreciation of the specific historical context of London as a global financial centre is fundamentally important.

The City of London

The choice of the Bank of England is not merely down to the institution itself; rather, it is the historical and geographical embedding of the Bank within London's financial district that is of interest here. In his exhaustive studies of the City of London, Kynaston (2011) makes it clear that the eighteenth-century City revolved around shipping and mercantile activities. Credit facilitated trade, and merchants such as Barings took on financial functions and would eventually be referred to as 'merchant banks'. Indeed, Kynaston is at pains to remind us that at this very same time the Bank of England was essentially a profit-making bank run by merchants on behalf of the mercantile rather than the banking community (Kynaston, 2011, p. 12). As Kynaston memorably puts it, the Bank of England, then, was 'the merchant bank supreme'. Mervyn King attests to this relationship between the Bank of England and sea-bound trade when he recalls that:

> In the early years of the Bank of England, there were unexpected shifts in the demand for money and credit resulting from uncertain arrival times in the port of London of ships laden with commodities from all over the world. The uncertainty derived from changes in the direction and speed of the wind carrying ships up the Thames to the port of London. Hence the Court Room of the Bank of England contained a weather vane which provided an accurate guide to these shifts in money demand – the weather vane is there to this day, and it still works.
>
> (King, 2001, p. 173)

Further, new banks needed to relocate to within ten-minutes' walk of the Bank of England and the latter enjoyed membership of what Geoffrey Ingham (1984) has called the 'City – Bank of England – Treasury nexus' in running the British economy. During this period, London emerged as World Financial Centre by usurping Amsterdam in the early part of the seventeenth century after the breakdown of Dutch and British diplomatic relations prevented London based banks from being a lender of last resort for banks such as the Royal Exchange Bank and Farelinks. The Napoleonic Wars had the further impact of unsettling the community of financiers who resided in Amsterdam, leading to migration to the emergent, yet much more stable, financial centre of London (Langley, 2002). The relationship between City of London, Bank of England and the Treasury served the interest of finance well during this period. Both the industrial revolution and the imperial expansion of Britain consolidated London's condition of a liquid source of global credit. The maturation of London as a financial centre saw the development of deep capital and money markets, with sterling denominated credit becoming the oil in the wheels of two-thirds of world trade (Langley, 2002).

Just as war had served to disrupt Amsterdam's preeminent position as a World Financial Centre, the First World War saw a large amount of financial business move to New York and although many customers from the colonies returned to London in 1918, London had been weakened to the extent that it was not able to manage the central European sovereign debt and banking crisis in 1931. London's position as a global financial centre fluctuated during the second half of the twentieth century, again buttressed by its ability, at different times, to command deposits which could be extended as credit elsewhere. Initially overshadowed by New York, in the 1950s and 1960s London established itself as an offshore market for dollar denominated accounts, circumventing both interest rate restrictions within the United States and capital controls on sterling leaving the United Kingdom[3] (Strange, 1994). And while there has been debate around the territorial status of the Eurodollar market (Amato and Fantacci, 2011), the more prosaic point here is that London once again became a locus for global credit practices. Nonetheless, London's position as the leading financial centre was by no means secure and during the 1970s structural changes in the global financial architecture, such as freeing up of capital controls, the revolution in informational technology, and global innovation in credit practices – such as disintermediation and securitization[4] – left London's financial centre increasingly antiquated and inefficient (Leyshon and Thrift, 1997). Reminiscent of the way that London returned to prominence with Eurodollar markets, the British state led efforts to revive London's competitiveness through a restructuring of the regulatory environment, known as the Big Bang,[5] which was completed in 1986.

In the period following the Big Bang, London has established itself as a leading centre for derivatives. Regulatory environment, position between the United States and the European Union and sophisticated legal, accountancy and marketing available in the City of London have contributed to this boon in London based derivative trading (Clark, 2002). In 2013, the United Kingdom (read London) had just under 50 per cent of the average daily turnover by notional value of global OTC interest rate derivatives denominated in US dollars.

At the same time, London had the greatest share of daily turnover by notional value of foreign exchange derivatives, for contracts denominated in euro *and* US dollars (House of Lords, Select Committee 2016). As Tony Norfield (2016) compellingly argues, London is a global financial power today on the basis of 'the relative size of the international assets and liabilities of banks operating in particular countries'. Norfield makes the point that both being able to borrow (liabilities) and lend (assets) are reflections of power because it is a global creditor yet also respected sufficiently by other global lenders. The argument I am developing, then, is that the geographical position of the Bank of England within the City of London, and the City's own position in global credit and derivative practices, should interest us precisely because geographers of money and finance have extensively investigated the many ways in which financial knowledge and services agglomerate or cluster in what are known as 'global financial centres' (Cook *et al.*, 2007). Clustering produces economies of scale, as well as reduced temporal and spatial frictions, due to a spatial proximity which is especially valuable to market participants and business organizations which are both relentlessly hungry for information and new contacts (Thrift, 1994). By way of suggestive metaphor, Gordon Clark (2005) considers money to 'flow like mercury', in no small part due to its distinct tendency to run together and pool.

Finance/security and credit

London's historical transformation from centre of world credit practices to global derivatives centre is important for our purposes precisely because of the relationship between security and the derivative. Derivatives are some 4,000 years old and are essentially a contract between two parties – about a future transaction relating to an underlying commodity or asset (Wigan, 2009). Some characteristic of an asset is traded without either of the parties needing to own the underlying asset. However, the price of such a derivative is determined by the price of the underlying. Arguably at the heart of the so-called 'innovations' in global finance that preceded the 2007–2009 Global Crisis (Engelen *et al.*, 2011), financial derivatives gained notoriety in the Anglo-American world with Warren Buffett's (2003) memorable and popular epithet that they were 'Financial Weapons of Mass Destruction'. And while this may be viewed as merely memorable rhetoric there is, however, an increasing understanding in both critical finance and security studies that the merging together of the worlds of derivative finance and security hints at something more meaningful and substantive (Amoore, 2011). Instead, and from the vantage point of the finance/security literature, Buffett's words seem particularly prescient (Martin, 2007). In other words, contemporary financial and security risk management cannot be easily isolated and are instead imbricated in a series of causal, instrumental and conceptual interrelations (de Goede, 2010). In such a way, the derivative logic is a security logic because one element of any object can be abstracted away from risk associated with ownership of the underlying object. As noted by authors such as Martin (2007) and Amoore (2013), the derivative has a 'security' logic precisely because the reward characteristics of the derivative are 'indifferent' to the underlying risk. For Martin (2007), this was a feature of imperial American war, oriented towards removing oil from underlying territory without ownership of sovereign Iraqi soil. On Amoore's terms, modern security operates through the data derivative, in which possible futures are first eviscerated from their underlying probabilities of occurring and second acted on in the present as if they had a reality.

More than this, derivatives are 'fungible globules of risk', securing by offsetting uncertainty and risk both temporally and spatially (Wigan, 2009). And, in the case of the credit derivatives which take centre stage in the analysis of Chapter 4, we must attend to the distinct spatiality of credit and debt practices. A credit derivative is a contract which exchanges the default risk of a loan or income stream. One can trade the risk of a mortgage without owning the bricks and mortar to which the mortgage is attached. Social relations of credit and debt can therefore become both extended and complicated. As Chris Harker (2017) has recently noted, credit and debt are topological[6] precisely because of the need to draw often disparate parties together within a creditor/debtor contract and relationship. In other words, the 'far becomes near' through the credit contract (Martin, 2011, p. 159). The primacy that London has held in derivatives markets over the 21 years this book covers means, then, that it has been drawn into, and embedded within, global relations of risk transfer and management. For example, this occurs in a completed market for credit risk, where default risk is spread to those nodes most able to bear it. A completed market for credit risk is one that is secure. A completed market, then, is not a circuit or a flat surface, but, instead, is a series of folds, with some areas bearing the weight of credit risk more than others (Allen, 2011). In keeping with discussions of security in the introduction, credit derivatives involve security in terms of the continuity of the processes of credit creation and the circulation of the very financial instruments that embody default risk (Langley, 2015, p. 30). Ultimately, the embeddedness of the Bank of England within the City of London, the idea that financial knowledge agglomerates and the significance of London for derivatives trading are all conceptual parts of an argument that the Bank of England is at the heart of a financial, cultural and informational cluster concerned with risk management through derivatives.

Conclusions

This chapter began by introducing the reader to the specific developments in the governance structures and regulatory responsibilities of the Bank of England over the period of study.

Then, this chapter situated the present study within a literature addressing power in central banking. Here I categorized this literature as being divided into four parts: functional, structural, social constructivist and performative. This study fits into the latter camp, but, takes the concept of performativity forward in ways not already explored in the existing literature.

Third, this chapter has foregrounded and justified the focus on the Bank of England on the basis of a unique set of historical circumstances. The emergence of the Bank as a research institute, the development of financial supervision powers and the embeddedness of the Bank in a financial centre oriented towards derivative finance marks out the Bank of England as being of particular interest to research exploring the relationship between speculation and security. Fourth and finally, this chapter foregrounded the importance of credit derivatives for a study of finance and security. The next chapter is the first of two which expound the two key theoretical pivots of the book, focusing first on money cultures.

Notes

1 Previously, the Bank of England had been carrying out stress testing but the results were never made public (Research Interview with former Bank of England employee, 22 November 2016).
2 With the notable exceptions of Langley (2015) and Conti-Brown (2017). Siklos (2017), for example, provides an excellent account of changing trajectories in central banking over the ten years since the crisis, but the account of financial governance hinges on its link to the 'real economy' and monetary policy tools.
3 The Bretton Woods international capital controls prevented British banks from extending sterling credit overseas, while in the United States, the interest earned on bank deposits was capped by 'Regulation Q' of the New Deal regulations (Nocera, 1994). Dollars placed in Eurodollar accounts could earn higher interest repayments while also being lent to the rest of the world.
4 Disintermediation refers to lending by non-bank institutions. Securitization refers to the process through which an issuer engineers a financial instrument by combining other financial assets and selling different tiers of the repackaged assets to investors.
5 There were three key regulatory changes within the Big Bang revolution:

   (a) the abolition of minimum fixed commissions on trades.
   (b) the end of the separation between those who traded stocks and shares and those who advised investors.
   (c) the acceptance of the ownership of UK brokers by foreign firms.

6 Here Harker notes that, following Nietzsche (1887), critical studies of debt have focused primarily on its 'infinite' or 'indefinite' temporality (Deleuze and Guattari, 1983; Lazzarato, 2012; Stimilli, 2017).

References

Aitken, R. 2007. *Performing Capital: towards a cultural economy of popular and global finance.* Basingstoke: Palgrave Macmillan.
Allen, J. 2011. 'Topological twists: Power's shifting geographies'. *Dialogues in Human Geography* 1(3), pp. 283–298.
Allen, J. and Pryke, M. 1999. 'Money cultures after Georg Simmel: mobility, movement, and identity'. *Environment and Planning D: Society and Space* 17(1): 51–68.
Amato, M., and Fantacci, L. 2013. *The End of Finance.* New York: John Wiley & Sons.
Amin, A., and Thrift, N. 2004. *The Blackwell Cultural Economy Reader.* Oxford: Blackwell.
Amoore, L. 2011. 'Data derivatives on the emergence of a security risk calculus for our times'. *Theory, Culture & Society* 28(6), pp. 24–43.

Amoore, L. 2013. *The Politics of Possibility: Risk and security beyond probability.* Durham NC: Duke University Press.

Bank of England. 2016. *The Financial Policy Committee's framework for the systemic risk buffer.* [pdf] Available at: www.bankofengland.co.uk/financialstability/Documents/fpc/srbf_cp260516.pdf (Accessed 1 June 2017).

Bank of England. Research Interview with former Bank of England Employee, 22 November 2016.

Bank of England, n.d *a*, 'Aims and Objectives'. [Online] Available at: www.bankof england.co.uk/financialstability/Pages/role/risk_reduction/srr/aims.aspx (Accessed 28 September 2017).

Bank of England, n.d *b*, 'Historical Financial Stability Report'. [Online] Available at: www.bankofengland.co.uk/archive/Pages/digitalcontent/historicpubs/fsr.aspx (Accessed 28 September 2017).

Beckert, J. 2016. *Imagined Futures: Fictional expectations and capitalist dynamics.* Cambridge MA: Harvard University Press.

Bernanke, B., Laubach, T., Mishkin, F.S. and Posen, A.S. 1999. *Inflation targeting.* Princeton NJ: Princeton University Press.

Best, J. 2008. 'Ambiguity, Uncertainty, and Risk: Rethinking Indeterminacy'. *International Political Sociology* 2(4), pp. 355–374.

Best, J., and Paterson, M. 2010. *Cultural Political Economy.* Abingdon: Routledge.

Bowman, A., Erturk, I., Froud, J. and Johal, S. 2012. 'Central bank-led capitalism'. *Seattle UL Rev.* 36, pp. 455–487.

Braun, B. 2015. 'Governing the future: the European Central Bank's expectation management during the Great Moderation'. *Economy and Society* 44(3), pp. 367–391.

Braun, B. 2016. 'Speaking to the people? Money, trust, and central bank legitimacy in the age of quantitative easing'. *Review of International Political Economy* 23(6), pp. 1064–1092.

Buffett, W. 2003. 'Letter to Berkshire Hathaway's shareholders', 21 February 2003. [pdf] Available at: www.berkshirehathaway.com/letters/2002pdf.pdf (Accessed 15 May 2015).

Butler, J. 1997. *Excitable speech: A politics of the performative.* Abingdon: Routledge.

Callon, M. 2007. 'What does it mean to say that economics is performative?'. In MacKenzie, D., Muniesa, F., and Siu, L. (eds.). *Do Economists Make Markets? On the Performativity of Economics.* Princeton: Princeton University Press, pp. 311–357.

Christophers, B. 2014. 'From Marx to market and back again: Performing the economy'. *Geoforum* 57, pp. 12–20.

Clark, G.L. 2002. 'London in the European financial services industry: locational advantage and product complementarities'. *Journal of Economic Geography* 29(4), pp. 433–453.

Clark, G.L. 2005. 'Money flows like mercury: the geography of global finance'. *Geografiska Annaler: Series B, Human Geography* 87(2), pp. 99–112.

Conaghan, D. 2012. *The Bank: inside the Bank of England.* London: Biteback Publishing.

Conti-Brown, Peter. 2017. *The power and independence of the Federal Reserve.* Princeton NJ: Princeton University Press.

Cook, G., Pandit, N., Beaverstock, J., Taylor, P. and Pain, K. 2007. 'The role of location in knowledge creation and diffusion: evidence of centripetal and centrifugal forces in the City of London financial services agglomeration'. *Environment and Planning A* 39(6), pp. 1325–1345.

Davies, H., and Green, D. 2010. *Banking on the future: the fall and rise of central banking.* Princeton NJ: Princeton University Press.

Deleuze, G., and Guattari, F. 1983. *Capitalism and Schizophrenia: Anti-Oedipus*, Trans. by Hurley, R., Seem, M. and Lane, H.R. Minneapolis: University of Minnesota Press.

Dodd, N. 2014. *The Social Life of Money*. Princeton NJ: Princeton University Press.

Engelen, E., Erturk, I., Froud, J., Johal, S., Leaver, A., Moran, M., Nilsson, A., and Williams, K. 2011. *After the great complacence: Financial crisis and the politics of reform*. Oxford: Oxford University Press.

Finnemore, M., and Sikkink, K. 1998. 'International norm dynamics and political change'. *International organization* 52(4), pp. 887–917.

Fischer, S. 2005. *IMF Essays from a Time of Crisis: The International Financial System, Stabilization, and Development*. Cambridge MA: MIT Books. [e-book] Available at: https//ideas.repec.org/b/mtp/titles/0262562162.html (Accessed 10 October 2013).

Former Bank of England employee. Research Interview, 22 November 2016. London.

Foucault, M. 1970. *The Order of Things*. New York: Pantheon Books.

Foucault, M. 2014. *Wrong-doing, truth-telling: the function of avowal in justice*. Chicago IL: University of Chicago Press.

du Gay, P., and Pryke, M (eds). 2002. *Cultural Economy: Cultural analysis and commercial life*. London: Sage.

Global Financial Stability Board. n.d. 'Our Mandate'. [online] Available at: www.fsb.org/about/ (Accessed 28 September 2017).

de Goede, M. 2003. 'Beyond economism in international political economy'. *Review of International Studies* 29(1), pp. 79–97.

de Goede, M. 2005. *Virtue, Fortune and Faith: A genealogy of finance*. Minneapolis: University of Minnesota Press.

de Goede, M. 2010. 'Financial Security'. In Burgess, J.P., (ed.) *The Routledge Handbook of the New Security Studies*. Abingdon: Routledge, pp. 100–109.

de Goede, M. 2012. *Speculative Security: The politics of pursuing terrorist monies*. Minneapolis: University of Minnesota Press.

Goffman, E. 1959. *The presentation of self in everyday life*. Garden City, NY: Anchor.

Graeme, G., and Wright, J. 2000. 'Open mouth operations'. *Journal of Monetary Economics* 46(2), pp. 489–516.

Hardy, C., and Thomas, R. 2015. 'Discourse in a material world'. *Journal of Management Studies* vol. 52(5), pp. 680–696.

Harker, C. 2017. 'Debt space: topologies, ecologies and Ramallah, Palestine'. *Environment and planning D: Society and Space* 35(4), pp. 600–619.

Harvey, D. 2006. *The Limits to Capital (Second Edition)*. London: Verso.

Harvey, D. 2010. *The Enigma of Capital and the Crises of Capitalism*. London: Profile Books.

Haas, P. 1992. 'Introduction: epistemic communities and international policy coordination'. *International organization* 46(1), pp. 1–35.

Holmes, D. 2009. 'Economy of Words'. *Cultural Anthropology* 24(3), pp. 381–419.

Holmes, D. 2014. *Economy of Words: Communicative imperatives in central banks*. Chicago IL: University of Chicago Press.

House of Lords Select Committee on European Union. 2016. *Brexit: Financial Services 9th Report of Session 2016–17* – HL Paper 81. [online] Available at https://publications.parliament.uk/pa/ld201617/ldselect/ldeucom/81/8102.htm (Accessed 10 September 2017).

Ingham, G. 1984. 'The City's Impact: The State, Dominant Class, and Financial System', in Ingham, G., *Capitalism divided?: the City and industry in British social development*. Basingstoke: Macmillan, pp. 128–151.

Ingham, G. 2004. *The Nature of Money.* Cambridge: Polity.

Jacobs, L.R., and King, D. 2016. *Fed Power: How Finance Wins.* Oxford: Oxford University Press.

Jessop, B. 2006. 'Spatial fixes, temporal fixes and spatio-temporal fixes'. In Castree, N., and Gregory, D. (eds.) *David Harvey: a Critical Reader.* Oxford: Blackwell, pp. 142–166.

Jessop, B. 2010. 'The 'Return' of the National State in the Current Crisis of the World Market', *Capital and Class 34*(1), pp. 38–43.

King, M. 2001. 'No Money, no Inflation', paper presented to the 'Festschrift in honour of Professor Charles Goodhart' held at the Bank of England on 15th November 2001. [pdf] Available at: www.bankofengland.co.uk/archive/Documents/historicpubs/qb/2002/qb020203.pdf (Accessed 9 February 2017).

Knafo, S. 2013. *The Making of Modern Finance: liberal governance and the gold standard.* Abingdon: Routledge.

Krippner, G. 2007. 'The making of US monetary policy: Central bank transparency and the neoliberal dilemma'. *Theory and Society* 36(6), pp. 477–513.

Kynaston, D. 2011. *City of London: the history.* London: Random House.

Langley, P. 2002. *World financial orders: an historical international political economy.* Abingdon: Routledge.

Langley, P. 2013. 'Anticipating uncertainty, reviving risk? On the stress testing of finance in crisis'. *Economy and Society* 42(1), pp. 51–73.

Langley, P. 2015. *Liquidity Lost: The Governance of the Global Financial Crisis.* Oxford: Oxford University Press.

Lazzarato, M. 2012. *The Making of the Indebted Man: An Essay on the Neoliberal Condition*, trans. Jordan, J.D. New York: Semiotext (e).

Lee, B. 2016. 'From Primitives to Derivatives', in Lee, B., and Martin, R. (eds.) *Derivatives and the Wealth of Societies.* Chicago Il: Chicago University Press, pp. 82–141.

Lewin, S. 2017. *Regulated organizations: responding to and managing regulatory change.* (Unpublished Doctoral Thesis Submitted to the London School of Economics).

Leyshon, A., and Thrift, N. 1997. *Money/Space: Geographies of monetary transformation.* Abingdon: Routledge.

Mann, G. 2010. 'Hobbes' redoubt? Toward a geography of monetary policy'. *Progress in Human Geography* 34(5), pp. 601–625.

Mann, G. 2013. *Disassembly Required: A Field Guide to Actually Existing Capitalism.* Edinburgh: AK Press.

Martin, R. 2007. An *Empire of Indifference: American War and the Financial Logic of Risk Management.* Durham, NC: Duke University Press.

Martin, R. 2011. 'Taking an administrative turn: Derivative logics for a recharged humanities'. *Representations* 116(1), pp. 156–176.

Maxfield, S. 1997. *The International Political Economy of Central Banking in Developing Countries.* Princeton: NJ: Princeton University Press.

McCormack, D. 2012. 'Governing economic futures through the war on inflation'. *Environment and Planning A* 44(7), pp. 1536–1553.

McCormack, D. 2015. 'Governing inflation: Price and atmospheres of emergency'. *Theory, Culture & Society* 32(2), pp. 131–154.

Nietzsche, F. 1887 [1996]. *On the Genealogy of Morals.* Oxford: Oxford Paperbacks.

Nocera, J. 1994. *A Piece of the Action: How the Middle Class Joined the Money Class.* New York: Simon and Schuster.

Nordhaus, W. 1975. 'The political business cycle'. *The Review of Economic Studies* 42(2), pp. 169–190.

Norfield, T. 2016. *The City: London and the Global Power of Finance*. London: Verso.

Siklos, P.L. 2017. *Central Banks into the Breach: From Triumph to Crisis and the Road Ahead*. Oxford: Oxford University Press.

Simmel, G. (1900) [2011]. *The Philosophy of Money*. Abingdon: Routledge.

Smart, G. 2006. *Writing the economy: Activity, genre and technology in the world of banking*. London: Equinox.

Stenfors, A. 2017. *Barometer of fear: An insider's account of rogue trading and the greatest banking scandal in history*. London: Zed Books.

Stimilli, E. 2017. *The Debt of the Living: Ascesis and Capitalism*. New York: SUNY Press.

Strange, S. 1994. 'From Bretton Woods to the Casino Economy'. In Corbridge, S., Martin, R., and Thrift, N., (eds.) *Money, Power, and Space*. Oxford: Blackwell, pp. 49–62.

Thrift, N. 1994. 'On the Social and Cultural determinants of International Financial Centres: the Case of the City of London'. In Corbridge, S., Martin, R., and Thrift, N. (eds.), *Money, Power, and Space*. Oxford: Blackwell, pp. 327–355.

Valdez, S., and Molyneux, P. 2010. *An introduction to global financial markets*. Basingstoke: Palgrave Macmillan.

Vogl, J. 2015. *The Ascendancy of Finance*. Cambridge: Polity.

Wigan, D. 2009. 'Financialisation and derivatives: Constructing an artifice of indifference'. *Competition & Change* 13(2), pp. 157–172.

2 Money cultures

Introduction: money, calculation and culture?

As controversial and contested as the ontology of money is, 'money' nonetheless has been identified by a number of analytic accounts as being anything that functions as a store of value, unit of account, medium of exchange and social relation of credit and debt (Dodd, 1994; Ingham, 1996; Fine and Lapavitsas, 2000; Zelizer, 2000). Crucial to these functional operations is money's ability to measure and quantify. For this reason, money, observes Georg Simmel, 'turned the world into an arithmetic problem' (Zelizer, 1997, p. 6). In the first part of his *Philosophy of Money* (1900), Simmel argues that money is 'characterized' by its 'complete indifference to individual qualities' and further, money 'measures all objects with merciless objectivity'. For Simmel here, calculation equates to the rationalization and homogenization of culture. In this book, I advance a cultural political economy account which disputes this a-cultural account when thinking about the calculation, pricing and transfer of risk in the form of financial instruments. Calculation and value are then seen as cultural processes (Zelizer, 1997; Muniesa *et al.*, 2017). The imperative, then, is to follow Simmel's (1900) further insight that questions concerning the ontology of money are less prescient than what the historical and cultural 'phenomenon of money reveals about human existence and the conditions of reflection on that existence' (Goodstein, 2017, p. 170). The route I take to pursue this is through cultural approaches to money and finance.

'Cultural economy' is a broadly conceived label for an interdisciplinary range of approaches including (but not restricted to) global political economy, human geography, business studies, anthropology and economic sociology (Amin and Thrift, 2002). As such, cultural economy can be thought of as the diverse responses of a wide range of scholars of the economy to the 'cultural turn' in social theory (Langley, 2015, p. 2). Such scholarship is provoked by a firm belief that something called 'culture is both somehow critical to understanding what is happening to, as well as to practically intervening in, contemporary economic and organizational life' (du Gay and Pryke, 2002, p. 1). The purportedly strict inter-disciplinary distinctions between cultural and political economy overlap and 'interact' because of 'the cultural dimensions of "the economy", the economic aspects of "culture" and the "political" character of both' (Zelizer, 2011, p. 377; Best and Paterson, 2010, p. 2); du Gay and Pryke (2002, p. 9) go onto argue that 'there is no reason to assume that these' normative and technical 'regimes are founded on any prior, general analytic distinction or opposition between "culture" and something else'.

On such an approach, some activity that may be thought of as purely 'quant-itative', such as calculation, is 'shaped by both culture and context' (Dodd, 2014, p. 297). Money is neither, to borrow a phrase from Viviana Zelizer (1997, p. 18), 'culturally neutral or socially anonymous'. This chapter will set out three steps towards an analytic of money culture and seeks to situate the argument in rela-tion to existing work in political economy, economic geography and economic sociology. The first section builds on the cultural turn in risk studies to propose a cultural economy of financial risk management. Building on this initial move, the second section attends to the spatiality of financial risk management. It is argued that risk is virtual in the sense that it only has reality in practice. Then, by drawing on geographical notions of functional space and mobility, this section introduces Randy Martin's (2015) recent work on movement and finance to argue that contemporary financial risk management operates through and hinges on the mobilization of risk in the form of financial instruments.

The third section engages with geographers who, inspired by the work of Simmel (1900), have thought about the relationship between movement of money and financial instruments and the cultural meanings attributed to money (Allen and Pryke, 1999; Langley, 2017). The argument developed then is that money cultures at the Bank of England have supervened on the mobilization of risk in the financial system.

Finance, risk and the cultural turn

Uncertainty about the future means that risk is inherent in financial agreements such as contracts (Esposito, 2011). At its earliest iteration, financial risk referred to the 'exposure to the possibility of *future* financial loss' (Christophers, 2017, p. 1119 *emphasis added*). For example, commodity derivatives have a 4,000-year lineage as they were designed to lock in prices and secure against the risk of price fluctuations for agricultural products (Wigan, 2009). Likewise, the aforementioned intimate relationship between credit and insurance services and seaborne trade promulgated the moniker 'merchant banking'. Merchants needed credit to fund operations that sought to yield profit in the future, while insurance was needed in the face of the uncertain future of weather and sea conditions (Lobo-Guerrero, 2010). Risk, then, emerged as a technology for governing the future (Yadav, 2008). The two faces of risk, of opportunity and threat, were key to understanding the functionality of finance in early capitalism (Wigan, 2009).

Risk in finance can be thought about using either one of two paradigms of risk. The first of these approaches is a 'sociological account' for which risk is 'viewed within a … narrative of phases of modernity and as a feature of the ontological condition of humans within' the contemporary world (Dean, 2010,

p. 207). For this approach, contemporary risks are the 'manufactured ... by-products of an industrial machine which needs a new politics to control it' (Hutter and Power, 2005, p. 1). In short, it is a principle which characterizes types of society and as such, is an actually existing global entity (Dean, 2010, p. 207). Accounts such as Watson (2007) are situated in the tradition of Ulrich Beck's *Risk Society* (1992). On this approach, risk is characterized as a very real threat to financial stability. Within this 'financial risk society' (Watson, 2007, p. 62), the unprecedented and traumatic stock market crash of 1987 could be taken as an example of the manifestation of the many and varied material risks associated with investing and trading securities.[1]

The second overarching approach to risk is anchored in a critical body of scholarship for which 'risk cannot be isolated as a tangible entity or event' (Amoore, 2013, p. 7). As Best (2010, p. 41) puts it, risks 'are human inventions, historically linked to the development of statistical and actuarial methods'. As such, 'risk management is performative', rather than descriptive, 'because the way organizations depict their risks has a significant effect on the way they will, eventually, react to events and other actors' and 'an influential risk management system will bring about institutionalized patterns of risk embodiment' (Millo and MacKenzie, 2009, p. 639). Much of the impetus for this conception of risk stemmed from the English language publication in 1991 of 'Lecture Four' of Foucault's *Security, Territory, Population* lecture series at the College de France in the late 1970s. Foucault here is preoccupied with the 'ensemble formed by the institutions, procedures, analyses and reflections, the calculations and tactics, that allow the exercise of this very specific albeit complex form of power' (1979, p. 20).

Critical accountancy studies seized upon the way that insurance, social security and public health work through 'logics of calculability and the management of populations at an aggregate level, notably through regulation in terms of statistical distributions about a mean' (O'Malley, 1992, p. 253).[2] For this line of reasoning, the governance of economic life through the assigning of probabilities to future states of the world involves considerable investment in 'intellectual technologies' that render aspects of existence amenable to inscription and calculation. Such 'governmentality' has a 'characteristically programmatic form, and that it is inextricably bound to the invention and evaluation of technologies that seek to give it effect' (Miller and Rose, 1990, p. 1). And indeed, such Foucauldian analysis has been made of the governance of risk in international finance. For Vikash Yadav (2008), derivative finance has long operated through 'a series of possible and probable events', evaluating comparative cost and specifying 'the optimal mean within a tolerable bandwidth of variation or compliance' (Yadav, 2008, p. 60). Crucially though, while on the one hand Yadav (2008, pp. 39–40) seeks to shed light on 'political economy of risk', on the other hand he nods to the cultural nature of such an endeavour when he argues that:

> the categories of risk are always only a possible instantiation of risk. Risk materializes wherever experts manage to locate a particular class of risk.

Of course, the risk assessment expert does not merely passively register risk and devise instruments against it; he also actively produces risk.

The argument, then, is that risk is produced, rather than discovered, and that this is a cultural phenomenon. The type of risks that are attended to, then, very much depend on culture and perception (Hood *et al.*, 2001). Indeed, critical cultural scholarship has long argued that risk is incorporated in popular financial culture through activities such as card games (Goggin, 2012). Similarly, the idea that risk is culturally gendered, in such a way that 'Lady Credit' or 'Fortuna' must be mastered, pervades western literature from the early modern period onwards through the work of authors and artists such as Defoe, Hogarth and Gilray (de Goede, 2005; Crosthwaite *et al.*, 2014). In *Wall Street Women*, Melissa Fisher (2012) argues that attitudes towards risk evince gendered patterns, whereby women trying to establish themselves in investment banking adopt the risk tolerant attitude of male traders. Finance, then, 'culturalizes risk by rendering it a calculable[3] gain from an expected outcome' (Martin, 2009, p. 111). But, this is not to say that I pursue the route of finding risk practices within cultural forms. Instead, the task here is to find the cultural forms within risk practices per se.

Indeed, Beck himself makes a cultural turn of sorts. In his *World at Risk* (2009), risk culture is a 'post-religious, quasi-religious belief', the very real risks attached to modern life. Here Beck contrasts 'European' risk culture with 'American' risk culture. For the former, risk issues such as 'climate change' and financial mobility have a key importance. For the latter, 'terrorism' is thought to be the fundamental risk issue. And, while intuitively there is something useful in Beck's formulation, he ascribes regional culture a homogeneity that is not necessarily there. For example, it is hard to say that policy makers in the United Kingdom have the same risk culture to financial regulation that the French do. Further, and critically, it makes little sense to argue that views on risk management are aligned within regulators and banks in the same jurisdiction, when interests and pay-offs are so clearly misaligned (Confidential Research Interview, 13 September 2016). Instead, I want to invoke 'contemporary risk culture' at the more granular and technical level. The realism about risk that Beck offers is not suitable for a critical account in which risk is a technology for governing the future (Yadav, 2008).

For our present purposes, risk cultures are the amalgam of ideas, practices and techniques employed by risk professionals in an institution *both* in private and *in* public. This is different to Black's (2002) conception of 'regulatory identity', which is created by 'communications between all those involved in the regulatory process', most notably between regulator and regulated. As such this appears to create a binary between the two parts of the relationship. Instead, the culture I refer to here is an attitude towards an underlying (virtual) entity, risk. Thus, the account offered here aligns risk culture more closely with a body of thought for which 'a set of shared values and supporting social institutions is biased towards highlighting certain risks and downplaying others' (Douglas and Wildavsky, 1983). This does not refer to cultures of behaviours in finance that could be described as 'risky', as Chappe *et al.* (2012) have it, but rather, refers to intentional attitudes to what is understood as risk. Douglas (1986, p. 67) argues that culture is 'the publicly shared collections of principles and values used … to justify behavior' and that cultures are products of organizations and social institutions. The 'cultures' that I discuss in this book, then, are the shared meanings that emerge *across both*, and as *commonalties between*, the public arena *and* behind the scenes. One important qualification here is to return to the issue highlighted in Chapter 1, that financial stability is a global regulatory phenomenon and issue, and so wider regulatory contexts have influenced, and been influenced by, financial cultures at the Bank of England (Lewin, 2017). Studying the Bank of England, then, does also give an insight into wider cultural developments in global risk management.

The association between profession and risk is explored by a sociologically inflected literature for which speculators perform the vital role of 'professional, mercenary risk takers'. As such, speculators are highly skilled 'knowledge workers' who 'interpret a vast, continuous stream of technical data to assess the uncertain futures of bonds, derivatives, commodities' (Wexler, 2010, p. 4). In such a way, organized exchanges of speculation 'bring future hazards under control, allowing banks to forge systemic plans' for firms and clients (Zaloom, 2004, p. 365). Speculators both 'keep under control' and 'escalate their risk' taking skills (Wexler, 2010, p. 4). For Knorr Cetina, speculators are 'co-present observers' in markets, developing a number of 'instruments, strategies and ethnomethods' which makes them closer to 'practical sociologists' than 'rational economic actors'. This sort of knowledge work involves 'assessing what others think and are up to, taking their perspective, imagining that they reflexively, too, expect and counteract our strategies' (Knorr Cetina, 2007, p. 487).

Here I think it is useful to think about risk as being virtual. This is not to conflate risk with computation, the digital or the algorithmic. Instead, this is a claim about the ontology of risk. As discussed in the previous section, risks can be conceived of as being performative. This does not mean that they do not matter; after all, risks come to bear on our decision making in the present. On LiPuma and Lee's (2005, p. 413) account of derivatives, risk is 'abstract' before it is converted or translated into an 'objectified' form through processes of detachment, classification and calculation. And although this is similar to the approach I develop here, there are some key distinctions. First, the distinction LiPuma and Lee draw between 'abstract' and 'objectified risk' obscures the reality that abstract (on their account) or 'virtual' risk has in practice (Arnoldi, 2004, p. 32). On Peter Pelzer's (2013) terms, risk can be a present state of 'what is to come'. In such a way, virtual risk can be acted on and mobilized before it 'crystalizes' or materializes as an instrument. This sense of a distinction between risk and crystallization of risk is essential if an account is to be faithful to contemporary financial risk management. Second, LiPuma and Lee argue that risk is 'detached from the social context that created the risk and the relations in which it is immersed'. This is in keeping with Arnoldi (2004) because these virtual risks are thought to be decoupled from productive processes. This may be because synthetic credit derivatives are fictitious or 'self-referential abstract replicas'; merely benchmarked to themselves rather than 'productive' processes (Rotman, 1987; Cloke, 2009; Maurer, 2002). For Adam Tickell (2000) this detachment from production means that derivatives are essentially volatile and speculative, and are thus both uncertain and dangerous.

There are however, influential political economy authors who are sceptical about the ability of financial derivatives to cleave themselves from the social context from which they originated, namely the purportedly 'productive' economy (Bryan and Rafferty, 2006; Leyshon and Thrift, 2007). For example, while it may be the case that Duncan Wigan (2009, pp. 159, 165) has argued that derivatives 'abstract from any linear relationship to underlying processes of real wealth creation', he still recognizes that 'indifference cannot be absolute since finance cannot unequivocally decouple from a real economy'. The Subprime Crisis demonstrates that purportedly abstract and 'fictitious' derivatives were still tangentially coupled to the bricks and mortar of the construction industry (Cloke, 2009). After all, Leyshon and Thrift (2007) have convincingly argued that this novel fourth circuit of financial innovation 'still requires the existence of mundane but predictable sources of income'. These 'mundane sources of income act as anchors to which the rest of the financial system is attached'. This means that some virtual risks, such as those attached to loan repayments, are not decoupled from the productive economy.

As de Goede (2004, p. 213) puts it, 'financial risk management does not just react to but creates particular definitions of insecurity because, instead of eradicating uncertainty from business ventures', such techniques identify, and invent, 'more and more possible uncertainties to be hedged'. If I read de Goede correctly, then her formulation of contemporary risk culture is close to what Langley (2015, p. 32) calls 'mechanisms of mitigation' in the sense that both authors focus on the conversion of life's 'contingencies and uncertainties' into calculable and tradable risks (de Goede, 2009, p. 307). Such contemporary mechanisms continue to provide the seemingly never-ending search for new and often mundane income streams, such as water bills, which are needed to fuel this financialized capitalization of 'almost everything' (Leyshon and Thrift, 2007; Allen and Pryke, 2013). And, de Goede is exactly right that such risk cultures are transformations in risk and capitalization practices that remain largely invisible to a wider audience. As MacKenzie (2009) argues in the context of 'valuation cultures', different groups within financial institutions make sense of, and form judgement on, financial instruments in contrasting ways. However, what interests me here is not so much the mitigation of uncertainty into risk, but the very process of distributing risks through functional space. It is the key argument of this chapter that we ought to read risk cultures through the posthumous work of Randy Martin (2015) on movement and furthermore combine this with Simmel's (1900) work on the relationship between movement, money and culture.

Functionally spatializing and mobilizing risk

The second strand of this argument focuses on the spatiality of financial risk management. In short, these are practices which are about movement – namely the mobilization of risk. This requires two additional ways of thinking about spatiality, both gleaned from political economists. The first geographical point here is to draw on Benjamin Cohen's distinction between physical and functional space – so that money is conceived of as abstract flows or networks, rather than 'spatial packages' (Cohen, 1998, pp. 16, 22). A second distinction is that made by Matthew Watson when he emphasizes the utility of bracketing of spatial mobility from functional mobility. Capital then, does not flow between the same markets in different financial centres, but between different markets for products that have different functions (Watson, 1999, p. 62).

Here I apply functional mobility to risk. For critical security scholar Louise Amoore (2011), crucial to the way in which the logic of the data derivative circulates in contemporary security practices is how 'the reward characteristics of the derivative are sustained in a way that is *indifferent* to the risks of individual underlying elements' (Amoore, 2013, p. 60 *emphasis added*). The derivative technique divorces attributes of an asset from ownership of the underlying asset – by way of a problematic but effective analogy, I can bet on the result of a horse race without owning the underlying racehorse. In such a way, I am indifferent to all the other considerations that may surround the horse if I did own it. In Amoore's (2011, 2013) writings, future possibilities are eviscerated from underlying probabilities under the auspices of anti-terrorism policing. The derivative is 'overwhelmingly indifferent to the occurrence of specific events' (Amoore, 2013, p. 64). Risk about the imagined future, then, is something that can be made actionable and offset in the present. And this can be applied to everyday life (Martin, 2002). As Amoore (2013, p. 61) elaborates: 'the risks of mortgage default, home repossessions, unemployment and a whole range of life choices are not treated as threats in and of themselves but as sets of relations that can be unbundled, reattached to other elements, and repriced'.

Randy Martin (2015) extends this argument further. If Amoore finds the financial logic emerge in security practices, Martin holds that the logic of both the data and financial derivative is an instantiation of a wider social logic evident in, and extrapolated from, practices traditionally seen as being beyond the economic, such as medicine, grammar and music. Rather than seeing the financial elsewhere, Martin inverts this thinking to argue that the broader 'elsewhere' finds one instantiation in finance. Abstractly, this social logic sees the 'transmission of *some characteristic* from an originating source to a consequent site, expression or manifestation' (Martin, 2012). If the financial derivative then, is a principle in which values are dispersed spatially and offset temporally 'as to distribute their volatilities and consequences' (Martin, Rafferty and Bryan, 2008, p. 129), then the social logic of the derivative refers 'not to a fixed relation between part and whole but to *a collection of attributes that are assembled together in relation to other discernible features of the bodies, or variables, or environmental conditions they encounter'*. The derivative is a 'complex process' or 'act of bundling attributes together' in terms of a 'lateral orientation, which is an effect of intercommensurability' (Martin, 2015, pp. 60, 75 *emphasis added*). For Martin, the social logic of the derivative is the spatial process of mobilizing together different attributes. For example, Martin (2015, p. 144) argues that dance has kinesthetic attributes that are derivative in character. Martin finds that:

> The rhythms and cadences of bodies in motion and the manner in which value circulates through society share mutually constitutive principles of association whose language is poorly articulated and more readily explained as a succession of ideas from exalted individuals. The turn to dance here is meant to make this language of social movement audible, perceptible, sensible, and legible.

And, here Martin gives us an account of hip-hop in which the culture was 'distributed across music, visual art, and dance and the corollary self-organization of youth into their own forms of collectives, whether they were named "gangs", "posses", or "crews"' (Martin, 2015, p. 186). Sampling in music has a derivative logic because it works through 'a derivative ethos for the production, dissemination, and representation of music' (Martin, 2015, p. 188). Martin then, attends to distribution, assembly, collection and dissemination – the full gambit of social oriented movements. Elsewhere Martin (2011, p. 160) argues that derivatives are the 'specifiable and tangible form what is made in accelerating motion'. The social logic of the derivative is such that derivatives can secure by dispersal, moving risk outwards and away in a way that stabilizes the system by relocating risk to areas best suited to bearing it. They allow a trader or client to embrace risk, holding it close. Martin and Amoore give us a means to think about virtual risks as things that can be mobilized, manipulated, moved, gathered and combined. Taking positions, that is to say, arbitraging, hedging or speculating, draws one towards risk or pushes risk away. In less succinct terms, arbitrage, hedging and speculation are about the functional mobilization of risk.

Movement and money cultures

Here I extend the argument further to argue that functionally mobilizing risk has implications for attributing money with social meanings (Allen and Pryke, 1999, p. 61). For example, in the post-Bretton Woods monetary system, the 'money culture' of territorially bound finance became disrupted by finance's novel spatiality and security claims (Cohen, 1998, p. 27; Allen and Pryke, 1999; Langley, 2002; Engelen *et al.*, 2011, p. 46). In the second part of the *Philosophy of Money*, Simmel (1900, p. 388) argues that money may quantify and calculate, but, it also turns 'objectively given quanta of value into a higher quantum of subjectively felt value by change in mere bearer'. In such a way, economic value, Simmel argued, is the 'objectification of subjective values'. Tellingly, geography features in Simmel's analysis because he develops the wider philosophical position that perception and cognition vary over time and place (Goodstein, 2017, p. 68). Simmel makes the case that:

> the formation of values develops with the distance between the consumer and the cause of his enjoyment. The differences in valuation which have to be distinguished as subjective and objective, originate from such variations in distance measured ... in terms of desire, which is engendered by the distance and seeks to overcome it.

Alongside distance, movement and motion are important categories in Simmel's thinking about money. As Simmel writes in an essay which attends to the relationship between money and the 'tempo of life':

> there is simply no clearer symbol than money for the character of the world as absolute movement. The meaning of money lies in it being given away; as soon as it rests, it is no longer money in its specific value and meaning.
> (Simmel, 1897, p. 234)

In other words, money is 'the purest realization of the principle of movement ... expression for all of the concrete and relative effects that money's position in practical life exercises on the determination of life's tempo' (Simmel, 1897, p. 234). While this does initially appear to conflict with his account of quantification that we encountered at the beginning of this chapter, it is important to remember that as a modernist philosopher, Simmel demonstrates 'the viability of multiple, conflicting interpretations of the phenomena that make up human life' (Goodstein, 2017, p. 147).

Financial geographers have been drawn to the spatiality of some of Simmel's observations. One pertinent idea in Simmel is that a social feature of money – such as circulation – appears as an objective property of objects themselves. This occurs through the interplay of 'subjective desire' and 'intersubjective processes of exchange' (Dodd, 2014, pp. 27–29). As Simmel (1900) writes, 'a claim may be considered subjective, while from the subject's point of view it appears to be objective'. This is experienced 'as something independent within our representation and as detached from the function by which it exists in us'. In such a way, 'money literally enriches the lived world' through the 'generative quality of the inter- and transsubjective relations it embodies and fosters' (Goodstein, 2017, p. 180). For Allen and Pryke (1999, pp. 55–60), following and updating Simmel's insights allows them to account for the way that the advent of financial derivatives changed cultural understandings of the pace and rhythm of money. In a slightly later article, these authors argue that the manner in which 'risks interact and the speed of their interaction suggest the emergence' of an intensely experienced 'monetized space-time' (Pryke and Allen, 2000, pp. 265, 281). Langley (2017) and de Goede (2017) have in turn developed this idea to think of 'spatial imaginaries' and, in particular, Langley highlights the way that 'flow charts of the securitization chain' produced a spatial imaginary of the distribution of risk and market completion for credit risk prior to the Global Financial Crisis. Arguing in the same vein, I make the case that the perceived mobilization of risk that the derivatives of the 1990s instantiated, itself facilitated an imperfect financial security through risk dispersal. Fundamental to these securitization techniques were the assumptions of probabilistic reasoning and normality (Foucault, 2007, pp. 35, 70, 87). That is, the risk of trading positions as conceived of in terms of falling into a normal distribution. In other words, the functional spatiality of derivatives and the moving of virtual risks significantly changed notions of financial security. In Part II of this book I develop this argument by tracing an emergence of *speculating on risk* in the development of contemporary investment risk management. At first the Bank of England was relatively ambivalent about the claims of the new financial risk management to secure imperfectly. The Bank took a calculated gamble on investment risk management and lacked precision in its identification of risks. In 2007, the Bank was reasonably relaxed that if it 'did not know' where risk was, then it probably had been 'dispersed beyond the regulated sector' (Tucker, 2007).

In Part III, I chart the development of *speculating for risk*, one of the post-crisis money cultures. And, here I highlight the important ways the tendency towards speculative techniques of securing the future has intensified through appeals to extreme macroeconomic conditions. There are two shifts here. The first is the shift from speculation as the attempt to 'prosper' from the financial stability provided by private risk management to a sense of speculation as knowing and anticipating. Second, and related is the shift away from assumptions of normality to what Amoore (2013, p. 65) calls 'mobile norms' that seek out conditions that go beyond a normal distribution. Importantly, this is not to argue that one money culture simply supplants another, but in some aspects the two coalesce and in others there is a period of contestation, such as that between practices of computing from historical data against subjective probabilities involved in forecasting (Author's Field-notes, 13 May 2016). The key distinction between this culture and what had preceded it was that this culture sought to quantify, specify and map the mobilization of risk with a much greater level of precision and granularity (Bank of England Research Interview, 23 August 2017).

Conclusion

The first of two theoretical chapters, the concern in this chapter has been to bring culture into our analysis of money and financial risk management. The cultural turn is necessary because risk is a product of reiterative calculative practices rather than something discovered by those practices. The second key theoretical step made in this chapter is one which spatializes financial risk management, by attending to the functional mobility of financial instruments, the virtual nature of risk and the way that risk is mobilized (Watson, 1999). Third, the chapter combines the work of Randy Martin and Georg Simmel to appreciate the way that the functional mobility of risk begets cultural understandings of money and risk.

In the following chapter, I go onto foreground the conception of financial performativity underpinning the notion of a money culture. If money culture names the change, then central banking as performed domain goes some way towards explaining the change. In particular, I argue that financial performativity must be conceptualized as layered and open to disruption, improvisation and drama. By linking together money culture with the performed domain, these concepts provide a grid which can be brought to bear on culture at the Bank of England over the period 1996–2017. This is the subject of the discussion presented in Parts II and III of the book respectively.

Notes

1 On one trading day – Monday 19 October 1987 – the Dow Jones Industrial Average fell by 508 points.
2 This literature clusters around *the Foucault Effect (1991)* project which was a reaction to the publication of the 'Governmentality lecture'. See Donzelot,1991; Ewald, 1991; Castel, 1991; Defert, 1991; Miller and Rose, 1990; O'Malley, 1992; Dean, 1999. See Rose *et al.* (2006) for an overview of governmentality and its legacy.
3 This calculative aspect has a significant role to play in the culturally specific distinction between 'speculation' and 'gambling' (See de Goede, 2005).

References

Allen, J., and Pryke, M. 1999. 'Money cultures after Georg Simmel: mobility, movement, and identity'. *Environment and Planning D: Society and Space* 17(1), pp. 51–68.

Allen, J., and Pryke, M. 2013. 'Financialising household water: Thames Water, MEIF, and "ring-fenced" politics'. *Cambridge Journal of Regions, Economy and Society* 6(3), pp. 419–439.

Amin, A., and Thrift, N. 2004. *The Blackwell Cultural Economy Reader*. Oxford: Blackwell.

Amoore, L. 2011. 'Data derivatives: on the emergence of a security risk calculus for our times'. *Theory, Culture & Society* 28(6), pp. 24–43.

Amoore, L. 2013. *The Politics of Possibility: Risk and security beyond probability*. Durham NC: Duke University Press.

Arnoldi, J. 2004. 'Derivatives: Virtual Values and Real Risks'. *Theory, Culture & Society* 21(6), pp. 23–42.

Beck, U. 1992. *Risk society: Towards a new modernity*. London: Sage.

Beck, U. 2009. *World at Risk*. Cambridge: Polity.

Best, J. 2010. 'The Limits of Financial Risk Management: Or what we didn't learn from the Asian Crisis'. *New Political Economy* 15(1), pp. 29–49.

Best, J., and Paterson, M. 2010. *Cultural Political Economy*. Abingdon: Routledge.

Black, J. 2002. 'Regulatory conversations'. *Journal of Law and Society* 29(1), pp. 163–196.

Bryan, D., and Rafferty, M. 2006. 'Financial derivatives: The new gold?'. *Competition & Change* 10(3), pp. 265–282.

Castel, R. 1991. 'From dangerousness to risk'. In Gordon, C., Burchell, G., and Miller, P. (eds.) *The Foucault effect: Studies in governmentality*. London: Wheatsheaf, pp. 281–298.

Chappe, R., Nell, E., and Semmler, W. 2012. 'On the History of the US Financial Culture'. *Geschichte und Gesellschaft. Sonderheft*, pp. 59–84.

Christophers, B. 2017. 'Climate Change and Financial Instability: Risk Disclosure and the Problematics of Neoliberal Governance'. *Annals of the American Association of Geographers* 107(5), pp. 1108–1127.

Cloke, J. 2009. 'An economic wonderland: derivative castles built on sand'. *Critical perspectives on international business* 5(1/2), pp. 107–119.

Cohen, B.J. 1998. *The Geography of Money*. Ithaca: Cornell University Press.

Confidential research interview with former risk manager at a large bank, 13 September 2016. London.

Crosthwaite, P., Knight, P., and Marsh, N. 2014. *Show me the money: the image of finance, 1700 to the present*. Manchester: Manchester University Press.

Dean, M. 2010. *Governmentality: Power and rule in modern society*. London: Sage.

Defert, D. 1991. 'Popular life and insurance technology'. In Gordon, C., Burchell, G., and Miller, P., (eds.) *The Foucault effect: Studies in governmentality*. London: Wheatsheaf, pp. 211–233.

Dodd, N. 1994. *The Sociology of Money: economics, reason and contemporary society*. Cambridge: Polity Press.

Dodd, N. 2014. *The Social Life of Money*. Princeton NJ: Princeton University Press.

Donzelot, J. 1991. 'The Mobilization of Society'. In Gordon, C., Burchell, G., and Miller, P., (eds.) *The Foucault effect: Studies in governmentality*. London: Wheatsheaf, pp. 169–179.

Douglas, M. 1986. *Risk Acceptability according to the Social Science*. Abingdon: Routledge.

Douglas, M., and Wildavsky, A. 1983. *Risk and culture: An essay on the selection of technological and environmental dangers*. Berkeley CA: University of California Press.

Engelen, E., Erturk, I., Froud, J., Johal, S., Leaver, A., Moran, M., Nilsson, A., and Williams, K. 2011. *After the great complacence: Financial crisis and the politics of reform*. Oxford: Oxford University Press.

Esposito, E. 2011. *The Future of Futures: The Time of Money in Financing and Society*. Cheltenham: Edward Elgar Publishing.

Ewald, F. 1991. 'Insurance and risk'. In Gordon, C., Burchell, G., and Miller, P., (eds.) *The Foucault effect: Studies in governmentality*. London: Wheatsheaf, pp. 197–210.

Fine, B., and Lapavitsas, C. 2000. 'Markets and money in social theory: what role for economics?'. *Economy and Society* 29(3), pp. 357–382.

Fisher, M. 2012. *Wall Street Women*. Durham NC: Duke University Press.

Foucault, M. 1979. 'On governmentality'. *Ideology & Consciousness* 6, 5–21.

Foucault, M. 2007. *Security, Territory, Population*. Basingstoke: Palgrave Macmillan.

du Gay, P., and Pryke, M. (eds.) 2002. *Cultural Economy: Cultural analysis and commercial life*. London: Sage.

de Goede, M. 2004. 'Repoliticizing financial risk'. *Economy and Society* 33(2), pp. 197–217.

de Goede, M. 2005. *Virtue, fortune, and Faith: A Genealogy of Finance*. Minneapolis: University of Minnesota Press.

de Goede, M. 2009. 'Finance and the excess. The politics of visibility in the credit crisis', *Zeitschrift für Internationale Beziehungen* 16, pp. 299–310.

de Goede, M. 2017. 'Banks in the Frontline: Assembling Space/Time in Financial Warfare'. In Christophers, B., Leyshon, A., and Mann, G. (eds.) *Money and Finance*

After the Crisis: Critical Thinking for Uncertain Times. New York: Wiley-Blackwell, pp. 117–144.

Goggin, J. 2012. 'Regulating (virtual) subjects: finance, entertainment and games'. *Journal of Cultural Economy* 5(4), pp. 441–456.

Goodstein, E.S. 2017. *Georg Simmel and the Disciplinary Imaginary.* Stanford CA: Stanford University Press.

Gordon, C., Burchell, G., and Miller, P., (eds.) *The Foucault effect: Studies in governmentality.* London: Wheatsheaf.

Hood, C., Rothstein, H., and Baldwin, R. 2001. *The government of risk: Understanding risk regulation regimes.* Oxford: Oxford University Press.

Hutter, B., and Power, M. (eds.). 2005. *Organizational encounters with risk.* Cambridge: Cambridge University Press.

Ingham, G. 1996. 'Money is a social relation'. *Review of Social Economy* 54(4), pp. 507–529.

Knorr Cetina, Karin. 2007. 'Markets as Definitional Practices: A Comment on Charles W. Smith'. *The Canadian Journal of Sociology* 32(4), pp. 487–490.

Langley, P. 2002. *World Financial Orders: an historical international political economy.* Abingdon: Routledge.

Langley, P. 2015. *Liquidity Lost: The Governance of the Global Financial Crisis.* Oxford: Oxford University Press.

Langley, P. 2017. 'Financial Flows: Spatial imaginaries of speculative circulations'. In Christophers, B., Leyshon, A., and Mann, G. *Money and Finance after the Crisis: Critical Thinking for Uncertain Times.* New York: Wiley-Blackwell, pp. 69–90.

Leyshon, A., and Thrift, N. 2007. 'The capitalization of almost everything: The future of finance and capitalism'. *Theory, Culture & Society* 24 (7–8), pp. 97–115.

Lewin, S. 2017. *Regulated organizations: responding to and managing regulatory change.* (Unpublished doctoral thesis submitted to the London School of Economics).

LiPuma, E., and Lee, B. 2005. 'Financial derivatives and the rise of circulation'. *Economy and Society* 34(3), pp. 404–427.

Lobo-Guerrero, L. 2010. *Insuring Security: biopolitics, security and risk.* Abingdon: Routledge.

MacKenzie, D. 2009. 'Beneath all the toxic acronyms lies a basic cultural issue', *Financial Times* 26 November, p. 12. [pdf] Available at: www.sps.ed.ac.uk/__data/assets/pdf_file/0004/36472/11473_PDFonly.pdf (Accessed 24 May 2017).

Martin, R. 2002. *Financialization of daily life.* Philadelphia: Temple University Press.

Martin, R. 2011. 'Taking an administrative turn: Derivative logics for a recharged humanities'. *Representations* 116(1), pp. 156–176.

Martin, R. 2012. 'A precarious dance, a derivative sociality'. *TDR/The Drama Review* 56(4), pp. 62–77.

Martin, R. 2015. *Knowledge LTD: Toward a Social Logic of the Derivative.* Philadelphia: Temple University Press.

Martin, R., Rafferty, M., and Bryan, D. 2008. 'Financialization, risk and labour'. *Competition & Change* 12(2), pp. 120–132.

Maurer, B. 2002. 'Repressed futures: financial derivatives' theological unconscious'. *Economy and Society* 31(1), pp. 15–36.

Miller, P., and Rose, N. 1990. 'Governing economic life'. *Economy and Society* 19(1), pp. 1–31.

Millo, Y., and MacKenzie, D. 2009. 'The usefulness of inaccurate models: Towards an understanding of the emergence of financial risk management'. *Accounting, Organizations and Society* 34(5), pp. 638–653.

Morris, J.H. 2016. *Field-notes* from participant observation at Financial Risk Management practitioner event in London, 13 May 2016.

Muniesa, F., Doganova, L., Ortiz, H., Pina-Stranger, A., Paterson, F., Bourgoin, A., Ehrenstein, V. 2017. *Capitalization: A Cultural Guide*, Paris: Presses des Mines.

O'Malley, P. 1992. 'Risk, power and crime prevention'. *Economy and Society* 21(3), pp. 252–275.

Pelzer, P. 2012. *Risk, Risk Management and Regulation in the Banking Industry: The Risk to Come*. Abingdon: Routledge.

Pryke, M., and Allen, J. 2000. 'Monetized time-space: derivatives–money's 'new imaginary'?'. *Economy and Society* 29(2), pp. 264–284.

Rotman, B. 1987. *Signifying Nothing: The Semiotics of Zero*. na.

Simmel, G. 1897. 'The Significance of Money for the Tempo of Life'. Cited in Goodstein, E.S. 2017. *Georg Simmel and the Disciplinary Imaginary*. Stanford CA: Stanford University Press.

Simmel, G. 1900 [2011]. *The Philosophy of Money*, Abingdon: Routledge.

Simmel, G. 1903. 'The metropolis and mental life'. In Wolff, K.H. (ed.) *The Sociology of Georg Simmel* reprinted in 1950, Free Press, New York, pp. 409–424.

Tickell, A. 2000. 'Dangerous derivatives: controlling and creating risks in international money'. *Geoforum* 31(1), pp. 87–99.

Tucker, P. 2007. 'A Perspective on Recent Monetary and Financial System Developments', speech given at Meryll Lynch, 26 April 2007. [pdf] Available at: www.bankofengland.co.uk/archive/Documents/historicpubs/speeches/2007/speech308.pdf (Accessed: 20 May 2017).

Watson, M. 1999. 'Rethinking capital mobility, re-regulating financial markets'. *New Political Economy* 4(1), pp. 55–75.

Watson, M. 2007. *The Political Economy of International Capital Mobility*. Basingstoke: Palgrave Macmillan.

Wexler, M. 2010. 'Financial edgework and the persistence of rogue traders'. *Business and Society Review* 115(1), pp. 1–25.

Wigan, D. 2009. 'Financialisation and derivatives: Constructing an artifice of indifference'. *Competition & Change* 13(2), pp. 157–172.

Yadav, V. 2008. *Risk in International Finance*. Abingdon: Routledge.

Zaloom, C. 2004. 'The productive life of risk', *Cultural Anthropology* 19(3), pp. 365–391.

Zelizer, V. 1997. *The Social Meaning of Money*, Princeton NY: Princeton University Press.

Zelizer, V. 2000. 'Fine tuning the Zelizer view'. *Economy and Society* 29(3), pp. 383–389.

Zelizer, V. 2011. *Economic lives: How culture shapes the economy*. Princeton NJ: Princeton University Press.

3 Central banking as a performed domain

Introduction: a very public currency

> Monetary policy makes for instant headlines: 'RATES HIKE!'. Macroprudential policy does not seem to scan so easily ... many people ... might find them rather opaque. In addition, there will be times when the recommendations ... cannot be revealed to a wider audience.
>
> (Paul Fisher, 12 March 2012)

As the above passage sets out, the increasingly transparent attempts by central banks to develop a 'public currency' in monetary policy (Holmes, 2016) has helped to garner a contrast with a purportedly secretive and arcane world of financial stability (Conti-Brown, 2017). In this chapter I challenge this binary by bringing the public performances of financial stability to the fore. An attention to money cultures at the Bank of England brings us to the interrelated features of narration and calculation in central banking. In Pierre Siklos' (2017, pp. 218–219) terms, 'words matter'.

From the vantage point of ethnographic research into monetary and financial governance, central banking involves at some stages 'writing the economy', and at others, the manipulation of an 'economy of words' (Smart, 2006; Holmes, 2009). Such research pays close attention to the processes of designing macroeconomic models, the internal lobbying for their introduction into methodology and reasoning, and the writing and printing process of inflation reporting. In particular, Smart (2006) goes into great detail about the interaction between the Bank of Canada and the financial press, even taking his reader inside the press 'lock up' where reporters receive the Monetary Policy Report two hours before its general release. In sum, in the monetary policy oriented literature there is a consistent argument that central bank staff employ 'open mouth operations' as a future oriented policy tool (Guthrie and Wright, 2000; Krippner, 2007; Holmes, 2014; Braun, 2015; Siklos, 2017). Considerably less attention has been paid to communication in the context of financial stability (see Morris, 2016).

There is, of course, a wider literature that is directly concerned with questions of financial performativity (Callon, 1998; MacKenzie, 2003, 2004a, 2004b, 2005, 2006a, 2006b, 2009; MacKenzie and Millo, 2003; de Goede, 2005;

Aitken, 2007; Callon *et al.*, 2007; Langley, 2008a, 2010, 2015; Brassett and Clarke, 2012; Clarke, 2012; Esposito, 2013; Braun, 2015). The most widely utilized entry point to this performativity literature is that which is commonly classified as the Social Studies of Finance (SSF). For such sociological approaches, ethnographic research is employed to make the case that the technical discipline of economics 'shapes' and 'formats the economy, rather than recording how it functions' (Callon, 1998, p. 2; see MacKenzie *et al.*, 2007). And, although Callon's own writings on performativity take an altogether different direction, he has provided inspiration for sociologists such as Donald MacKenzie (2006a) and Knorr Cetina and Preda (2005) (cited in Langley, 2010, p. 74). What MacKenzie (2004a) terms 'Austinian Performativity' holds for circumstances in which the 'reflexive use of the model' in some way leads to the world 'gradually conforming' to its depiction within the model. MacKenzie's work makes the case most effectively when analysing how the Black-Scholes-Merton formula, used in the pricing of options, itself employed assumptions that were initially unrealistic but became increasingly realistic due to changes in the reality it sought to represent (MacKenzie and Millo, 2003).

At the analytical foundations of this conception of the performative is J.L. Austin's pragmatic analysis of language in which a speech act, such as a chairman opening a board meeting, is said to bring about the effect which it names. In such a situation, one is actually doing something, opening the meeting, rather than merely reporting the event of a meeting of a board of directors (Austin, 1962). When Butler reads Austin, she draws a distinction between the illocutionary, which 'brings something into being', such as a judge convicting a defendant, and the perlocutionary, which 'alters an ongoing situation' (Butler, 2010, p. 151). As Christophers points out, it is the perlocutionary which is associated with the most prominent work in SSF. In other words, financial theories actively 'contribute' to the world they seek to theorize (Christophers, 2014, p. 18).

A further concept that authors in SSF have appropriated, drawing on Callon's reading of Deleuze, is that of *agencement* (Callon, 2006, p. 13). This concept refers to an economic actor which is not necessarily an individual human being alone, but rather, a relational sum of parts. An agencement can include humans, but also 'equipment, technical devices and algorithms' (Callon, 2005, p. 4; cited in Hardie and MacKenzie, 2007). On this analysis, the actor's characteristics are constituted by the agencements of which they are made up (Hardie and MacKenzie, 2007, pp. 57–58). The performativity of economics for SSF is thus one in which economics is not merely textbook theory, but models and devices found 'at large' and 'in the wild' (Callon, 2007).

However, the performative account provided by authors such as MacKenzie (2003), does not exhaust the types of performativity at play in finance *tout court*. Instead, performativity has alternatively been construed as the reiterative practices through which 'a discursive operation produces the effect that it names' (Butler, 1993, p. 2). For example, Clarke and Robert's recent article on overlapping gendered performances argues that we can see that 'masculinity' is performed in at least two distinct ways by the current Bank of England Governor, Mark Carney (Clarke and Roberts, 2014, p. 6). Within critical studies of finance, the application of this approach is most commonly associated with the work of Marieke de Goede (2005) on stock markets and the history of speculation, and later developed in Paul Langley's work both on everyday financial subjectivities (2008a) and liquidity in the Subprime Crisis (Langley, 2010; see also Thrift, 2000; Aitken, 2007; Brassett and Clarke, 2012). The common object of interest here is how the category of performativity can be utilized within broader Foucauldian concerns with the interstices of power, knowledge and subjectivity. As Langley explains, de Goede's (2005) approach is initially 'derived from the work of Judith Butler which is itself grounded in a Foucauldian reading of power and Derrida's deconstructionist engagement with Austin' (Langley, 2010, p. 74). Such an approach attempts to displace discourse in favour of matter; a move from discursive practices of meaning making to material practices (de Goede, 2005, p. 7). However, if we read de Goede's (2012) more recent contribution on *Speculative Security*, we find that her reading of Butler is now through Bialasiewicz *et al.* (2007) which now recognizes the distinction between discursive and non-discursive phenomena but maintains that 'discourses constitute the objects of which they speak'. Consequently, the researcher's attention is refocused on processes of materialization whereby 'discourse stabilizes over time to produce the effect of boundary, fixity and surface' (de Goede, 2012, p. 32).

At this stage of the debate, it is important to note that not all accounts of performativity sit in one or the other of the two camps presented above. There are a number of accounts that, in somewhat different ways, attempt to overcome the existing bifurcation. Importantly for the arguments being developed in this book, Douglas Holmes (2014) explicitly focuses on the 'performative apparatus' of the central bank (2014, p. 53). As he does so, Holmes' work shows that the monetary governance of central bank practitioners has long worked with the assumption that talking about future intentions on interest rates can be just as important as actual rate decisions. This is because policy discourse shapes market expectations. Holmes' (2009, 2014) approach is particularly interesting because he is seemingly providing some kind of third way between Austin and Butler. As Holmes later emphasizes in his own reading of MacKenzie *et al.* (2007), 'it is this kind of interweaving of "words" and "action" – of representations and interventions – that the concept of "performativity" is designed to capture' (MacKenzie *et al.*, 2007, p. 5; cf. Holmes, 2014, p. 23).

Benjamin Braun's (2015) study of the European Central Bank (ECB) is broadly consistent with Holmes' earlier study because Braun conceptualizes this central bank as a 'communicative apparatus' in which inflationary 'expectations are performative effects of carefully crafted arrangements' (Braun, 2015, pp. 369, 371). Indeed, Braun outlines a very similar conceptualization of performativity because he explicitly seeks to bring together the work of Callon (1998) and Holmes (2014). If there is a discernible difference, however, it lies in the way that Braun analyses aspects of ECB performativity through Goffman's (1959) almost theatrical sense of dual performances. On such an account, there is set of understandings and practices behind the closed doors of the central bank, and another performance that is staged at the front of house for consumption in the public domain (Braun, 2015, p. 371).

The most established attempt to overcome the Austinian-Generic bifurcation is provided by Chris Clarke (2012) when he points out that, like generic performativity, Austin's 'understanding of the performative embraces the contingent and historicised nature of performative utterances'. For Clarke, the two seemingly competing conceptualizations of performativity thus contain a common emphasis, such that 'further reflection … might show how they both constitute a valid and useful understanding of performative finance, especially perhaps when used together' (Clarke, 2012, p. 268). In line with this argument, Clarke goes onto to propose the notion of overlapping or 'layered performativities'.

The remainder of the chapter explores and elaborates the layering of performances through an analysis of the financial stability press conferences of the Bank of England. To begin, I make the case that both Austinian and Generic performativity are present in these acts of governing financial stability, both through the technical device of the stress test and the reiterative and ritualistic practices which foreshadow the authority of the Bank. These latter practices help the Governor to pass a verdict on the state of the financial system. Thereafter, I attend to two further, lively, features of the layering of performativity at the press conferences. One is the emergence of counter-performativity or misfires. Misfires have a performative force, what Derrida (1988) characterized as 'force de rupture'. This then is when an 'utterance gains force through breaking with prior positions' (Butler 1997, p. 145). Second, I attend to creative responses to difficult questions from journalists, which I analyse through Thrift and Dewsbury's (2000) reading of Deleuze. The response of improvisation to disruption of the conventions of the press conference is the corollary of the relation between misfire and improvisation that I elaborate in later chapters.

The layered performativities of financial stability

Financial stability reports appear twice a year, aim to highlight developments affecting the stability of the financial system, and have been released through press conferences since 2011. The press conference is also used to announce the results of the stress tests which initially emerged as an urgent response to the Global Financial Crisis (see Langley, 2013). Stress testing works with a wider macroprudential idea that regulators need to identify systemic weaknesses caused by collective behaviour (Baker, 2013, p. 316), but it is also a technique which identifies how much extra regulatory capital could be needed to absorb low probability/high-impact macroeconomic shocks. The stress testing exercise has now become an annual event, and is incorporated into one of the two FSR press conferences.

Bringing about financial stability

When we unpack a heated debate in a FSR press conference, we can see that the central bank believes that the stress test exercise can contribute to changes in the financial system. During the June 2014 press conference, in which the Bank of England outlined a loan income cap to dampen a new housing bubble, Paul Mason, a television journalist, asked in an accusatory tone whether the Bank's financial stability policies are ineffective, describing the Bank as the 'Bank of Zero'. Both Governor Mark Carney and Deputy Governor Andrew Bailey appeared to find this remark provocative and felt it necessary to respond. The point at issue is Mason's blunt claim that there has been 'zero impact from the stress test'. Carney and Bailey responded as follows:

MARK CARNEY: There's no reason to come to the conclusion that the stress test is zero. As Andrew Bailey just outlined, a 35 per cent house price shock – it's a stress scenario, it's not a prediction, just to be clear. But in conjunction with a 6 per cent increase in the unemployment rate – stress scenario, not a prediction – a sharp increase in interest rates and a three-year recession, do banks and building societies in this country have balance sheets today that are resilient enough to withstand that type of stress? And if they don't, the PRA and the FPC will consider actions that those institutions need to take to address them. So it would be a big mistake to look at the stress test, which we're undergoing right now, and conclude that this is anything other than a very serious exercise that may have consequences for some banks and building societies.

ANDREW BAILEY: Can I add one point on the zero impact, to challenge it? A year ago at this press conference we were discussing the FPC's recommendation on capital. Today if you look at the *Financial Stability Report*, the FPC has essentially closed its recommendation on capital. And the reason it's closed its recommendation on capital is because of the actions that have been taken in the interim period on adjusting and raising capital and adjusting the capital position of the banking system in this country. That is not a zero impact. It is also in my view an essential component of supporting a durable recovery. So I really do push back on this zero impact point.

(Press Conference Questions and Answers, June 2014)

So, what Carney and Bailey's respective responses to the question reveal, is that the stress test itself was said to have a 'very serious' impact on the financial system. The stress test itself encourages financial institutions to hold more and better quality regulatory capital, thereby improving their capital adequacy in the face of future shocks and difficulties. Put simply, an anticipatory test for essentially prudent capital provisioning brings about the prudent provisioning of capital. And, as both Langley (2013) and Geithner (2014) argue, effective stress testing can generate confidence. Thus, it can be said that stress testing has the perlocutionary effect of altering an ongoing situation because, as Bailey argued, 'actions ... have been taken to adjust(ing) the capital position of the banking system'.

Within this line of argument, we are, in Langley's terms, faced with an ascription of 'agency to calculative devices of risk' (2008, p. 472), or to the agencement of which it is a part. The agency of technical devices is important within the Bank of England's stress testing programme, because at its heart we find the RAMSI collection of models which arrive at an estimate of the resilience of banks and banking in a stress scenario (Alessandri *et al.*, 2009). According to Bank of England staff, RAMSI is comprised of a set of equations and algorithms that model each component of the largest UK banks' income, dependent on the composition of their balance sheets (Burrows *et al.*, 2012). However, all this is not to do away with human agency or action. As the Bank of England readily concedes, RAMSI 'is in no sense perfect' because 'the simplicity of much of RAMSI means it must be combined with human judgement' (Burrows *et al.*, 2012, p. 4). What we encounter through the stress test is a distributed agency of an agencement of humans and technology that work on the future in a particular way.

Building on a seemingly Austinian approach to the stress test, what I now seek to do is to make the case that, as Clarke (2012) argues, the more generic form – the performance of the central banker – is also present in financial stability governance. The role that generic performativity has in the press conference is to establish an authority context between Bank staff and the journalists who are present and will be reporting on the event.

Rituals and conventions

To invoke de Goede's (2005) argument concerning the ritualistic reiteration of the discourses of the Dow Jones Index, the way in which both inflation forecasts and FSRs are released, communicated and taken up from press conferences are almost ritualistic events. From an anthropological perspective, LiPuma (2016) succinctly writes that 'the objectification of the social and the structure of practice is tied to the performativity inherent in ritual'. We see this ritualistic aspect overtly in central banking when we draw on Graham Smart's insights from one of the editors of the monetary policy report at the Bank of Canada, that: 'the whole thing is a pretty structured, cohesive process, twice a year. Now they know what to expect, and we know what to expect' (in Smart, 2006, p. 167). So, the FSR is produced and released twice a year. At each publication of an FSR, the Bank of England hosts a press conference, at which the Governor of the Bank and the Chairperson of the FPC are joined by three other members of the FPC, typically Deputy Governors and the Head of Financial Stability. The five committee members sit behind four desks, each desk has a Bank of England emblem on it.

The opening to the press conference is consistently of the following form, with Nils Blythe welcoming the press and talking through the FPC line-up present in the meeting. The Governor then welcomes the press:

NILS BLYTHE: Good morning everyone and welcome to the financial stability report press conference, on my left is Andrew Bailey, Deputy Governor for financial regulation. On my far right is Spencer Dale, the Bank's Director for Financial Stability and Risk. Next to him is John Cunliffe, Deputy Governor for Financial Stability, and next to me is the Governor of the Bank of England, Mark Carney.

GOVERNOR: Thank you very much Nils. Good morning everybody.

The 'Question and Answers' format also remains the same and is quite regimented between the Bank and the journalists who are present. The journalists address Mervyn King or Mark Carney as 'Governor', and are given the microphone for one question, before returning the microphone to the Governor for his response. The Governor can then choose to answer the question himself, or nominate one of the other FPC members to respond to the question. It is clear that the authority of the Governor is a strong theme during the press conference as he is both the centre of proceedings and a sort of gate-keeper by determining who answers which question. However, delegation within the press conference also brings into light the contributions of other high-ranking officials within the Bank.

With the ritualistic reproduction of conventions and practices, we have a situation suggestive of a performed economic domain (Clarke, 2012, pp. 263–265). When King or Carney is interpolated as the 'Governor' or sits behind a desk with the Bank's emblem on it, there is something both reiterative and authoritative about his position in relation to the immediate audience, the journalists. In other words, it is the cultivation of a certain type of subject. When a question is asked, it is the Governor who is given the microphone, and he who decides whether he will answer the question, or whether it will be delegated to another FPC member. The press conference highlights for us the generic performativity at play in central banking. And, when taken alongside the results of the stress test, this ritualistic and reiterative performative overlaps with the propensity for central bank statements to shape and format the economy through the news media present in the press conference (Velthuis, 2015).

Writing the financial system

The question then becomes one of what is the significance of these rituals and conventions for the economy? In other words, how do the Bank Governor and FPC members format the economy in these press conferences? In this section I provide three extracts from the beginning of the press conferences. This part of the press conference is archived on the Bank's website as a separate document to the podcast of the conference, or indeed the FSR itself. Within his opening remarks, the Governor of the Bank provides a verdict on the state of the financial system, and any changes since the previous report and conference. These verdicts are reported by the press, and conveyed to the public domain. The work of Holmes (2014) and Braun (2015) suggests that these verdicts should shape public and market expectations.

In this first example, Governor King is speaking in the context of 'deteriorating' economic conditions in the Eurozone, where seemingly unresolvable large sovereign debts are causing investors in sovereign bonds much concern. Notably, the Governor's opening statement confers the social status of 'deterioration' for levels of financial stability:

> Since we last met, the outlook for financial stability has deteriorated. The crisis in the euro area has generated a great deal of uncertainty around the economic outlook and exposed severe vulnerabilities in the European banking system. The fortunes of the United Kingdom economy, and in particular our financial system, have inevitably been affected.
>
> (King, June 2012)

Moving along further to 2013 and the second example, the new Governor, Mark Carney, delivers a more optimistic verdict on an emergent recovery in the UK economy:

> In the six months since the June Financial Stability Report an economic recovery has taken hold in the UK. Confidence has returned and credit conditions have eased further ... liquidity conditions remain robust.
>
> (Carney, November 2013)

For the third example, Carney's opening remarks at the publication of the first FSR of 2014 are even more effusive, with the 'recovery' being described as 'broadening' and developing into a so-called 'durable expansion'. Despite this, Carney still warns against possible points of future fragility which may undermine the purported expansion:

> With the recovery in the UK economy broadening and gaining momentum in recent months, the Bank of England is now focused on turning that recovery into a durable expansion.
>
> (Carney, June 2014)

Up to this point I have briefly illustrated how both Austinian and Generic performativity coalesce and feed off each other in the financial stability press conference. This prompts us towards a layered account of performativity. In the following section I argue that there is a further layering at play.

Lively practices

The argument being developed here is that even though some key aspects of financial performativity are anchored in the mere reproduction of models and meaningful statements, more is needed. In other words, the issue is what are other sources of the performative force of the central bank?

Governor Mark Carney gives us a clue to locating the performative force when he refers to the mandate that the FPC has been given by Parliament: 'Our role – given to us by Parliament – is to manage risks to financial stability, including the build-up of unsustainable levels of leverage, debt or credit growth' (Carney, June 2014). An initially tempting analytical route to go down then is to conceptualize members of the FPC as 'petty sovereigns' in the sense articulated by Judith Butler (2004). In *Precarious Life*, Butler is trying to capture the managerial power behind many of the sovereign decisions over life made during the war on terror. The analogy that could be developed here is to decisions such as changes in interest rates, or indeed when to inject money into the economy through quantitative easing. Alternatively, if an unnoticed but fundamental agency is key for Butler, then an alternative explanation for the discursive force of the FPC could be that it is an instance of Bourdieu's 'habitus', where the high-ranking officials are an embodiment of established contexts of authority. Here habitus refers to the 'lasting dispositions, trained capacities and structured propensities to think, feel and act in determinant ways' (Wacquant, 2005, p. 316). A second approach using Bourdieu would be to draw on *Language and Symbolic Power* (1991) and his characterization of the 'legitimate language' that needs to be in place for a performative utterance to be valid. Thus Bourdieu argues that a spokesperson is endowed with the full power to act on behalf of the group and 'must conduct himself in accordance with the social essence which is thereby assigned to him' (Bourdieu, 1991, pp. 105–106).

However, I want to suggest that none of these potential routes adequately capture what is at play here. First, although we might agree with Butler that throughout the process of delegation within the Bank of England press conference, 'power precedes them and constitutes them as sovereigns', there are still compelling grounds to break the analogy. For, as Butler argues, petty sovereigns have minimal accountability because they 'do not offer either representative or legitimating functions' (Butler, 2004, p. 62). Given that members of the FPC at the press conference both represent the Bank and explain and legitimize policy, they cannot be considered petty sovereigns. Second, it is possible to critique Bourdieu's formulation of 'habitus' by aligning the argument with those made by Butler, to reject the formulation in which 'utterances are functionally secured in advance by the "social positions" to which they are mimetically related'. Instead then, there are instances where 'an utterance gains force through breaking with prior positions' (Butler, 1997, p. 145). Third, and to return to *Language and Symbolic Power*, 'the act of naming' is said to structure 'the perception which social agents have of the social world' (Bourdieu, 1991, p. 106). The issue with this is that Bank of England committee members have perceptions about the social world prior to entering the Bank of England and committee members do disagree about policy, rather than sharing one structured view.

And, as such, accounts in which institutions and social conventions 'structure' behaviour do not really help us. The entry point for analysis must be different. As geographers Thrift and Dewsbury (2000, p. 414) argue, a 'major apprehension' with generic performativity is the lack of creativity and 'free play' which ultimately prioritizes restrictive discursive operations. For example, the gendered subjects that we encounter in Butler (1993) 'unconsciously' foreclose an analysis of the variable nature of social action and change by conforming to a 'self-identical principle' (Thrift and Dewsbury, 2000, p. 414). The implication, then, is that if generic performativity is about a performance of something, then perhaps the consequence is to lose touch with the liveliness and potential for disruption from the 'performance' of central banking.

It is quite possible to analyse the financial stability press conferences of the Bank of England in order to identify and illustrate a third and equally important layer of performativity; that which I will term 'lively practices'. I coin this as an umbrella term for a field of disruption, and improvisation. And, to draw out each of these two different and lively practices, I take insights from two social theorists. First, for Derrida, the ruptures intrinsic to communication have the potential to disrupt seemingly regimented conventions. Second, I transpose Deleuzian ideas from Thrift and Dewsbury (2000) to look at creative improvisations with unknown outcomes which again disrupt the repetition of established discursive operations. The argument being built here is that such lively practices, and in particular, disruptions or misfires to performativity have an implication for the risk culture at the Bank of England.

Derrida and misfire

In this section I attend fully to the category of misfire. Derrida's seminal engagement with Anglo-American philosopher John Searle is important because it attends to the slippages in communication that do not appear to be captured by Holmes' (2014) idea of a negotiated performativity. Indeed, there is no mention of Derrida in the communicative imperatives of Holmes' *Economy of Words*. Butler writes that 'in "Signature, Event, Context", Derrida (1988) argued that we can only think the process of iterability by understanding the rupture or failure that characterizes every interstitial moment within iteration' (Butler, 2010, p. 152). In other words, for Derrida, a sign or mark that was not repeatable would not be able to function as 'an element in a language'. And, this repeatability of the mark means that while two identical marks are the same, there is also a difference because there are two of them (Loxley, 2007, pp. 77–78). There is then, 'an irreducible difference to the structure of the mark'. This difference or absence has both spatial and temporal dimensions (May, 1997, p. 100). On the one hand, it is spatial because the consequence of language being a formal system of differences is that the meaningfulness of any given element in language is only by reference to other elements that are not present. On the other hand, it is temporal because the intention to mean something cannot ever be 'fully present to itself' (May, 1997, p. 100).

As Loxley puts it, performativity as the 'simple conformity to constitutive rules can be put into question by the recognition that institutions are themselves' necessarily implicated in 'an iterability they cannot simply contain' (Loxley, 2007, p. 89). So, for Butler, if it is both true that a financial 'theory tends to produce the phenomenon', but also 'that it can sometimes fail to produce what it anticipates, then it seems we have opened up the possibility of "misfire" at the basis of performativity itself' (Butler, 2010, pp. 152–153). And, while such lively practices are referred to in the literature as 'misfires' (see Callon, 2010), this seemingly lower status is not fairly warranted because such difference is embedded at the heart of every performative utterance. Misfires have a performative force, what Derrida (1988) characterized as 'force de rupture'. This then is when an 'utterance gains force through breaking with prior positions' (Butler,1997, p. 145). Misfire, rather than merely signalling the breakdown of performativity, instead has a dynamism that leads to improvisation and change. As such, a misfire has a 'violent' force precisely because the force is 'not derived from conformity to prior' conditions or conventions (Loxley, 2007, p. 104). The importance of this category will be made clear at the beginning of Chapter 6. In short, the key shift in money culture with which this book is preoccupied is stimulated by a misfire. This can be seen through the corollary and response to misfire, namely improvisation.

Deleuze and improvisation

Improvisation enters the picture through the work of Gilles Deleuze. Deleuze's interest in performativity is anchored in the way that repetition can be contrasted to a pure difference in which 'risky, creative and experimental' actions can anticipate but 'not know ... their outcomes' (Williams, 2003, p. 16). A Deleuzian alternative of the kind suggested by Thrift and Dewsbury (2000) is one which is sensitive to the creativity of performance, rather than the ritualistic performance of existing categories and symbolism. To make this point, Thrift and Dewsbury suggest we think in terms of possibility and representation for generic performativity, and the virtual, and practice for a more Deleuzian variant of performance (Deleuze, 1968, p. 263). Thrift and Dewsbury read Deleuze as arguing that 'the realisation of the possible operates' through 'imitation and resemblance', in this case the repetition of discursive operations. Because 'there are many possibles, any realization of any one of them necessarily limits these potential possibles to only one'. To take this further, and to relate to Deleuze's work on difference (1968), 'the possible comes to completion only by ... filling the hollow or gap that difference resides in, (and so) nothing new is created'. In contrast to representation, in which 'we know the outcome', with difference we can only speculate (Thrift and Dewsbury, 2000, p. 416).

The example I utilize here demonstrates improvisation by one of the speakers, Andrew Haldane, (then) the Bank of England's Executive Director of Financial Stability. Haldane faces a difficult question, and I have selected it because it is not an obvious question related directly to an event, but instead draws together statements made by Haldane and Mark Carney over the reforms to banking conventions in the Basel III Capital Accord:

BEN CHU (*Independent*): A question for Andy Haldane. In your recent 'Dog and the Frisbee' speech you seem to suggest that the thrust of the Basel III approach which is the emphasis on complexity might be misconceived. Mark Carney, who we now know is going to be the next Governor of the Bank of England, suggested that your concerns were uneven and not based on a full appreciation of the facts. Are we looking at a misunderstanding there or is it a fundamental difference on the philosophy of how you regulate the banking sector?

ANDREW HALDANE: Just a couple of points on that if I can, Ben. So on the Basel III question just to be absolutely clear what I said in the speech you mentioned. There's no question in my mind – and I've said it repeatedly – that Basel III was a significant improvement over Basel II, in particular in clarifying and simplifying and raising the numerator of the capital ratio, okay. But the part it left untouched was the denominator, which is risk-weighted assets and concerns we have about its opacity, about its complexity, about its inconsistency – in fact exactly the things we discuss in today's Report … on to the second point, I mean if you, as I know you have, if you were to put Mark and I's speech cheek by jowl, you would find not so much as a fag paper of difference between them on the regulatory reform agenda. The particular issue you mention actually concerned the leverage ratio. And guess what? The country – one, that has a leverage ratio, and two, has been one of the biggest supporters of it because it protected them from the storms we've had over the last few years – was indeed Canada, and has indeed been Mark. So I think, insofar as there's anything at all, there is complete consistency on what we want by way of the future regulatory agenda, and improving risk weights are one element of that.

(Press Conference Questions and Answers, November 2012)

At this stage, although confirmed, Carney had not started working at the Bank of England. In light of its unpredictable nature, I characterize the response as improvisation by Haldane, as to not create any friction between himself and the incoming Governor Carney. Haldane has to be resourceful in his answer. This can be contrasted to the following extract, where the respondents seemingly have a response prepared in advance for a question regarding Paul Tucker's future as Deputy Governor after he was overlooked for the Governor's job in favour of Mark Carney. Haldane then, makes use of what he has available, evidence of Carney's record as Governor of the Bank of Canada, to defuse a politically charged question in a way that does not undermine or critique the future Governor. This can be contrasted to the much more scripted seeming response of King and Tucker to a question about Tucker's future.

CHRIS GILES (*The Financial Times*):   'I'm sorry, we've all been terribly British about this so far, but I do think that we have to ask Paul Tucker if he would comment on his future after the recent appointment of Mark Carney. But I also wanted to ask another question – a proper question –'

MERVYN KING: 'You asked one. Paul will answer that, and then you can come back to your second question next time round. Paul.'

PAUL TUCKER: 'I'm the Deputy Governor for Financial Stability. There's a job of work to be done; I'm doing it.'

MERVYN KING: 'Next question.'

(Press Conference Questions and Answers, November 2012)

The latter exchange conveys a sense of a pre-meditated shutting down of an avenue of discussion as quickly as possible, without any elaboration. King immediately hands over to Tucker, seemingly confident in the answer Tucker will provide. This can be compared to the former passage which was a much longer and effusive discussion and rejection of a politically charged question. Haldane appears to be thinking on his feet and improvising, rather than citing an answer he has rehearsed. This, then, is another lively practice. The account of improvisation here mirrors but is very distinct from the account of Bowman *et al.* (2012, p. 466) who attend to the 'emergence of improvisation, bricolage, and a return to tacit knowledge' in central banking following the crisis. In particular, this is the strategic improvised response to changing material conditions. As Engelen *et al.* (2011) argue, improvisation is a 'parallel mode of acquiring knowledge and involves building up structures by fitting together events'. While for these authors improvisation has primarily emerged in the use of policy tools 'changing the balance sheets of market actors', in the account I am providing here improvisation comes in the form of communicative responses to misfire and counter-performativity.

Conclusions

This chapter has sought to establish the different layers of performativity at play in the context of central banking and financial stability governance. I have made the case that the Bank of England does believe that the technical device of stress testing, including the RAMSI suite of models and algorithms, has altered the financial system. However, the stress testing example can be presented alongside certain ritualistic features of the press conferences to illustrate that layered performativities is a useful concept. But, rather than being completely satisfied with an explanation that meaning laden conventions determine the efficacy of central bank performativity, this chapter engages with improvisation and misfire. This is the thought that current studies of performativity of finance under-appreciate the way that performance is as much about the delivery and the way something is said, as it is its linguistic content and meaning.

This chapter has presented three existing approaches to performativity found in work in the SSF, cultural economy and cultural anthropology. These are Austinian performativity, generic performativity and layered performance. By analysing press conference transcripts and video recordings, this chapter supports Clarke's (2012) view that performativities can be overlapping. The technical device of the stress test may have an impact on bank reserve capital, but the results of the exercise are presented through a convention laden press conference. Furthermore, the chapter has argued that to understand the performativity of the economy we must add an additional layer, a layer that is generally marginalized by Generic and Austinian performativity – lively practices. And here I analyse texts and video recordings through Derrida and Deleuze. These authors provide rich theoretical tools with which we can think about the disruption and improvisation of central banking and financial stability. This has been both illustrated and teased out using the more or less discrete and concrete example I have studied. The account of performativity outlined here links the concept of money cultures by thinking about the relationship between misfire and improvisation in central banking. The following chapter is the start of Part II of the book, in which I chart the development of the money culture of *speculating on risk* at the Bank of England.

References

Aitken, R. 2007. *Performing Capital: Towards a Cultural Economy of Popular and Global Finance*. Basingstoke: Palgrave Macmillan.

Alessandri, P., Gai, P., Kapadia, S., Mora, N., and Puhr, C. 2009. 'Towards a framework for quantifying systemic stability'. *International Journal of Central Banking* 5(3), pp. 47–81.

Austin, J.L. 1962. *How To Do Things With Words*. Oxford: Clarendon.

Baker, A. 2013. 'The new political economy of the macroprudential ideational shift'. *New Political Economy* 18(1), pp. 112–139.

Bank of England. 2011. Financial Stability Report Press Conference June 2011. [pdf] Transcript available at: www.bankofengland.co.uk/publications/Documents/fsr/2011/conf110624.pdf (Accessed 4 February 2014).

Bank of England. 2012a. Financial Stability Report Press Conference June 2012. [pdf] Transcript available at: www.bankofengland.co.uk/publications/Pages/fsr/2012/fsr31.aspx. Podcast: http://download.world-television.com/boe/boe_20120629.mp3 (Accessed 4 January 2014).

Bank of England. 2012b. Financial Stability Report Press Conference November 2012. [pdf] Transcript available at: www.bankofengland.co.uk/publications/Pages/fsr/2012/fsr32.aspx. Podcast: http://download.world-television.com/boe/boe_20121129.mp3 (Accessed 5 January 2014).

Bank of England. 2013. Financial Stability Report Press Conference November 2013. [pdf] Transcript available at: www.bankofengland.co.uk/publications/Pages/fsr/2013/fsr34.aspx. Podcast: http://download.world-television.com/boe/boe_20132811.mp3 (Accessed 10 January 2014).

Bank of England. 2014. Financial Stability Report Press Conference June 2014. [pdf] Transcript available at: www.bankofengland.co.uk/publications/Pages/fsr/2014/fsr35.aspx. Podcast: http://download.world-television.com/boe/boe_20140626.mp3 (Accessed 10 January 2014).

Bialasiewicz, L., Campbell, D., Elden, S., Graham, S., Jeffrey, A., and Williams, A. 2007. 'Performing security: The imaginative geographies of current US strategy'. *Political Geography* 26(4), pp. 405–422.

Bourdieu, P. 1991. *Language and Symbolic Power*. Cambridge: Polity Press.

Brassett, J., and Clarke, C. 2012. 'Performing the sub-prime crisis: trauma and the financial event'. *International Political Sociology* 6 (1), pp. 4–20.

Braun, B. 2015. 'Governing the future: the European Central Bank's expectation management during the Great Moderation'. *Economy and Society* 44(3): pp. 367–391.

Burrows, O., Learmonth, D., McKeown, J., and Williams, R. 2012. 'RAMSI – a top-down stress-testing model', Bank of England Financial Stability Paper No. 17. [pdf] Available at www.bankofengland.co.uk/financialstability/Documents/fpc/fspapers/fs_paper17.pdf. (Accessed 20 October 2013).

Butler, J. 1993. *Bodies That Matter: On the Discursive Limits of Sex*. Abingdon: Routledge.

Butler, J. 1997. *Excitable Speech: A Politics of the Performative*. New York: Routledge.

Butler, J. 2004. *Precarious Life*. London: Verso.

Butler, J. 2010. 'Performative agency'. *Journal of Cultural Economy* 3(2), pp. 147–161.

Callon, M. 1998. *The Laws of the Markets*. Oxford: Blackwell.

Callon, M. 2005. 'Why virtualism paves the way to political impotence: a reply to Daniel Miller's critique of the Laws of the Markets'. *Economic Sociology: European Electronic Newsletter* 6(2), pp. 3–20.

Callon, M. 2006. 'What does it mean to say that economics is performative?'. CSI Working papers series 005:1–58. [pdf] Available at: https://hal.archives-ouvertes.fr/file/index/docid/91596/filename/WP_CSI_005.pdf. (Accessed 10 June 2016).

Callon, M. 2007. 'Performative economics', in MacKenzie, D., Muniesa, F., and Siu, L. (eds.) *Do Economists Make Markets?* Princeton NJ: Princeton University Press, pp. 311–357.

Christophers, B. 2014. 'From Marx to market and back again: performing the economy', *Geoforum* 57(1), pp. 12–20.

Clarke, C. 2012. 'Financial engineering, not economic photography'. *Journal of Cultural Economy* 5 (3), pp. 261–278.

Clarke, C., and Roberts, A. 2016. 'Mark Carney and the gendered political economy of British central banking'. *The British Journal of Politics and International Relations* 18(1), pp. 49–71.

Conti-Brown, P. 2017. *The power and independence of the Federal Reserve*. Princeton NJ: Princeton University Press.

Deleuze, G. 1968. *Difference and Repetition*. London: Bloomsbury.

Derrida, J. 1988. 'Signature, event context', in *Limited Inc*, Evanston, IL, Northwestern University Press, pp. 1–23.

Engelen, E., Erturk, I., Froud, J., Johal, S., Leaver, A., Moran, M., Nilsson, A., and Williams, K. 2011. *After the great complacence: Financial crisis and the politics of reform*. Oxford: Oxford University Press.

Esposito, E. 2013. 'The structures of uncertainty: performativity and unpredictability in economic operations'. *Economy and Society* 42(1), pp. 102–129.

Fisher, P. 2012. 'Policy making at the Bank of England: the Financial Policy Committee', speech given at University of Warwick, London Alumni Group, 12 March 2012. [pdf] Available at: www.bankofengland.co.uk/archive/Documents/historicpubs/speeches/2012/speech550.pdf (Accessed 20 July 2017).

Geithner, T. 2014. *Stress Test: Reflections on Financial Crises*. New York: Crown Publishers.

de Goede, M. 2005. *Virtue, Fortune, and Faith: A Genealogy of Finance*. Minneapolis: University of Minnesota Press.

de Goede, M. 2012. *Speculative Security: The politics of pursuing terrorist monies*, Minneapolis: University of Minnesota Press.

Guthrie, G., and Wright, J. 2000. 'Open mouth operations'. *Journal of Monetary Economics* 46(2), pp. 489–516.

Hardie, I., and MacKenzie, D. 2007. 'Assembling an economic actor: the agencement of a Hedge Fund'. *The Sociological Review* 55(1), pp. 57–80.

Holmes, D.R. 2009. 'Economy of words'. *Cultural Anthropology* 24(3), pp. 381–419.

Holmes, D.R. 2014. *Economy of words: Communicative imperatives in central banks.* Chicago Il: University of Chicago Press.

Holmes, D.R. 2016. 'Public currency: Anthropological labor in central Banks', *Journal of Cultural Economy* 9(1), pp. 5–26.

Knorr Cetina, K., and Preda, A. (eds) 2005. *The Sociology of Financial Markets.* Oxford: Oxford University Press.

Krippner, G.R. 2007. 'The making of US monetary policy: Central bank transparency and the neoliberal dilemma'. *Theory and Society* 36(6), pp. 477–513.

Langley, P. 2008a. *The Everyday Life of Global Finance: Saving and Borrowing in Anglo-America.* Oxford: Oxford University Press.

Langley, P. 2008b. 'Sub-prime mortgage lending: a cultural economy'. *Economy and Society* 37(4), pp. 469–494.

Langley, P. 2010. 'The performance of liquidity in the subprime mortgage crisis'. *New Political Economy* 15(1), pp. 71–89.

Langley, P. 2013. 'Anticipating uncertainty, reviving risk? On the stress testing of finance in crisis'. *Economy and Society* 42(1), pp. 51–73.

Langley, P. 2015. *Liquidity Lost: The Governance of the Global Financial Crisis.* Oxford: Oxford University Press.

LiPuma, E. 2016. 'Ritual in Financial Life'. In Lee, B., and Martin, R. (eds.) *Derivatives and the Wealth of Societies.* Chicago Il: University of Chicago Press, pp. 37–81.

Loxley, J. 2007. *Performativity.* Abingdon: Routledge.

MacKenzie, D. 2003. 'An equation and its worlds: bricolage, exemplars, disunity and performativity in financial economics'. *Social Studies of Science* 33(6), pp. 831–868.

MacKenzie, D. 2004a. 'Physics and finance: s-terms and modern finance as a topic for science studies', in Amin, A., and Thrift, N. (eds.) *The Blackwell Cultural Economy Reader.* Oxford: Blackwell, pp. 101–120.

MacKenzie, D. 2004b. 'The big, bad wolf and the rational market: portfolio insurance, the 1987 crash and the performativity of economics'. *Economy and Society* 33(3), pp. 303–334.

MacKenzie, D. 2005. 'Mathematizing risk: models, arbitrage and crises', in Hutter, B., and Power, M (eds.) *Organizational Encounters with Risk.* Cambridge: Cambridge University Press, pp. 167–189.

MacKenzie, D. 2006a. 'Is economics performative? Option theory and the construction of derivatives markets'. *Journal of the History of Economic Thought* 28(1), pp. 29–55.

MacKenzie, D. 2006b. *An Engine, Not a Camera: How Financial Models Shape Markets.* Cambridge, MA: MIT Press.

MacKenzie, D. 2009. *Material Markets: How Economic Agents Are Constructed.* Oxford: Oxford University Press.

MacKenzie, D., and Millo, Y. 2003. 'Constructing a market, performing theory: the historical sociology of a financial derivatives exchange'. *American Journal of Sociology* 109(1), pp. 107–145.

MacKenzie, D., Muniesa, F., and Siu, L. (eds.) 2007. *Do Economists Make Markets? On the Performativity of Economics.* Princeton, NJ: Princeton University Press.

May, T. 1997. *Reconsidering Difference: Nancy, Derrida, Levinas, Deleuze.* Pennsylvania: Pennsylvania State University Press.

Morris, J.H. 2016. 'The performativity, performance and lively practices in financial stability press conferences'. *Journal of Cultural Economy* 9(3), pp. 245–260.

Siklos, P.L. 2017. *Central Banks Into the Breach: From Triumph to Crisis and the Road Ahead*. Oxford: Oxford University Press.

Smart, G. 2006. *Writing the economy: Activity, genre and technology in the world of banking*. London: Equinox.

Thrift, N. 2000. 'Performing cultures in the new economy', *Annals of the Association of American Geographers* 90(4), pp. 674–692.

Thrift, N., and Dewsbury, J.D. 2000. 'Dead geographies: and how to make them live'. *Environment and Planning D: Society and Space* 18(4), pp. 411–432.

Velthuis, O. 2015. 'Making monetary markets transparent: the European Central Bank's communication policy and its interactions with the media'. *Economy and Society* 44(2), pp. 316–340.

Wacquant, L. 2005. 'Habitus', in Beckert, J., and Zafirovski, M (eds.) *International Encyclopaedia of Economic Sociology*. Abingdon: Routledge, pp. 315–319.

Williams, J. 2003. *Gilles Deleuze's Difference and Repetition: A Critical Introduction and Guide*. Edinburgh: Edinburgh University Press.

Part II
A money culture of speculating on risk

4 Completing credit markets?

Introduction: financial weapons of destruction?

As Dick Bryan and Michael Rafferty (2006a) put it, derivatives are on some occasions lauded for their elegance and flexibility, other times despised as a form of speculation, or simply not very well understood. Derivative practices per se have a long history, stretching back 4,000 years, and were originally developed to insure against, or transfer, the risks associated with price fluctuations in agricultural commodity markets such as wheat (Wigan, 2009). Since then, they have become the preserve of financial traders. Derivatives are an agreement between two parties, which establishes the price to be paid for a particular commodity in a future transaction between those same parties. More specifically, they can be in the form of futures, forwards, options or swaps. The incentive to trade commodity derivatives is to lock in the future price of some goods in question, in order to 'buy certainty' and thereby gain a measure of security against an uncertain future (Bryan and Rafferty, 2007, p. 136; Esposito, 2011). Derivatives, then, are concerned with making parties secure in the face of an uncertain future. This logic of the derivative also makes it possible to unbundle and purchase the risk of possessing an asset, without actually buying the underlying asset to which the derivative refers. In terms of financial security, some 'reward characteristic' becomes 'indifferent' to the risk of holding the underlying elements (Amoore, 2013, p. 60). This is security in the form of dislocation from risk. Conceivably, derivatives thus ensure that 'the attributes of any asset' can be 'configured as universally recognizable and generic and therefore tradable', irrespective of the market for the asset itself (Bryan and Rafferty, 2006a, p. 52). Buyers of derivatives are therefore often said to be taking positions which may be 'covered' (i.e. related to their holdings of underlying assets), or 'uncovered'. Such contracts are written and traded in two types of markets: on exchanges, where largely standardized derivatives are mainly traded in terms of price; and (ii) more informally, on 'over-the-counter' (OTC) markets, in which they tend not to be standardized.

Until the mid-1980s, derivatives were widely accepted to be instruments that helped to create commodity price certainty over time. However, more recently the speculative (in the sense of taking on uncertainty for profit) aspect of derivatives have come to the fore. Derivatives allow parties within the contract to 'take on a maximal risk exposure without committing much money' (Durand, 2017). The last 30 years or so has seen the development of an array of financial contracts, which perform a far more heterogeneous array of functions and are typically written and traded on OTC markets. This has included the development of credit derivatives. Risk is inherent in credit relationships because lenders might end up losing their loans upon default, while investors lose out when bonds default. The rationale behind credit derivatives then is to sell on the risk without relinquishing the underlying loan. Derivatives have thus moved away from the idea that 'the value of the derivative derives from the price of the underlying commodity and are an adjunct to trade in these commodities' (Bryan and Rafferty, 2006a, p. 40). And, if derivatives of any kind serve to 'unbundle funding – and, thus, "liquidity risk"– from the underlying risk to which an agent is seeking exposure via a particular contract, then credit derivatives unbundle "credit risk" or "default risk" from the funding of credit-debt relations' (Tucker, 2007a, p. 22).

Credit derivatives were developed by globally facing investment bank J.P. Morgan in 1992 and were traded by the major investing houses in the New York swap market (Goodhart *et al.*, 1998, p. 91). The market was initially dominated by a select number of swap houses who consequently developed significant exposures to each other and several large customers. There was, then, a clear motivation to develop further instruments to allow diversification in the international debt markets, primarily those markets based in London. In particular, securitization of illiquid assets such as mortgage repayments became a core part of the financial industry over the next decade. For some commentators, such as Warren Buffett (2003), credit derivatives could be pithily thought of as being akin to 'Financial Weapons of Mass Destruction'. Despite unease in certain quarters, the volume of credit derivatives outstanding accelerated dramatically during the first years of the new millennium (MacKenzie, 2007). For individual financial market intermediaries, seeking to cover credit risk in their asset portfolio or deciding to take a position on particular risks, participation in credit derivatives markets has a clear rationale. In this vein, for example, credit derivatives were widely held to have 'come of age' as tools of risk management by the late 1990s, especially as credit default swaps (CDSs) had successfully contained the fall-out from the Enron default in 1997 and mitigated against Russia's sovereign debt default (Cloke, 2009). This suggested that credit derivatives could indeed contribute to financial stability. At the level of the financial system as a whole, moreover, the growth of credit derivatives came to be regarded as a positive development by regulatory authorities on the grounds that these contracts enabled the transfer and dispersal of risk 'away from highly leveraged institutions' (Greenspan 2007: p. 371). In short, the successful management of risk by each intermediary institution – i.e. internal risk management – was equated with an advance in collective security through the successful management of 'systemic risk' (Collier and Lakoff, 2008). In such a way, credit derivatives were thought to contribute to financial stability.

Collateralized Debt Obligations (CDOs) are structured credit instruments made by bundling up the risk characteristics of an array of underlying assets, and in the run-up to the Global Financial Crisis tended to include subprime mortgages; that is, loans to people who were considered to be a bad credit risk. When a mortgage originating institution writes a mortgage loan, a possible option is to securitize that asset. It is a derivative because the mortgage repayment is separated from the underlying asset of the house. This means that the institution sells the mortgage repayment to a 'shell' company (SPV) that has been set up in order to pool and sell on the mortgage repayments to investors. In other words, the financial institution can take the mortgage repayments connected to the asset in question and pool these repayments with those other repayment streams that are connected to other assets. This process creates, effectively, one large (bundle) of 'promised future cash flows from a wide range of different sources' (Christophers, 2009, p. 819). Further, this asset bundle can be segmented into different orderly sections. It is typical for the cash flows, in this case mortgage repayments, to be grouped by their perceived riskiness. This will create a safe group (or tranche), a middle tranche and a risky tranche. This tranching creates a liability/reward structure, through which losses accrue to the tranches in terms of highest risk first. This structure is the 'who owes what and to whom' of the derivative contract. As Christophers eloquently explains, these 'tranches – the CDOs – are then sold on separately, paying different interest rates, to different sets of investors … with different appetites for risk' (Christophers, 2009, p. 819).

So to unpack Figure 4.1, a number of:

> assets are pooled, packaged and sold by their owner to a shell of a company (a Special Purpose Vehicle), specially created by its originator for the purposes of structuring the assets, thereby recreating them anew as asset-backed securities, and issuing notes on these new securities to fund the operation.
>
> (Lozano, 2015, p. 60)

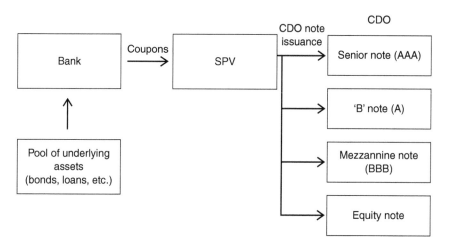

Figure 4.1 How CDOs work.

Source: www.actuarial-files.com/content/risk/creditderivatives.html.

These notes reflect the aforementioned tranching based on perceived levels of risk.

On the other hand, CDSs are an agreement whereby a bondholder, of say a company, pays a premium for someone else to take on the risk of default. The swap is a derivative because ownership of the underlying company does not change hands. This can metaphorically be thought of as being close to an insurance policy against default. The premium is paid for an agreed period of time and if the bond has not defaulted in this time, the premium taker (CDS seller) can keep the payments and has nothing to pay. Should the bond default during this time period, then the bondholder (CDS buyer) 'hands over the bond in return for its face value' (Valdez and Molyneux, 2010, p. 430). The CDS seller has to pay the face value to the CDS buyer. This again is the liability structure.

In this chapter, I illustrate the theoretical account of the money culture of *speculating on risk*, by showing examples of where the Bank of England was historically aware of both the positive and negative risks associated with credit derivatives. I go onto argue that the nature of the problems with credit derivatives changed over time. At some times the Bank was concerned with systemic risk or complexity and at other times – including the height of the Global Financial Crisis – the Bank focused on valuation difficulties. I argue that as the volume of credit derivatives issued increased during the first half of the 2000s, the Bank was increasingly aware of the way that investment risk management was becoming more and more complex. The Bank was less certain where risk was being distributed and aggregated.

Bank of England thinking on credit derivatives

This section begins by turning to the financial stability archive that I compiled from unstructured materials on the Bank of England website. At the forefront of analysis of documents from 1998 to 2003 is a considerable regulatory ambivalence in which the Bank of England consistently acknowledges both the positives and negatives of credit derivatives. The upside and downside risks are seemingly presented on an even footing. The Bank, therefore, seems to take a broad-brush and relatively unrefined approach to risk.

In a 1998 book published in association with the Bank of England, for instance, derivatives were viewed primarily as a 'new technology for risk management' and were thought to possibly 'turn out to be the most significant financial innovation of the 1990s'. In this early text we see the emergence of a significant idea: 'this new credit risk management tool should make the global allocation of risk more efficient ... the new instruments make *credit markets complete*' (Goodhart *et al.*, 1998, p. 94). This is the idea that 'in particular, credit default products' constituted the height of a sophisticated credit market that efficiently distributed risk to those most suited to bear it. The hope here was that it would make systemic collapse less likely. Later, of course, and in the context of the post-2007 crisis, it became common for regulators to acknowledge that credit derivatives did not distribute risks and thereby reduce systemic risk, but created systemic risks that were effectively concentrated in certain key institutions such as Bear Stearns and AIG. Moreover, it was later argued that the securitization boom of 2002–2007 was driven by the notion that market completion 'enhances (market) liquidity' (Nesvetailova, 2010, p. 128).

What we find in the Bank of England archives, then, is an initial example of the legitimization of credit derivative practices, highlighted by the association of 'improper' application of risk management techniques with 'gambling'. Nonetheless, in the financial stability publication, and when thinking about derivatives, such a normative statement about the 'proper' status of calculation also lay in tension with an admission of 'the difficulties involved in pricing credit derivatives' (Goodhart *et al.*, 1998, p. 94). The Bank conceded that 'the evaluation of credit risk is more complicated than the evaluation of market risk' (Goodhart *et al.*, 1998, p. 94). Indeed, here the Bank attempted to bypass the tension of its position over improper financial behaviour, deferring to the opinion of an industry expert: as Paul Varotsis writes in a recent BBA volume on credit derivatives, 'the lack of a scientific pricing method has never been a deterrent to trading (BBA 1997)' (Goodhart *et al.*, 1998, p. 94).

I characterize this as the 'valuation difficulty' within a technique of calculation. In drawing together a tentative and broad-brush conclusion on credit derivatives the Bank wrote that:

> Some of the risks previously confined to the banking sector might spread to other economic sectors via credit derivatives, and some commentators question whether this might be undesirable. We think that it would be an advantage, because non-financial institutions are not a source of systemic risk. If some banking risks can be unloaded onto non-banks, this should decrease systemic risk, rather than increase it. But third parties should be aware of the risks they are taking on.
>
> (Goodhart *et al.*, 1998, p. 96)

Therefore, in this early Bank of England publication, credit derivatives were described from a regulatory perspective as being potentially 'a new beast to be tamed' (Goodhart *et al.*, 1998, p. 91). The implication, in short, was that the allocation of credit risk ought not to be left solely to the pre-emptive logic of the derivative. Taming implies a docility and a discipline which would 'not allow things to escape', or be 'abandoned to themselves' (Foucault, 2007, p. 45). Indeed, later the document explained the various facets of the disciplinary reasoning behind this argument:

> While they may be used for more efficient risk management, they may also increase *systemic risk* if applied improperly. For example, a bank 'gambling on resurrection' could take on concentrated credit risk positions much more quickly than through the traditional lending process. Second … if there are improper internal capital allocations, then the writing of credit derivatives among a limited number of banks could lead to a 'cascading' of credit risk

among the market participants, with systemic consequences if there is default in this group.

(Goodhart *et al.*, 1998, p. 95)

However, here the Bank of England argued that '*caveat emptor* should apply', i.e. the goods are *subject to defects*, rather than prohibited *because* of these defects. Events are therefore *allowed to happen*, and although they are not completely abandoned, 'laissez faire is indispensable at a certain level' (Foucault, 2007, p. 68). In the 1998 publication, then, there was qualified optimism about the potential benefits of credit derivatives. Two aspects are particularly important: (a) the hope that the new instruments may lead to market completion and thus make systemic collapse less likely; (b) a worry over the difficulties that arise in valuing derivatives. In an elaboration on its initial take on credit derivatives, within a year they were primarily being viewed in more unequivocal terms as a 'risk unbundling' technology with 'significant economic benefits' (FSR, 1999a, p. 104). Indeed, it is interesting that in 1999 the Bank of England considered credit derivatives to be 'a serious alternative to central counterparties' as a means of controlling counterparty credit risk (FSR, 1999a, p. 124). There was also a recognition that credit derivatives created 'another level of complexity' for credit risk models because 'credit derivative technology uses a different and more complicated form of probabilities than those traditionally used in portfolio theory' (FSR, 1999a, p. 112).

Similarly, in both 2000 and 2001, the potential benefits of credit derivatives were no longer presented alongside issues with pricing or valuation. Instead, enthusiasm for credit derivatives was still tempered, but this time with issues about systemic risk. As such, credit derivatives were viewed as a positive development because they 'diversified risk by broadening the population of investors in credit risk' (FSR, 2000b, p. 16). The hope here was that risk was dispersed and systemic collapse would be much less likely. However, the Bank of England maintained that 'financial stability authorities need to follow' developments in credit risks 'closely' (FSR, 2000b, p. 16). The 'cash flows associated with derivatives' were 'generally not seen as a material problem in overall liquidity management'; however, concerns were raised for dynamic hedging to occur in 'abnormal conditions ... when the relationships between prices of financial instruments can alter suddenly' (FSR, 2000b, p. 108). In 2001, Clementi's speech reiterated the attractiveness of the risk management function of credit derivatives:

In a wider sense the development of these markets for the transfer of credit risk is highly desirable. The institution best placed to originate a loan is not necessarily best placed to bear the risk. Markets in credit risk allow financial institutions to diversify their exposure across different sectors and geographic regions while retaining customer relationships ... if they work well, markets in credit risk transfer have the potential to enhance financial stability and efficiency by ensuring that exposures to shocks are diffused throughout the system with no single player excessively exposed.

(Clementi, 2001a, p. 11)

However, alongside this, the FSR maintained that 'there is also the possibility that they could deliberately or inadvertently concentrate' risk because 'market participants can set limits on their own counterparty exposures but not on the aggregate exposures that the whole market might have to a particular counterparty' (FSR, 2001a, p. 140).

FSR 2002a is a particularly important document, because it discusses the role of 'relatively novel means of credit risk transfer' played in 'the aftermath of the Enron default; and that ... credit default swaps, have performed as intended' (and dispersed risk). It is important to note that even then, the other, negative account was still present. The Bank warned that:

> It is more difficult now to assess where risk is ending up. Greater use of credit derivatives by international banks to manage credit risk is also bringing into the credit arena some challenges already encountered in accounting measurement of interest rate and exchange rate risk.
>
> (FSR, 2002a, pp. 10–11)

The salient questions, Andrew Crockett, Howard Davies and others reminded us, were both of locating where 'certain risks are lodged' and asking 'whether they have been correctly priced?' (Crockett, 2003a, p. 46). As Crockett summarized, 'there are signs that credit transfer has, overall, been a stabilising factor, but there are concerns about whether some of the buyers of credit risk have properly assessed the risks they have taken on' (Crockett, 2003a, p. 46). The analysis serves to highlight ambivalence at the heart of the ability of credit derivatives to disperse risk and make systemic collapse less likely. Close inspection of the Bank of England archive, during the formative period in which the trade in credit derivatives was expanding, suggests that the potential to act as a device for credit risk management (and thus security logic more broadly) was inseparable from a fear about the various dangers associated with these calculative techniques at the heart of structured credit. Having a system where risk was mobilized required the Bank of England to take a gamble on financial risk management techniques. In the remainder of the chapter I plot the way statements about credit derivatives increasingly focused on the purported complexity of derivatives. There was, then, a sharpening of the Bank's approach to risk in the run-up to the crisis.

Focusing on a problem with complexity

To return to the archived texts, and returning to 2003, the financial stability reports document a sense of a period of change in which there was:

> a redistribution of credit risk, both within the banking sector and to non-bank financial institutions – not only via well-established mechanisms such as syndication and securitisation, but also via credit derivatives and structured credit products sold to non-bank investors. The credit markets – and so the capacity to manage credit risk – have continued to develop during 2003.
>
> (FSR, 2003b, p. 25)

Against the backdrop of the apparent maturing of markets for credit risk, however, both the 2003 financial stability reports and speeches by two senior staff members acknowledged that innovation had 'brought increasing complexity to the financial sector' (Crockett, 2003a, p. 46). FSR 2003a warned, for instance, that:

> there is specifically a danger that the riskiness of some innovative investment products designed to enhance yield might be underestimated or misunderstood, given the complexity of the payoffs; there is often a small probability of a very large fall in value.
>
> (FSR, 2003a, p. 11)

So, in 2003 there was a clear sense of the ambivalence highlighted in the previous section of this chapter. The middle of the first decade of the new millennium also saw the Bank very neatly knit credit derivatives into a broader narrative of the recent course taken by global finance. Indeed, there was a rather triumphalist tone about this particular portrayal of credit derivatives. Consider, for example, the following from a speech by Deputy Governor Large in 2003:

> I would like to mention complex financial instruments.… We have all read alarmist stories but Alan Greenspan often makes the point that one may over estimate some of the risks and underestimate the benefits. Shocks such as the Asian Financial Crisis[1] … have been successfully absorbed by the financial system. The fact is that they have not triggered a systemic financial crisis and the instruments themselves contribute to flexibility or resilience in the system. They enable financial institutions such as banks to transfer or diversify risk to a wide variety of participants including mutual funds and insurance companies and hence reduce concentration.
>
> (Large, 2003, pp. 7–8)

However, later in the same speech, Large went on to suggest that the Bank and its staff were also still fully aware of the tension between efficient risk transfer, (leading to market completion and thus enhancing financial stability and security), and concerns about complexity, transparency, and thus, and explicitly, pricing:

> We need to understand the implications and threats of these instruments. We start by breaking down the whole area of complex instruments into a more granular form … firstly there is the question of opacity and data. It is very hard to know both where risks have been transferred from and who is now on the receiving end. A dilemma of today's world is that despite attempts to improve transparency the new instruments themselves can actually make it more opaque. Second there are questions of pricing and evaluation.
>
> (Large, 2003, p. 8)

The Bank of England's ambivalence about credit derivatives was yet again present in 2004. In the June FSR the 'holding of other bank's credit derivatives' was seen as a good thing because 'CDSs may aid a bank facing a liquidity shock', but may 'not help the banking system as a whole in the case of a system wide liquidity shock, as CDSs are 'inside' rather than 'outside' assets' (FSR, 2004a, p. 64). Likewise, while 'products such as credit default swaps' were said to 'facilitate the transfer of credit risk to those agents able to bear and manage it most efficiently', at the same time they presented:

> Multiple challenges for prudential regulation. One of these challenges is part of a wider issue, which is how to assess the risks that arise in the trading book when it acts as the conduit for the dispersion of risks ... credit derivatives, while often a tool for reducing concentrations of credit risk, may also create direct credit exposures.
>
> (FSR, 2004b, p. 75)

If, during the first half of the 2000s, both facets of risk – and the way that credit derivatives secured in a fragile way – were clearly present in financial stability reports, this later developed into a preoccupation with downside risks. Initially, this focused on the risk associated with the increased complexity of credit derivatives. In 2007, the central bank's statements became more squarely centred on the creation of 'new and ever more complex financial instruments' in an era of innovation. The emergence of 'exotic' synthetic instruments which invested in tranches of CDOs were cause for concern because they were thought to be 'highly sensitive to small changes in the correlations of underlying returns which we do not understand with any great precision' (King, 2007, p. 5). Complexity was a key theme in FSR 2007a and by the release of FSR 2007b it was thought to be a source of uncertainty. As Bank Governor King argued:

> Ever more complex instruments are designed almost every day. Some of the important risks that could affect all instruments – from terrorist attacks, invasion of computer systems, or even the consequences of a flu pandemic – are almost *impossible to quantify*, and past experience offers little guide.
>
> (King, 2007, p. 5 *emphasis added*)

Increased complexity meant that faith in the risk management provided by credit derivatives became increasingly speculative. And yet, this gamble was hardly seen as such. In 2007 Paul Tucker admitted that:

> given the variety of vehicles and their use of risk transfer instruments, it has become commonplace that 'we' no longer know where risk lies. Most often, the 'we' is the official sector, and in particular bank regulators. But 'we' might just as well be the management of banks and dealers.
>
> (Tucker, 2007, p. 7)

However, alongside this he argued that he was 'not so sure' that this was 'a bad thing'. Tucker made two points that are worth mentioning. First, Tucker (2007a, p. 7) argued that 'derivative markets in interest rates, exchange rates and equity prices have existed – on-exchange and over-the-counter – for approaching two decades. We have not known where those risks are for quite a long time'. Second, Tucker (2007a, pp. 8–9) makes the case that:

> if we 'no longer know where the risk is', that implies that it has been dispersed beyond the regulated sector ... if risks were widely and evenly distributed across savings institutions internationally, a very nasty shock causing a sharp fall in asset markets would not obviously destabilise the financial system ... so it would seem that there is a good deal to welcome in the greater dispersion of risk made possible by modern instruments, markets and institutions.

Tucker still qualified this bullish statement by saying that, 'there are most certainly qualifications to such an apparently alluring conclusion ... the banking system retains risk in a number of ways, both pre- and post-risk transfer, and its aggregate balance sheet has in fact expanded' (Tucker 2007a, pp. 8–9). Despite this, it does seem clear that there was a culture in which the Bank of England is nonplussed by not being able to visualize risk in any comprehensive way. Alongside this, other anxieties were still present in statements about credit derivatives, especially those reporting developments in the US subprime mortgage sector in which the number of defaults on mortgages was rapidly increasing. For example:

> market contacts have pointed to the recent volatility of prices in the synthetic US sub-prime markets as suggestive of how, during a period of stress, prices in the cash and derivative markets may become disconnected, causing the correlation assumptions underpinning hedging to break down and crystallising basis risks.
>
> (FSR, 2007a, p. 47)

By 2007, emerging fragilities in the global financial system started to become the focus of FSRs discussing credit derivatives. Investors bought these financial instruments assuming that the credit ratings attached to the 'Mortgage-Backed Securities' were accurate reflections of this risk involved and subprime mortgage loans tripled 'between 2000 and 2006, reaching US$1.17 trillion' (Broome, 2014, p. 189). However, this seemingly 'everyone wins' scenario did not last forever.

As Langley suggests, the calculative devices of what was known as 'Internal Risk Management' failed because they:

> failed, in their own terms, to price default risk effectively; securitization enabled so-called 'risk spreading' among investors, but intensified the

contraction of lending once uncertainties became apparent and liquidity dried up; and interest-only and adjustable rate mortgage products sharply exposed borrowers to uncertainties over interest rates and house prices and lenders to rapidly rising default rates.

(Langley, 2008b, p. 472)

It is FSR 2007b which highlighted the crystallization of concerns about the pricing of credit derivatives because it argued that 'price moves a long way outside the range of historical experience confounded pricing models' (FSR, 2007b, p. 19). The Bank of England forecasts went as far as saying that that 'the greatest vulnerability facing the financial system is a significant increase in the probability of risk pricing uncertainty' (FSR, 2007b, p. 15). As more and more of these subprime borrowers defaulted on their mortgages during the mid-2000s, financial institutions became increasingly unsure of how to value the credit derivatives on their own, or other banks', balance sheets (Broome, 2014, p. 189). In 2007, BNP Paribas publicly conceded that there was a valuation problem for assets related to subprime lending. At this point, credit derivatives, which nobody could value, were deemed too risky and close to a gamble by BNP Paribas. In particular, it is important not to underestimate the significance of BNP Paribas for the Bank of England's understanding of credit derivatives. As this French bank publicly admitted that it was unsure how to calculate industry wide exposures to credit derivatives, the following excerpt from a Bank of England document suggested that:

The announcement by BNP Paribas in early August that it was temporarily suspending redemptions from several funds, demonstrated *the global spread of valuation difficulties*. These events highlighted how inadequate information about the location of exposures in global credit markets could translate into sharply heightened uncertainty about counterparty risk.

(FSR, 2007b, p. 7 *emphasis added*)

Indeed, in the same FSR, the Bank of England reported that the market for mortgage-backed securities and CDOs became illiquid:

BNP Paribas suspended redemptions from three money market funds for two weeks in August because they did not feel they could fairly value their positions ... as money market funds had previously been assumed to be low risk, this came as a further adverse shock to investors' expectations. In the absence of reliable information and confidence on the part of both buyers and sellers, markets in ABS largely shut and CDO issuance came to a near halt.

(FSR, 2007b, p. 19)

The difficulty with pricing credit derivatives remained at the heart of financial stability discourses in 2008. Following the collapse of Lehman Brothers due to this bank being overexposed to credit derivative products, significantly overleveraged and unable to find buyer or bail-out agreement with public authorities, the Bank of England argued that:

> valuation uncertainty rose sharply, particularly for more complex products where informational problems were most acute, as end-investors lost confidence in credit rating methodologies.
>
> (FSR, 2008b, pp. 8–9)

Indeed, 'illiquidity and uncertainty ... led to a lack of price discovery, amplifying uncertainty about asset values and mispricing'. The Bank maintained that there remained significant variation and inconsistencies between the prices of US subprime RMBS tranches (FSR, 2008b, p. 12). Going into 2009, and both the intensification of the Global Financial Crisis and the public bail-out of distressed financial institutions, the downside risk associated with credit derivatives seemingly reverted further and further towards a concern with the complexity of financial innovation. The textual analysis demonstrates that when the Bank of England was concerned about credit derivatives, the issue was almost exclusively the perceived complexity of the CDO chains. As Andrew Haldane of the Bank of England argued:

> Financial innovation often took a particular form – structured credit – with risk decomposed and then reconstituted like the meat in an increasingly exotic sausage. The result was a *complex* interlocking set of claims. With each restructuring of ingredients, the web branched and the dimensionality of the network multiplied ... end-investors in these instruments were no more likely to know the name of the companies in their portfolios than the name of the cow or pig in their exotic hot dog.
>
> (Haldane, 2009, p. 16 *emphasis added*)

What I want to advocate here is that it was around this risk associated with credit derivatives – the complexity which made them increasingly more and more of a gamble regarding their efficacy as a risk management tool – that the Bank of England focused efforts to consolidate the risk dispersal aspect of the derivatives. This can be thought of as a response to the misfire of credit derivatives, counter-performative because rather than dispersing risk in a stabilizing way, they instead concentrated risk in a destabilizing manner. Further, and to reiterate the argument about functional spatiality, Engelen *et al.* (2011) provide a telling account of the mobilization of risk in the years leading up to the Global Financial Crisis. If financial innovation 'built up (structures) by fitting together events', risks were concentrated in the centre of circuits, rather than being dispersed chains (Engelen *et al.* 2011, pp. 56–63). And, the complexity of such derivatives obfuscated (or at least was thought to have) the concentration of credit risk at a few systemically important financial institutions and entities.

Conclusions

As we have seen, credit derivatives emerged in the New York swaps markets in the early 1990s and were originally traded by a small number of institutions. More innovations occurred in international debt markets housed in London as market participants tried to diversify the intense concentrations of risk that were developing. Credit derivatives were thought to move risk in a way that traded it away from the core hubs of the financial system. Such derivatives, then, were treated by regulators as a significant development with the potential to 'complete' credit markets. At the same time however, regulators were clearly aware of significant downside risks associated with the products, meaning that the derivatives secured imperfectly. This overriding ambivalence in Bank of England statements persisted through to the early 2000s, and the Bank became increasingly concerned with the complexity of credit derivatives. Less sure of where risks were going and the liability structure of securitized debt products, investment risk management became increasingly speculative, in terms of a gamble about something uncertain. Indeed, Paul Tucker argued that an inability to see where risks were could well be a sign that risk had been diversified.

By the mid-2000s, the Bank of England raised its growing anxieties with the valuation of credit derivatives. In 2007 the French Bank BNP Paribas signalled that credit derivatives were far too speculative, and suspended trading these products. Suddenly credit derivatives became illiquid and led to a general freeze in inter-bank lending (Nesvetailova, 2010). The geography of finance here suggests that the mobilization of risk had concentrated risk rather than dispersing it and moreover, did so in a way that was not immediately visible (Engelen *et al.*, 2011). As will be developed in Chapters 6 and 7, this functional spatiality of finance would have consequences for Bank of England money cultures, risk management and financial stability techniques.

Note

1 The crisis was triggered by a series of currency devaluations that spread through many Asian markets beginning in the summer of 1997. The currency markets first failed in Thailand as the result of the government's decision to no longer peg the local currency to the US dollar (US$). Fears about the fundamentals of many Asian economies saw attempts to withdraw foreign direct investment. Such contagion led to extreme instability in financial markets. See Yadav (2008) for an overview of how risk technologies contributed to the crisis and Best (2010) for a critique of the policy lessons distilled from this episode of instability.

References

Amoore, L. 2013. *The Politics of Possibility: Risk and security beyond probability.* Durham NC: Duke University Press.

Bank of England. 1999. Financial Stability Review, June 1999 (a). [pdf] Available at: www.bankofengland.co.uk/archive/Documents/historicpubs/fsr/1999/fsrfull9906.pdf (Accessed 20 September 2013).

Bank of England. 2000. Financial Stability Review, December 2000 (b). [pdf] Available at: www.bankofengland.co.uk/archive/Documents/historicpubs/fsr/2000/fsrfull0012.pdf (Accessed 20 September 2013).

Bank of England. 2001. Financial Stability Review, June 2001 (a). [pdf] Available at: www.bankofengland.co.uk/archive/Documents/historicpubs/fsr/2001/fsrfull0106.pdf (Accessed 20 September 2013).

Bank of England. 2002. Financial Stability Review, June 2002 (a). [pdf] Available at: www.bankofengland.co.uk/archive/Documents/historicpubs/fsr/2002/fsrfull0206.pdf (Accessed 20 September 2013).

Bank of England. 2003a. Financial Stability Review, June 2003. [pdf] Available at: www. bankofengland.co.uk/archive/Documents/historicpubs/fsr/2003/fsrfull0306.pdf (Accessed 20 September 2013).

Bank of England. 2003b. Financial Stability Review, December 2003. [pdf] Available at: www.bankofengland.co.uk/archive/Documents/historicpubs/fsr/2003/fsrfull0312.pdf (Accessed 20 September 2013).

Bank of England. 2004a. Financial Stability Review, June 2004. [pdf] Available at: www. bankofengland.co.uk/archive/Documents/historicpubs/fsr/2004/fsrfull0406.pdf (Accessed 20 September 2013).

Bank of England. 2004b. Financial Stability Review, December 2004. [pdf] Available at: www.bankofengland.co.uk/archive/Documents/historicpubs/fsr/2004/fsrfull0412.pdf (Accessed 7 November 2013).

Bank of England. 2007a. Financial Stability Report, 26 April 2007. [pdf] Available at: www.bankofengland.co.uk/publications/Documents/fsr/2007/fsrfull0704.pdf (Accessed 6 November 2013).

Bank of England. 2007b. Financial Stability Report, 25 October 2007. [pdf] Available at: www.bankofengland.co.uk/publications/Documents/fsr/2007/fsrfull0710.pdf (Assessed 1 November 2013).

Bank of England. 2008a. Financial Stability Report, 1 May 2008. [pdf] Available at: www.bankofengland.co.uk/publications/Documents/fsr/2008/fsrfull0804.pdf (Accessed 1 November 2013).

Bank of England. 2008b. Financial Stability Report, 28 October 2008 (b). [pdf] Available at: www.bankofengland.co.uk/publications/Documents/fsr/2008/fsrfull0810.pdf (Accessed 25 October 2013).

Best, J. 2010. 'The Limits of Financial Risk Management: Or what we didn't learn from the Asian Crisis'. *New Political Economy* 15(1), pp. 29–49.

Broome, A. 2014. *Issues and Actors in the Global Political Economy*. Basingstoke: Palgrave Macmillan.

Bryan, D., and Rafferty, M. 2006. *Capitalism with derivatives: A political economy of financial derivatives, capital and class*. Basingstoke: Palgrave Macmillan.

Bryan, D., and Rafferty, M. 2007. 'Financial derivatives and the theory of money'. *Economy and Society* 36(1), pp. 134–158.

Buffett, W. 2003. 'Letter to Berkshire Hathaway's shareholders', 21 February 2003. [pdf] Available at: www.berkshirehathaway.com/letters/2002pdf.pdf (Accessed 15 May 2015).

Christophers, B. 2009. 'Complexity, finance, and progress in human geography'. *Progress in Human Geography* 33(6), pp. 807–824.

Clementi, D. 2001. 'Recent Developments in securities markets and the implications for financial stability', speech given to the Euromoney International Bond Congress at the Queen Elizabeth II Conference Centre in London, 21 February 2001. [pdf] Available at: www.bankofengland.co.uk/archive/Documents/historicpubs/speeches/2001/speech 113.pdf (Accessed 25 October 2013).

Cloke, J. 2009. 'An economic wonderland: derivative castles built on sand'. *Critical perspectives on international business* 5(1/2), pp. 107–119.

Collier, S., and Lakoff, A. 2008. 'The vulnerability of vital systems: how "critical infrastructure" became a security problem'. In Cavelty, MD and Kristensen KS, (eds.) *The Politics of Securing the Homeland: Critical Infrastructures, Risk and Securitisation.* New York: Routledge, pp. 17–39.

Crockett, A., Ridley, A., Lamfalussy, A., and Davies, H. 2002. 'International Standard Setting in Financial Supervision', lecture given at Institute of Economic Affairs, London, 5 February 2003. [pdf] Available at: https://iea.org.uk/wp-content/uploads/2016/07/upldbook347pdf.pdf (Accessed 30 August 2017).

Durand, C. 2017. *Fictitious Capital: How Finance is Appropriating our Future*, Trans. David Broder. London: Verso.

Engelen, E., Erturk, I., Froud, J., Johal, S., Leaver, A., Moran, M., Nilsson, A., and Williams, K. 2011. *After the great complacence: Financial crisis and the politics of reform.* Oxford: Oxford University Press.

Esposito, E. 2011. *The Future of Futures: The Time of Money in Financing and Society.* Cheltenham: Edward Elgar.

Foucault, M. 2007. *Security, Territory, Population.* Basingstoke: Palgrave Macmillan.

Goodhart, C., Hartmann, P., Llewellyn, D., Rojas-Suarez, L., and Weisbrod, S. 1998. *Financial Regulation: Why, how and where now?* Abingdon: Routledge.

Greenspan, A. 2007. *The Age of Turbulence.* London: Allen Lane.

Haldane, A. 2009. 'Rethinking the Financial Network', speech given at the Financial Student Association, Amsterdam 28 April 2009. [pdf] Available at: www.bankofengland.co.uk/archive/Documents/historicpubs/speeches/2009/speech386.pdf (Accessed 11 October 2013).

King, M. 2007. 'Speech' given at the Bank of England, 23 January 2007. [pdf] Available at: www.bankofengland.co.uk/archive/Documents/historicpubs/speeches/2007/speech300.pdf (Accessed 12 October 2013).

Large, A. 2003. 'Financial Stability: Maintaining Confidence in a Complex World', speech given at City of London Central Banking Conference, National Liberal Club, 17 November 2003. [pdf] Available at: www.bankofengland.co.uk/archive/Documents/historicpubs/speeches/2003/speech205.pdf (Accessed 10 October 2013).

Lozano, B. 2015. *Of Synthetic Finance: Three Essays of Speculative Materialism.* New York: Routledge.

MacKenzie, D. 2007. 'The material production of virtuality: innovation, cultural geography and facticity in derivatives markets'. *Economy and Society* 36(3), pp. 355–376.

Nesvetailova, A. 2010. 'The crisis of invented money: Liquidity illusion and the global credit meltdown'. *Theoretical Inquiries in Law* 11(1), pp. 125–147.

Tucker, P. 2007. 'A Perspective on Recent Monetary and Financial System Developments', speech given at Meryll Lynch, 26 April 2007. [pdf] Available at: www.bankofengland.co.uk/archive/Documents/historicpubs/speeches/2007/speech308.pdf (Accessed 20 May 2017).

Wigan, D. 2009. 'Financialisation and derivatives: Constructing an artifice of indifference'. *Competition & Change* 13(2), pp. 157–172.

Yadav, V. 2008. *Risk in International Finance.* Abingdon: Routledge.

5 A fatal flaw

Introduction: revisiting the number that killed us

If, before the Global Financial Crisis, credit derivatives were viewed with suspicion as 'weapons of mass destruction', then a second and contemporaneous financial security technique that became viewed with outright contempt following the crisis was the regulatory use of Value-at-Risk (VaR) calculations by financial institutions. Indeed, Pablo Triana (2012) has memorably described VaR as 'a liar' and 'the number that killed us'. In contrast to this hyperbolic discourse, VaR had a relatively mundane genesis. The technique was first developed and deployed in the early 1990s by financial institutions such as J.P. Morgan to measure market risk (Goodhart *et al.*, 1998). VaR tells a trader or institution what losses are probable from a particular set of trading conditions under normal circumstances. So, to use Triana's example:

> a one-day 95 percent VaR of $50 million' means that a firm 'would be expected to lose more than $50 million only 12 days out of a year's 250 trading days.
>
> (Triana, 2012, pp. xi–xii)

Regulatory uses of VaR have to be considered within a wider history of regulatory thought and practices. Sian Lewin makes the case that prior to 1988, there was no international regulatory consensus on how banks should manage their balance sheets risks. Capital was fairly 'simplistic and fragmented', with the typical requirement being for banks to hold a minimum capital ratio, calculated very simply as a ratio of capital to total assets (Lewin, 2017). In the UK, this had only been a requirement since the Banking Act of 1987. It was becoming clear that the levels of risk being taken and traded were not being measured or estimated in a way that matched up to the complexity of the financially engineered 'fungible globules of risk' that emerged in New York and were documented in the previous chapter (Wigan, 2009). There was, from a regulatory perspective, growing disquiet about the risks being taken in relation to low levels of regulatory capital (Goodhart, 2011).

From the late 1980s onwards, however, capital adequacy, that is to say the amount of regulatory capital banks have to hold in reserve to absorb losses, was set by standards negotiated through the BIS Basel Committee on Banking Supervision. Under the terms of the 1988 Basel Accord the amount of a certain quality regulatory capital was to be held depending on the ratios to credit default 'risk weighted' assets. As Langley (2015, p. 127) explains:

> all government bonds held on the asset side of a bank's balance sheet were given a zero percent risk-weighting, loans to major economy banks had a 20 percent risk-weighting, and corporate loans came with a 100 percent risk-weighting that required the full 8 percent of their value had to be held as so-called 'regulatory capital'.

Value-at-Risk emerged within a specific regulatory context. Crucially, Basel I did not discuss or cover market risk, instead focusing on credit default risk. Only later did a measure for market risk become part of a regulatory context of capital accords. The initial impact of the Basel I was that aggregate levels of global bank capitalization did rise, but in the following decade these levels lapsed. Banks were able to exploit the rules to take on increasingly riskier, and potentially profitable, assets without setting aside additional regulatory capital. Critically, in the 1990s there were changing perceptions about the potential for technology to support the applications of finance theory, challenges to regulatory conservatism and an 'institutional climate of financialization' (Power, 2007, p. 72). The Basel Committee set to work on incorporating market risk into the existing Basel Accord, but did so in a relatively unsophisticated way when compared to what was going on in financial institutions like J.P. Morgan (Goodhart, 2011). As such, the calculative device of Value-at-Risk first emerged as a measurement tool 'inside dealing floors' to ascertain the level of market risk associated with specific trading decisions (Triana, 2012, p. xv). Here Lockwood (2015, p. 272) provides a detailed account of the germination of Value-at-Risk at J.P. Morgan, such that:

> as financial markets became increasingly globalized, (J.P. Morgan) wanted to be able to apply the concepts of value and risk to portfolios of assets that were denominated in different currencies and subject to different interest rates. This would allow them to measure the riskiness of the portfolio as a whole and 'manage' it through quantitative limits and off-setting investments, or hedges.

The existing regulations were cast as outdated and clumsy when compared to the innovative new derivative methods for diversifying risks that had been developed within financial institutions. Consequently, J.P. Morgan released VaR as part of its *Risk Metrics* into the public domain, arguing that their aim was to:

> establish a benchmark for market risk measurement. The absence of a common point of reference for market risks makes it difficult to compare different approaches to and measures of market risks. Risks are comparable only when they are measured with the same yardstick.
>
> (J.P. Morgan, 1996)

VaR was, effectively, being presented as 'a credible internal code of conduct' for market risk measurement (Tett, 2009, p. 39). This was, it has to be said, a highly political process. Following the release of VaR in 1993, the (think-tank) Institute for International Finance and the financial industry representative group The Group of Thirty both critiqued the existing Basel regulations on capital adequacy and championed the technical merits of the Value-at-Risk device (Yadav, 2008, pp. 78–79).

For Michael Power, 'the significant change' occurred in 1996 when the Basel Committee moved towards the formalization of a philosophy whereby 'banks regulate capital according to their own models, subject to regulatory oversight' (Power, 2005, pp. 581–582). It was then that an amendment was made to the capital accord to incorporate market risks, by the Basel Committee, in which they advocated the adoption of industry led measures of risk, such as VaR (Lewin, 2017). In accordance with the 1996 Amendment, banks were to develop their own internal VaR risk models for regulatory purposes (Lockwood, 2015, p. 274).

In 2004, the Securities and Exchange Commission in the United States formally adjusted its 'net capital rule' and agreed that VaR could be used to calculate the 'costliness, affordability and leverage of trading positions' (Triana, 2012, p. *xxxiv*). Importantly, VaR acts on and brings forth a distinct formulation of financial stability, the idea that stability can be achieved by each institution managing its own level of market risk independently. Basel II introduced a three 'pillar' system that, while continuing to specify minimum capital requirements, added guidelines on supervision for national regulators and new information disclosure standards for banks. Andrew Baker argues that for a substantial period, financial stability was promoted through a view that the private and individual pricing of risk would determine aggregate risk (Baker, 2013, p. 115).

The contours of this chapter are three-fold. First, I present the case that when Bank of England publications are analysed, it becomes clear that while it was a standard of accuracy which initially drove the adoption of VaR, this standard was later disavowed in response to sustained criticism of VaR in the early 2000s. This critique of VaR held that it actually served to increase market volatility by leading to the widespread and simultaneous cutting of positions. This I characterize as a critique of the Bank culture of *speculating on risk*. In many ways, this makes Value-at-Risk an important case study of how central banks deal with counter-performativity (MacKenzie, 2005). While initially the Bank of England did not respond to this critique, it later did defend the use of VaR in 2002. The second section provides examples from the archive that the Bank of England modified a discourse so that in order to justify continued use of VaR, there had to be a subtle yet significant shift in the standard regulating the use of VaR. Through these intertwined processes the Bank of England sought to engender a shift in the epistemic standard applied to VaR, from a standard of accuracy to a standard of precision. Due to the role of an article in FSR 2002b written by Phillipe Jorion, I have analysed this shift as hinging on a public facing economist acting as a technical expert. The shift to precision was made through appeal to 'smoothing mechanisms' in the Basel version of VaR.

Third and finally, I make the case that despite this shift to precision, and according to Bank of England statements, the extreme events of the Global Financial Crisis undermined the assumption of normality with the VaR calculation. And from this point of view, the inaccuracy of this assumption created a regulatory blind-spot, an ignoring of extreme macroeconomic conditions. Here then, we see a renewed criticism of the accuracy of VaR and a second moment in which Bank understandings of VaR had to encounter the way that using VaR to manage risk was something of a gamble. Further still, here, the Bank of England did take on board this critique of VaR.

The relationship between VaR and accuracy

Bank of England statements about VaR are instructive for analysing the institution's conceptualization of financial risk. What detailed archival research into VaR reveals is that when we study the adoption of the technical devices of financial economics for regulatory purposes, the idea of different epistemic standards is salient. By epistemic standards I refer to the epistemic rules or 'grammars' that operate within a particular technical discipline at a particular time (Amoore, 2014, pp. 3–4). The contemporary relationship between science, mathematics and finance is important here (de Goede, 2001). In other words, there are different standards or 'grammars' of knowledge at play in different instances. For example, the first empirical chapter outlined that 'the lack of a scientific pricing method has never been a deterrent to trading' (Goodhart *et al.*, 1998, p. 94). Similarly, a discussion of setting a level for capital adequacy ratios in a financial stability report reveals that 'we should of course be under no illusion that the ratios chosen in 1988 were arrived through a scientific process' (FSR, 2000b, p. 155). These two historical and textual examples serve to illustrate that a 'true' value does not always need to be produced in the sense of scientific standards of knowledge. In this section I focus on the role of accuracy in early Bank of England statements concerning Value-at-Risk and the measurement of risk.

While I must clarify that I am not arguing that financial risk management developed in a linear fashion, I do want to argue that a standard of accuracy was historically important for the widespread use of VaR. Alongside this we could also add efficiency (Triana, 2012, p. *xxxiii*), and usefulness, as other important factors in the proliferation of VaR before the Subprime Crisis (Millo and MacKenzie, 2009a, p. 640). However, a wide range of Bank of England documents supports Gillian Tett's assertion that originally 'VaR was primarily concerned with measuring market risk' (Tett, 2009, p. 58). While in 1997 there was an admission that the Bank of England was 'not yet convinced that risk management has evolved sufficiently to capture all elements of specific risk in an empirically-proven manner', the Bank was 'ready to review promptly if and when the industry can provide convincing evidence that specific risk is being modelled adequately' (FSR 1997: 80). In this period, the Bank seemed very open to the contribution that the financial industry could make in developing regulatory techniques.

Only a little later, trading activities and markets were evaluated in terms of the level of VaR in the respective markets. This allowed risk to be measured, 'recognized' and probability assigned to it (Clementi, 1999, p. 3). In such a way, the Bank of England now took the position that it was possible for risk to be 'captured accurately' and with 'greater sensitivity', so that 'if risks appear(ed) to be higher than the capital set aside to back them ... or whether a higher figure is needed' (Clementi, 2001, p. 3). Consequently, regulators hoped to 'align regulatory capital more closely with the underlying risks' (FSR, 2001a, pp. 99–100). And while it has since been argued that 'risk modelers' claims to objectivity and accuracy are contestable because VaR does not 'neutrally describe market dynamics', this was not how VaR was being presented at the time (Lockwood, 2015, p. 721).

The first step in the epistemic standard of accuracy was a realism about risk, in which claims were made about there being 'actual riskiness' or 'specific risk'. This provided a foundation for the use of VaR as a measurement of market risk exposure and market risk in trading activities, which frequently happened in FSRs. For example, the following was written during a period in which the bursting of the dotcom bubble and the collapse of LTCM brought market risk to prominence:

> Average value at risk (VaR) – the maximum amount which, on the basis of relatively recent price movements and within a specified level of confidence, an institution would expect to lose on its positions over a given trading period – generally declined for the trading books of major US securities firms between annual reporting dates in 1999 and 2000. Given that volatility of many markets in 2000 was relatively high, lower reported VaRs suggest that securities firms might have reduced the size of their market risk positions.
>
> (FSR, 2001a, p. 65)

Similarly, in the second FSR of 2001, the Bank of England was clearly thinking in terms of VaR:

> As measured by average Value-at-Risk as a proportion of shareholders' (equity) funds, market risk in trading activities was higher for a number of LCFIs in H1 2001 than in 2000, perhaps partly because of higher historical volatility in financial markets. But, according to published data, exposures remained a fraction of shareholders' equity and below 1999 levels. Since then, market participants, taken as a whole, appear to have avoided large trading losses in spite of the large movements in some prices since 11 September.
>
> (FSR, 2001b, p. 82)

Moving forward three years to 2004, we can find further examples where the Bank was content to use VaR as the straightforward measurement of market risk when the Bank of England argued that:

> market risk in the banking book is not accounted for on a mark-to-market basis. In practice, when interpreting banks' disclosures, it can be unclear whether some financial instruments are located in the trading book or elsewhere. Proposed changes in accounting standards may resolve this, which would be welcome. Trading book assets of most large UK-owned banks account for around 10% of total assets. As measured by average value-at-risk (VaR), in most cases market risk in these portfolios decreased marginally during 2003.
>
> (FSR, 2004, p. 68)

Millo and MacKenzie (2009a) credit Michael Power (2007) with the insight that the growth of risk management in the last two decades is related to a 'gradual convergence between risk calculation and risk management'. For Millo and MacKenzie, the shift from 'descriptive knowledge (risk calculation) into (practice-oriented) risk management' would have the consequence of organizational actors that gradually shift resources towards communicating and coordinating action, thus paying relatively less attention to merely calculating risk levels (Millo and MacKenzie, 2009a, p. 639). The idea then, is that usefulness, for example making communication clearer, became a more significant factor in model based risk management than accuracy alone. What I want to do here is to problematize this 'gradual convergence', and focus on a significant transformation in the technique of VaR, and how this was dealt with in an inventive and imaginative manner.

As we have already seen, VaR was developed as part of J.P. Morgan's *Risk Metrics* and championed as an internal code of conduct within the investment banking industry (Tett, 2009). The decision to incorporate VaR into legislation such as the 'net capital rule' of the Securities and Exchange Commission meant that, effectively, investment banks were governing the costliness, affordability and leverage of (their own) trading positions (Power, 2005, pp. 581–582).

Speculating on risk: long-term capital management (LTCM)

The collapse of LTCM in 1998 helped to illustrate the speculative nature of the reliance on Value-at-Risk calculations to secure financial stability. Long Term Capital Management was an extremely high profile and highly leveraged hedge fund which operated through arbitrage 'between international price differences of the same or similar financial instruments' (de Goede, 2001, p. 158). By leveraged, I mean the borrowing of capital to increase the potential return on investments. Leverage can magnify both profits and losses. On its own, financial arbitrage generally tends to generate very small profits and so to earn substantial returns, LTCM became increasingly leveraged. In 1998, LTCM was committed to more than 20,000 transactions and conducted business with over 75 counter-parties (de Goede, 2001, p. 160). The default by Russia on its sovereign debt obligations triggered a series of price movements that led to the collapse of LTCM. Due to the interconnected nature of the hedge fund and the fact that it held 5 per cent of the total global fixed-income market, the US Treasury bailed out LTCM in September 1998 (Investopedia, n.d). The failure of LTCM raised important questions about the use of the Black-Scholes-Merton pricing model but importantly, highlighted volatility issues when VaR was used as a bench-mark for the cutting of trading positions. If all market participants use the same model to gauge when positions should be cut, this will lead to herding behaviour and a volatile rush for the exit at the same time (de Goede, 2001; MacKenzie, 2005; Triana, 2012). According to Donald MacKenzie, the 'events of 1998 … suggested a reflexive loop that was counterperformative rather than performa-tive' because VaR brought about the instability it was seeking to avoid (Mac-Kenzie, 2005, p. 186). In other words:

> When a VaR limit is breached, traders are typically asked to cut down posi-tions (by risk managers) until their exposure (to risk) is reduced back below their VaR limit. In a quest to reduce risk, traders are forced to sell some of their portfolio into the market. If many firms do this concurrently, massive volatility and crashing prices may rapidly ensue … the end result: massive liquidations leading to additional massive liquidations (as VaR gets breached over and over again) causing huge losses and potentially a system wide breakdown.
>
> (Triana, 2012, p. 29)

In such a way, and as MacKenzie presciently points out, VaR can be counter-performative by increasing instability. As *The Economist* magazine argued in 1998:

> value-at-risk models implicitly assumed that banks could always get out of their positions: they made no allowance for liquidity risk. Unfortunately, the exit has been well and truly jammed as everybody scrambled to get out of the same positions at the same time. Intermediaries, mostly investment banks, became less willing to bid for assets. With liquidity reduced, volatil-ity tended to rise and prices to fall, in turn forcing the banks to sell even more.

In 1999, very soon after the collapse of LTCM, the Bank of England was relat-ively uncritical of the role of VaR in the global economic turbulence around this particular crisis, as VaR was still described as 'almost the industry standard measure' (FSR, 1999a, p. 130). In FSR 1999b (p. 138), the Bank reported that 'Merton-style models … accurately estimate Value at Risk for portfolios of US dollar denominated international bonds over rolling twelve month periods between 1988 and 1998'. The study was somewhat negative in its conclusions since 'the models used in the study yield far more 'exceptions' than they document'. Similar in this lack of serious scrutiny were both FSRs from 2000 as neither had much to say about VaR (FSR 2000a, 2000b).

By early 2002 the Bank of England acknowledged the critique of VaR as it reports that critics, 'such as *The Economist* newspaper', argue 'that VaR-based capital requirements experienced sharp increases during the Summer of 1998, leading to forced position cutting and increased volatility' (FSR, 2002, p. 123). I will go onto make the case that in 2002 the Bank of England engaged with this critique of VaR, but presented a rebuttal of the argument. The argument I am forwarding in the following section is that, when faced by the allegation that volatility destabilization was caused by VaR, the Bank of England made an important improvisation to justify continued use of VaR – it disavowed the calculative device's own accuracy. And, while it could be argued that this intervention lacked 'real' force because financial regulation was the responsibility of the FSA, I would argue that the ability of the Bank to shape mainstream opinion, and of its staff to move into other regulatory bodies and institutions, was still significant. Crucial for this reading of an intervention by the Bank of England is an article by Professor Phillipe Jorion[1] in FSR 2002, entitled 'Fallacies about the effects of market risk management systems'. At this point it can be asked, what is a form of economic governance that disavows its own accuracy?

The answer I forward here is that the technique of VaR had to be seen to be stabilizing through an improvised argument. For this interpretation of a fundamental shift, a key document is the Jorion penned chapter of FSR 2002, because the article in question purported to show that:

> Capital requirements should be constructed so as to be reasonably 'smooth' over time, be they for market or credit risk. This fact has escaped most of the literature on Value-at-Risk, where the focus has been near-exclusively on developing accurate 1-day volatility forecasts … Other important objectives, beyond accuracy, are the average level of capital as well as fluctuations in capital requirements.
>
> (Jorion, 2002, p. 116)

Jorion improvised a shift from accuracy to one of precision because he argued there are other 'important objectives beyond accuracy' (Jorion, 2002, p. 116). Later Jorion argued that 'the quest for accuracy in VaR measures, which would dictate fast-moving systems, should take second place to stability in the market risk charge' (Jorion, 2002, p. 125). From this we can plausibly infer that precision was viewed to be useful. Millo and MacKenzie (2009b) focus on the idea that usefulness can be as important to sustain an inaccurate model. As Millo and MacKenzie (2009b, p. 111) found from an interview with an American regulator in 2001:

> it was more important to approve a financial risk management system that was acceptable by virtually all market participants, albeit being unreliable

under infrequent extreme conditions, than to have a system whose most market participants had complaints about its usefulness.

So, we can infer that VaR was still viewed as having considerable utility by the Bank of England. And, as we will see, it is the drive towards usefulness, in the form of a stabilizing mechanism, that saw the Bank of England shift the focus of VaR usage from accuracy to precision. Similarly, Langley, drawing on the history of science, argues that it is a positive affective charge which then sustains the performative force of precise techniques (Langley, 2013a, pp. 55, 67).

Improvisation occurred in the way that calculations were drawn up and completed, data was plotted into graphs and lines were drawn. It is the comparison between the lines within charts 4 and 5 – in Figures 5.1 and 5.2 – which was crucial to explain the precision brought about through the market risk charge of the VaR calculation used in Basel II. Further still, in this document, the different VaR calculations (Basel Market Risk Charge and Daily VaR) were included and had a role to play (see Figures 5.1 and 5.3). The improvisation set out by Jorion lay with the 'smoothing mechanism' that Jorion found in the Basel Market Risk Charge. Capital and risk calculations using the Basel model of VaR were 'not volatile' (as alleged), but 'smooth'. This is important, because it prioritized a capital charge based on an average over 60 days, rather than accuracy (Jorion, 2002, pp. 116, 126).

Quite literally, the transformation in interpretation of a set of data was drawn from 'P Jorion's calculations' (Figure 5.3). The transformation derived from the technician's ability to calculate, interpret data and make inferences (i.e. the graphs showing 'smooth' curves for the capital charges under the Basel version of VaR) and to explain the significance of this data. Capital and risk calculations using the Basel model of VaR were not volatile (as alleged by VaR's critics), but smooth. Jorion's interpretation is the 'authentic' interpretation of the data, as opposed to the 'fallacies' which are his target in this part of the FSR. The display of the calculative process and use of data that Jorion provided established the authenticity of this technical improvisation. The lines on the graph contributed to the epistemic shift, because the smoothness of these lines was at stake in the moving of the epistemic standard away from accuracy to precision (Figures 5.2 and 5.3). The stability sought for then, was a case of achieving the same results given the same inputs. This differs somewhat from the idea that the intended target is being recorded. In other words, this is a matter of reliability or precision, rather than accuracy. This follows Lorraine Daston's general point about scientific practices; that other admirable methodological qualities are just as desirable as accuracy (Daston, 1995, p. 8; Amoore, 2013, p. 67; see Langley, 2015, p. 166).

Public facing economists are becoming more and more prominent, and here I think it is possible to view such economists as technical experts in the contemporary age (See Miller and Rose, 1990). Academic economists such as Ben Bernanke and Paul Krugman have both a prominent role and high profile in public life, be that through sovereign institutions such as the Federal Reserve,

The Market Risk Charge is then computed as the higher of the previous day's VaR, or the average VaR over the last 60 business days, times a 'multiplicative' factor k:

$$MRC_t = Max(k\frac{1}{60}\sum_{t=1}^{60}VaR_{t-i},VaR_{t-1}) \qquad (2)$$

where k is to be determined by local regulators, subject to an absolute floor of 3[21].

Apparently, the effect of these rules on the MRC has not been fully appreciated. This is the first paper, to our knowledge, that specifically analyzes the time-series behavior of the market risk charges. By now, there is an enormous literature on VaR, derived from statistical time-series techniques that narrowly focus on 1-day VaR accuracy issues[22].

Here, two smoothing mechanisms are involved. The first is the requirement that the model be based on at least a year of historical data. More precisely, the 'average life' of weights on past observations must be at least six months. This requirement can be traced to the observation of Jackson et al (1997) that short windows can lead to inaccurate VaR. But, as we will show, this requirement also has the effect of creating VaR measures that are very stable over time. The second mechanism consists of taking the average VaR over 60 days.

Modelling daily VaR

Let us examine first the requirement of a minimum window for computing daily VaR numbers. With the historical-simulation method, the window must be at least one year. Requiring at least 250 days seems reasonable as this would yield an expected 2.5 observations in the left tail. But then, as shown by Pritsker (2001), the VaR risk forecast will not be very responsive to changes in recent volatility, due to the fact that each observation in the 250-day window has a relatively small weight of 1/250. We need to have several observations below the previous quantile to start moving VaR measures.

Alternatively, consider parametric VaR models based on the standard deviation. Such models can accommodate time-variation in risk more easily. More recent models mix historical simulations with parametric volatility modeling[23]. Consider, for instance, a simple RiskMetrics-type Exponentially Weighted Moving Average (EWMA) forecast. The conditional variance forecast is:

$$h_t = \lambda h_{t-1} + (1-\lambda)r_{t-1}^2 \qquad (3)$$

where λ is the decay factor and r the rate of return on the asset.

With a dollar position of W_0, VaR can be computed as $VaR=W_0 \times 2.33\sqrt{h}$, at the 99% level assuming a conditional normal distribution. This could be extended to other parametric distributions, however, with a different multiplication factor.

Replacing recursively, this yields geometrically declining weights

$$h_t = (1-\lambda)[r_{t-1}^2 + \lambda r_{t-2}^2 + \lambda^2 r_{t-3}^2 \dots] \qquad (4)$$

The average life is the weighted sum of number of days

$$\sum_{i=1}^{\infty} i \times [(1-\lambda)\lambda^{i-1}] = 1/(1-\lambda) \qquad (5)$$

For example, the average life of the RiskMetrics model with λ=0.94 is 16.7 days, or 0.067 years, assuming a 250-day year. This is not allowed under the Basel rules, however. We need λ to be at least 0.992 to achieve an average life of half a year. Alternatively, banks could use a moving average over one year, with equal weights within the window

$$h_t = \frac{1}{250}\sum_{i=1}^{250} r_{t-i}^2 \qquad (6)$$

Chart 3 and Chart 4 compare the evolution of daily VaR models for the DM/US$ rate since 1980. First, note that the historical-simulation model generally yields a higher 99% VaR than the other models. This reflects the well-known observation that daily financial series have tails fatter than the normal[24].

In Chart 3, the EWMA with λ=0.94 is indeed very volatile, due to the higher weight on recent data. This

21: Ignoring the specific risk charge, which is explained in more detail in the Basel Amendment (1996).

22: See Hendricks (1996), Jackson et al (1997), Christoffersen (1998), Lopez (1999), among others.

23: See for instance Boudoukh et al (1998) and Hull and White (1998).

24: See Hendricks (1996).

Figure 5.1 Jorion article (a).

Source: Bank of England, Financial Stability Review: December 2002, pp. 121–123.

is not relevant, however, since such fast-moving models are not allowed under the Basel rules. Chart 4 shows that the normal-MA model based on a moving window of 250 days is much smoother. The historical-simulation method is more volatile, but still much smoother than the EWMA model with decay of 0.94. Finally, the EWMA with λ=0.992, which is the minimum decay allowed under Basel rules, is nearly as smooth as the normal model.

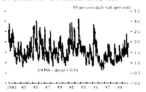

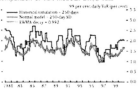

The fact that banks are constrained to use slow-moving VaR forecasts explains the finding by Berkowitz and O'Brien (2002) that banks' VaR forecasts can be beaten by a simple GARCH model applied to the history of P&L. At first sight, these findings are surprising since GARCH models have no information on changing positions. One interpretation is that "these results may reflect substantial computational difficulties in constructing large-scale structural models of trading risks for large, complex portfolios". Another interpretation, however, is that the banks' structural models are simply hamstrung by the Basel requirements. And, this may be a rational outcome since the purpose of these VaR

models is to produce a smooth capital requirement and not necessarily to measure next day's risk with utmost accuracy.

Which VaR is binding?
The market risk charge is composed of the maximum of two terms. Which of these terms in Equation (2) will be binding? The first term, which is three times the 60-day average, will in general be higher than yesterday's VaR, and thus will be binding. The bank would have to experience an enormous increase in the previous day's VaR for it to become the dominant factor.

To see this point, assume that VaR is stable at VaR for the last 60-day period, except for a spike on the last day. The second term in Equation (2) will be binding when

$$VaR_{t-1} > 3\frac{1}{60}[VaR_{t-1} + 59 VaR_0]$$ (7)

which implies

$$VaR_{t-1} > (3 \times 59/57) \times VaR_0 = 3.11 \times VaR_0$$ (8)

This could happen in one of two ways. Assuming stable risk factors, this could be achieved if the exposure W_t, or size of positions, is multiplied by a factor greater than 3.1. Alternatively, with constant exposures, this could also be achieved by an increase in the volatility of risk factors $\sqrt{h}$. The latter is much less likely, however.

Table 2 displays the required latest return, expressed in terms of volatility, such that the second term is binding, for various values of the decay parameter for the EWMA model, as well as the 250-day MA. Lower values for λ imply greater weight on the last observation. Hence, a smaller movement is required for the latest observation to be binding.

Model	EWMA, Decay (λ)					MA
Parameters	0.92	0.94	0.96	0.98	0.992	250 days
Required return	10.4σ	12.0σ	14.7σ	20.8σ	32.9σ	46.3σ

The table shows, for instance, that with λ=0.94 we require a shock twelve times the daily standard deviation. This happened only once in our equity and currency sample, during the crash of October 19, 1987.

Figure 5.2 Jorion article (b).

With the lowest decay allowed, λ=0.992, we need a
movement of 32.9 times the standard deviation for the
latest VaR to be binding. With a simple moving average
over the last year, the required move implies a factor of
46.5. It is highly unlikely that an exogenous shock to
volatility could induce yesterday's VaR to be binding.
Therefore, in what follows, we will assume that the
market risk charge is driven by three times the average
VaR. This is not to say, however, that the second term
in the market risk charge is useless. It serves to catch
banks that suddenly increase their positions.

Evaluation of the Basel market risk charge
The contention is that VaR-based capital
requirements experienced sharp increases during
Summer 1998, leading to forced position cutting.
The question is: how did the increased volatility of
financial markets affect the Basel capital
requirements?

Chart 5 displays movements in the market risk charge
for a fixed position in the exchange rate between the
dollar and the DM (now the euro). Note how smooth
the lines are compared to those in the previous graph.
This is due to the averaging over the last 60 days. The
figure does not include the normal-EWMA model
with decay of 0.94 since it is not allowed. The graph
shows no evidence of sharply higher market risk
charge during 1998. The fluctuations in market risk
charges in 1998 are actually lower than over the rest
of the sample period.

Chart 5:

Market risk charge: DM/$ rate

Source: P Jorion's calculations.

One could argue that volatility was confined to other
markets, however. So, we turn to US equities. Chart 6
plots the MRC for a fixed position in US stocks. There
is some evidence of an increase in the MRC during
1998, but not out of line with the history of the last
20 years.

Chart 6:

Market risk charge: US equities

Source: P Jorion's calculations.

Chart 7 gives more detail for 1998. The graph shows
that the increase in the MRC was very slow. It was
barely noticeable for the normal model with a
250-day MA and for the EWMA with decay of 0.992.
There is a greater increase for the historical
simulation method, but due to the averaging process,
the MRC only reaches a peak by the end of
November, by which time the crisis was over.

Chart 7:

Market risk charge in 1998: US equities

Source: P Jorion's calculations.

Finally, Chart 8 plots the MRC for a short position in
10-year Treasury notes. Again, there is no evidence of
sharp movements in the MRC for the HS and MA
models. While the 1980s were much more volatile
than the 1990s for Treasuries, 1998 was certainly not
an eventful year in terms of the Basel market risk
charge. In conclusion, it seems inappropriate to
blame increases in VaR models for position cutting.

Objective functions for VaR models
The previous section indicates that smoothness in the
VaR-based capital charge is a desirable property. This
has been largely ignored in the VaR literature, which
has focused on purely statistical issues such as bias
and bunching.

Figure 5.3 Jorion article (c).

media profile, or some combination of the two. As Graham Smart has it, economists in the (central) Bank of Canada 'collaborate in creating specialized written knowledge' and apply 'this knowledge in formulating and implementing' public policies (Smart, 2006, p. 7). Central bank economists then play a role in promulgating an 'economy of words', by negotiating the tension between statements designed to format the economy, with how the statements play out in the wild of a national economy (Holmes, 2014).

It is important to acknowledge that this is not the only account of improvisation within a technical discipline. Conceptualizing this as a modality of knowledge provides an extension of existing scholarship in the SSF. Authors such as Mallard (2007) and Holmes (2014), themselves drawing on the history of science, conceptualize ruptures or improvisation as 'experiments'. This is a promising line of enquiry, because it acknowledges the technical modality of expertise present in central banking. Here it becomes clear that 'the significance of an experiment never lies only in the technical achievement of the test itself' (Mallard, 2007, p. 157). Aspects such as location, design, form of intervention and the social practices used to disseminate results are also pertinent to the financial stability reporting of the Bank. However, as Engelen *et al.* (2011, p. 51) are at pains to establish, improvisation differs from experimentation because in experimentation 'a scientist creates events (changing the world) by means of structures', whereas the bricoleur improvises by creating structures by means of events.

For Miller and Rose (1990), the 'governmentality of economic life' has increasingly involved experts, expertise and expert knowledge. As such, governance from the sort of distance one would expect from a central bank has come to rely in crucial respects upon expertise, namely 'the social authority ascribed to particular agents and forms of judgement on the basis of their claims to possess specialized truths and rare powers' (Miller and Rose, 1990, p. 2). As Miller and Rose (p. 8) phrase it nicely, expertise is a 'complex amalgam of professionals, truth claims and technical procedures'. This, however, still does not adequately capture the logics at play in the relevant Bank of England publications. In this chapter I have attempted to unpack the black box of expertise to see how it functions within public policy. In particular, Foucault captures this operation of power when he says that:

> but as the establishment of a relation, in medical discourse between a number of distinct elements, some of which concerned the status of doctors, others the institutional and technical site from which they spoke, others their position as subjects perceiving, observing, describing, teaching etc. it can be said that this relation between different elements ... is effected by clinical discourse: it is this, as a practice, that establishes between them all a system of relations that is not really given or constituted a priori; and if there is a unity, if the modalities of enunciation that it uses, or to which it gives place are not simply juxtaposed by a series of historical contingencies, it is because it makes constant use of this group of relations.
>
> (Foucault, 1972, p. 59)

I am consequently treating this article in FSR 2002b by Jorion, and the system of relations bound up with it, as a 'threshold of positivity' (Foucault, 1972, p. 193). Taken together are a system of distinct elements such as the professional status of Professor Jorion, the institutional site of the central bank and the calculating subject. Erin Lockwood (2015, p. 747) has argued that VaR's 'status as an objective practice used by financial experts lies at the heart of its authority', and, indeed, this appears to have been borne out by the regulatory narrative produced after the collapse of Long Term Capital Management. If we follow Lockwood's argument further, then VaR's claim to 'objectivity and technicality is itself an act of political power because it depoliticizes decisions'. This much is true. However, Lockwood's excellent account stops short of fully interrogating the process through which a problematic risk management tool was retained. Certainly, in the case of the Bank of England's narrative, it was not that VaR had to be tweaked, as clearly shown by Lockwood (2015, p. 747) in the case of the Basel Committee, but rather that this changed the terms against which VaR was evaluated. The shift to precision *was* a depoliticization through technicality that we find in Lockwood's account and the acceptance, retention and rejection of Value-at-Risk *are* all connected to power and political economy, yet these actions also relate to regulatory culture. Likewise, this *does* relate to the reframing of uncertainty through probabilistic calculations, but as I will argue later, this is also about money cultures and later a shift in these terms towards more subjective probabilities and a possibilitisc risk calculus. In the final section of this chapter, I draw on FSR statements and comments by Andrew Haldane following the Global Financial Crisis to make the case that the Bank raised issues with the assumptions of normality in the VaR calculation. This I interpret as a moment in which Bank understandings of VaR coalesced around the way that VaR was counter-performative.

Speculating on risk (again): Global Financial Crisis

This subtle shift in the regulatory discourse helped to sustain the use of VaR for regulatory purposes throughout the first half of the decade. Of interest here is a 2005 Bank of England working paper which proposes to carry out stress testing using VaR models. The authors of this paper detailed that they:

> adopt a different approach to perform macroeconomic stress tests on the UK banking system and investigate whether the conclusions arising depend on the choice of stress test and on the fragility variable used. We attempt to account for the dynamics between banks' write-off to loan ratio and key macroeconomic variables using a parsimonious vector autoregression (VAR) model.
>
> (Hoggarth *et al.*, 2005)

This relatively uncritical attitude to VaR techniques argues that:

> 'unlike most existing stress testing work on links between the business cycle and the fragility of the banking system, a direct measure of banks' fragility

– the write-off ratio on loans – is employed. The advantage of the VAR is that it estimates how write-offs change in the quarters following adverse business cycle shocks implying that the stress test is conditional on the historical correlation among the variables in the multivariate model.

(Hoggarth *et al.*, 2005)

This working paper, while a minor publication, does pay some testament to the resilience of discourses about the utility of Value-at-Risk. However, within just two years critical attention soon returned to the accuracy of the calculation. In the period prior to the Subprime Crisis, the Bank of England raised issue with the accuracy of the statement of risk by the model:

As noted in previous FSRs, disclosed Value-at-Risk (VaR) measures have remained relatively stable in recent years while the trading revenues of the major UK banks and LCFIs have risen strongly. One explanation for this is that current measures of VaR may be understating risk due to the combined effects of their largely backward-looking nature and the recently benign financial market conditions. This highlights the need (which is recognised by most financial firms) to examine VaRs under stressed market conditions.

(FSR, 2007, p. 33)

The following year the Bank of England reiterated the point that the estimation of market risk may well have been too low because:

Backward-looking models take time to respond to sudden changes in market conditions. This can be true of models used for pricing assets, but also those used to manage market risk. As noted in previous Reports, in benign financial conditions, Value-at-Risk models may understate the risk that is actually being taken. These models are based on estimates of the volatility of asset returns and the correlations between them. A change in either of these estimates can have a considerable impact on a firm's Value-at-Risk.

(FSR, 2008, p. 47)

The events of the Subprime Crisis, and subsequent Global Financial Crisis, revealed two significant developments involving the risks associated with credit derivatives. First, systemic risk became concentrated at several large financial institutions, in particular insurance giant AIG, which had become drastically overexposed to credit default swap contracts. Second, risks that were being taken by financial institutions were seriously under-priced. Following BNP Paribas's abstention from CDO trading due to the difficulty with pricing its positions, anxiety in markets threatened to undermine the fragile and uncertain circulations of global finance which supported advanced liberal societies and lifestyles (Langley, 2013b). Due to the series of problems that emerged in this period, it became widely recognized that on its own, VaR was unable to account for high-impact/low probability events, so-called 'tail-risks'. As the (now) Chief Economist at the Bank of England Andrew Haldane (2012, p. 16) noted:

> The simplicity of VaR has led to its ubiquitous use in finance (Jorion (2006)). But VaR suffers a fatal flaw as a risk management and regulatory measure: it is essentially silent about risks in the tail beyond the confidence interval. For example, even if a trader's 99% VaR-based limit is $10 million, there is nothing to stop them constructing a portfolio which delivers a 1% chance of a $1 billion loss. VaR would be blind to that risk and regulatory capital requirements seriously understated.

In the above quoted speech from Andrew Haldane, VaR was described as being 'silent about risk' and 'blind to risk', as a measure of potential losses and responsible for the 'understating' of risk. In other words, the accuracy of VaR again became the focus of much recrimination in the regulatory community. The fundamental issue is, as de Goede argues, that the assumption of normality is that it is constructed into the 'very mathematical models which are supposed to measure it' and is thus a normative claim not 'of how things *are*, but how things *ought to be*' (de Goede, 2001, p. 160). The problem with this, simply put, is that 'financial markets are not normal' (Triana, 2012, p. 19). VaR then had an inaccurate assumption of normality and further, had a blind-spot of extreme events and economic shocks. In such a way, Value-at-Risk could only ever secure imperfectly. The Bank was unwilling or unable to improvise and retain VaR because the assumption of normality could not be salvaged. The events of the Global Financial Crisis showed that VaR was not as useful as previously thought.

Conclusions

The regulatory acceptance and use of Value-at-Risk emerged in the 1990s and worked on financial stability as something which could be privately managed within individual institutions. It was hoped that on a piecemeal basis this would contribute to an aggregate of stability. Bank of England thinking about VaR provides a window into institutional attitudes towards risk management in money and finance.

I have argued in this chapter that such internal risk management was considered to be a form of financial security. More than this, I have made the case that Value-at-Risk contributed to a money culture of *speculating on risk*. An analysis of Bank of England publications suggests that the adoption of VaR was viewed as a result of its purported accuracy as a standard of technical knowledge. This led to its consistent use as a measure for market risk in Bank of England documents. In this chapter I have developed the case that widespread use of VaR can increase market volatility (de Goede, 2011; MacKenzie, 2005; Triana, 2012). In such a way, VaR is seen as being counter-performative by ushering in instability. I have used archival research to characterize two episodes of failure of Value-at-Risk as periods in which VaR was being understood as securing imperfectly. In the first instance, the global financial volatility at the end of the 1990s was viewed as a situation in which widespread use of the same measure of risk increased volatility due to mass position cutting. And while the Bank at first did not respond to this critique, it later did in FSR 2002. Here misfire was offset by improvisation. In the face of this difficulty and the retention of thinking that VaR was useful, the Bank of England attempted to shift the epistemic standard away from accuracy to one of precision through improvisation. And, here I have focused on an article written by Phillipe Jorion who used calculations about the stability of the VaR calculated market risk charge to argue that VaR should be appraised in terms of a standard of knowledge of precision. The shift to precision was made through appeal to 'smoothing mechanisms' in the Basel version of VaR. Here I have placed emphasis on the role of public facing economist as technical expert. The change was prompted by improvisation, or the changing relations and elements within the discursive field, as professional status of a professor, institutional site of a central bank and the technocrat as calculating subject all came together.

And, while this subtle alteration in discourse sustained the use of VaR as the main regulatory tool for measuring market risk and requisite regulatory capital held as insurance against potential downturns, risk management would be severely reappraised following another period seen to be one of extreme failure. The instability was seen to lie within the under-pricing and concentration of risk that VaR oversaw during the early 2000s. In particular, inadequacies with the assumption of normality within the VaR calculation, and the fact that it did not take into account extreme combinations of events, led to renewed criticism of the accuracy of the likely losses and level of market risk attached to trading strategies. Moreover, this time it was the Bank of England that was raising the critique. As Andrew Haldane argued, 'the fatter the tails of the risk distribution, the more misleading VaR-based risk measures will be' (Haldane, 2012, p. 16). Following the Subprime Crisis, it has become widely recognized that on its own, VaR is unable to account for high-impact/low probability events, so-called tail-risks. To address this, the Bank of England recognized the need to modify and supplement the VaR with both a modification to VaR (towards use of stressed VaR) and the introduction of another technique, stress testing. Stress testing is a significant add-on because it includes the demand for 'extreme but plausible' scenarios. These two notable changes will be discussed in full in Chapters 6–8. This chapter and the ones that follow, then, are a response to Lockwood's (2015, p. 749) call for 'further inquiry into the nature and scope of expert authority in global finance to better identify the conditions under which that authority should be seen as legitimate and decisive'.

Note

1 Jorion is Professor of Finance at University of California at Irvine and has published over 100 text books on financial risk management and the core text book on Value-at-Risk.

References

Amoore, L. 2013. *The Politics of Possibility: Risk and security beyond probability.* Durham NC: Duke University Press.

Amoore, L. 2014. 'Security and the incalculable'. *Security Dialogue* 45(5), pp. 423–439.

Baker, A. 2013. 'The new political economy of the macroprudential ideational shift'. *New Political Economy* 18(1), pp. 112–139.

Bank of England. 1997. Financial Stability Review, Autumn 1997. [pdf] Available at: www.bankofengland.co.uk/archive/Documents/historicpubs/fsr/1997/fsrfull9710.pdf (Accessed 1 February 2014).

Bank of England. 1998. Financial Stability Review, Autumn 1998. [pdf] Available at: www.bankofengland.co.uk/archive/Documents/historicpubs/fsr/1998/fsrfull9811.pdf (Accessed 1 February 2014).

Bank of England. 1999a. Financial Stability Review, June 1999. [pdf] Available at: www. bankofengland.co.uk/archive/Documents/historicpubs/fsr/1999/fsrfull9906.pdf (Accessed 1 February 2014).

Bank of England. 1999b. Financial Stability Review, November 1999. [pdf] Available at: www.bankofengland.co.uk/archive/Documents/historicpubs/fsr/1999/fsrfull9911.pdf (Accessed 1 February 2014).

Bank of England. 2000a. Financial Stability Review, June 2000. [pdf] Available at: www. bankofengland.co.uk/archive/Documents/historicpubs/fsr/2000/fsrfull0006.pdf (Accessed 5 February 2014).

Bank of England. 2000b. Financial Stability Review, December 2000. [pdf] Available at: www.bankofengland.co.uk/archive/Documents/historicpubs/fsr/2000/fsrfull0012.pdf (Accessed 7 July 2014).

Bank of England. 2001a. Financial Stability Review, June 2001. [pdf] Available at: www. bankofengland.co.uk/archive/Documents/historicpubs/fsr/2001/fsrfull0106.pdf (Accessed 8 July 2014).

Bank of England. 2001b. Financial Stability Review, December 2001. [pdf] Available at: www.bankofengland.co.uk/archive/Documents/historicpubs/fsr/2001/fsrfull0112.pdf (Accessed 7 February 2014).

Bank of England. 2002. Financial Stability Review, December 2002. [pdf] Available at: www.bankofengland.co.uk/archive/Documents/historicpubs/fsr/2002/fsrfull0212.pdf (Accessed 11 February 2014).

Bank of England. 2004. Financial Stability Review, June 2004. [pdf] Available at: www. bankofengland.co.uk/archive/Documents/historicpubs/fsr/2004/fsrfull0406.pdf (Accessed 11 February 2014).

Bank of England. 2007. Financial Stability Report, 26 April 2007. [pdf] Available at: www.bankofengland.co.uk/publications/Pages/fsr/2007/fsr21.aspx (Accessed 14 February 2014).

Bank of England. 2008. Financial Stability Report, 1 May 2008. Available at: www. bankofengland.co.uk/publications/Documents/fsr/2008/fsrfull0804.pdf (Accessed 17 February 2014).

Clementi, D. 1999. 'The Basel Accord-Systemic Issues', speech given at the Bank of England 2 December 1999. [pdf] Available at www.bankofengland.co.uk/archive/ Documents/historicpubs/speeches/1999/speech63.pdf (Accessed 2 May 2016).

Clementi, D. 2001. 'Recent Developments in securities markets and the implications for financial stability', speech given to the Euromoney International Bond Congress at the Queen Elizabeth II Conference Centre in London, 21 February 2001. www.bankof

england.co.uk/archive/Documents/historicpubs/speeches/2001/speech113.pdf (Accessed 18 February 2014).

Daston, L. 1995. 'The Moral Economy of Science'. *Osiris* 10, pp. 3–24.

Davies, H., and Green, D. 2008. *Global Financial Regulation*. Cambridge: Polity.

Engelen, E., Erturk, I., Froud, J., Johal, S., Leaver, A., Moran, M., Nilsson, A., and Williams, K. 2011. *After the great complacence: Financial crisis and the politics of reform*. Oxford: Oxford University Press.

Foucault, M. 1972. *The Archaeology of Knowledge*. Abingdon: Routledge.

de Goede, M. 2001. 'Discourses of scientific finance and the failure of long-term capital management'. *New Political Economy* 6(2), pp. 149–170.

Goodhart, C. 2011. *The Basel Committee on Banking Supervision: A History of the Early Years, 1974–1997*. Cambridge: Cambridge University Press.

Goodhart, C., Hartmann, P., Llewellyn, D., Rojas-Suarez, L., and Weisbrod, S. 1998. *Financial Regulation: Why, how and where now?* Abingdon: Routledge.

Haldane, A. 2009. 'Why Banks Failed the Stress Test', speech given at the Marcus-Evans Conference on Stress-Testing, 13 February 2009. [pdf] Available at: www.bankofengland.co.uk/archive/Documents/historicpubs/speeches/2009/speech374.pdf (Accessed 1 June 2014).

Haldane, A. 2012. 'Tails of the unexpected', speech given at 'The Credit Crisis Five Years On: Unpacking the Crisis', conference held at the University of Edinburgh Business School, 8 June 2012. [pdf] Available at: https://pdfs.semanticscholar.org/55bd/31941afbbd1072b0b022971b3ab479db6c0d.pdf (Accessed 2 May 2015).

Hoggarth, G., Sorensen, S., and Zicchino, L. 2005. 'Stress tests of UK banks using a VAR approach', Bank of England Working Paper no. 282. [pdf] Available at: www.bankofengland.co.uk/archive/Documents/historicpubs/workingpapers/2005/wp282.pdf (Accessed 1 September 2017).

Holmes, D.R. 2014. *Economy of words: Communicative imperatives in central banks*. Chicago Il: University of Chicago Press.

Investopedia. n.d. 'Long-Term Capital Management', [online] Available at: www.investopedia.com/terms/l/longtermcapital.asp (Accessed 14 December 2016).

Jorion, P. 2002. 'Fallacies about the effects of market risk management systems', in Bank of England 2002 *Financial Stability Review*, December 2002, pp. 115–128. Available at: https://merage.uci.edu/~jorion/papers/riskfall.pdf (Accessed 1 May 2014).

J.P. Morgan. 1996. *RiskMetrics – Technical Document, Fourth Edition*. J.P. Morgan: New York.

Langley, P. 2013a. 'Anticipating uncertainty, reviving risk? On the stress testing of finance in crisis'. *Economy and Society* 42(1), pp. 51–73.

Langley, P. 2013b. 'Toxic assets, turbulence and biopolitical security: Governing the crisis of global financial circulation'. *Security Dialogue* 44(2), pp. 111–126.

Langley, P. 2015. *Liquidity Lost: The Governance of the Global Financial Crisis*. Oxford: Oxford University Press.

Lewin, S. 2017. *Regulated organizations: responding to and managing regulatory change*. (Unpublished Doctoral Thesis Submitted to the London School of Economics).

Lockwood, E. 2015. 'Predicting the unpredictable: Value-at-risk, performativity, and the politics of financial uncertainty'. *Review of International Political Economy* 22(4), pp. 719–756.

MacKenzie, D. 2005. 'Mathematizing Risk: Models, Arbitrage and Crises'. In Hutter, B., and Power, M (eds.) *Organizational Encounters with Risk*. Cambridge: Cambridge University Press, pp. 167–189.

Mallard, A. 2007. 'Performance testing: dissection of a consumerist experiment'. *The Sociological Review 55*(2), pp. 152–172.

Miller, P., and Rose, N. 1990. 'Governing economic life'. *Economy and Society* 19(1), pp. 1–31.

Millo, Y., and MacKenzie, D. 2009a. 'The usefulness of inaccurate models: Towards an understanding of the emergence of financial risk management'. *Accounting, Organizations and Society* 34(5), pp. 638–653.

Millo, Y., and MacKenzie, D. 2009b. 'The Practicalities of Being Inaccurate: Steps Towards the Social Geography of Financial Risk Management'. In Clark, G.L., Dixon, A.D. and Monk, A.H.B. (eds). *Managing financial risks: from global to local.* Oxford: Oxford University Press, pp. 95–119.

Power, M. 2005. 'The Invention of Operational Risk'. *Review of International Political Economy* 12(4), pp. 577–599.

Power, M. 2007. *Organized Uncertainty.* Oxford: Oxford University Press.

Smart, G. 2006. *Writing the economy: Activity, genre and technology in the world of banking.* London: Equinox.

Tett, G. 2009. *Fool's Gold: The Inside Story of JP Morgan and How Wall St. Greed Corrupted Its Bold Dream and Created a Financial Catastrophe.* New York: Free Press.

The Economist. 1998. 'The Risk Business', 15 October 1998. [online] Available at: www.economist.com/node/172042 (Accessed 5 June 2017).

Triana, P. 2012. *The number that killed us: A story of modern banking, flawed mathematics, and a big financial crisis.* New York: John Wiley & Sons.

Wigan, D. 2009. 'Financialisation and derivatives: Constructing an artifice of indifference'. *Competition & Change* 13(2), pp. 157–172.

Yadav, V. 2008. *Risk in international finance.* Abingdon: Routledge.

Part III

A money culture of speculating for risk

6 Putting risk under a microscope

Introduction: misfire at Threadneedle Street

> That social reality does not follow the scripts laid out by 'performativity theories' suggests that the observation of performative effects has more to do with a temporary alignment of theory and reality than with the actual conflation of epistemology and ontology that performativity theory implies.
>
> (Engelen, 2009, p. 129)

The unparalleled turmoil of the Global Financial Crisis prompted a number of geographers to attend to the failings of financial risk management at a variety of scales, spanning from the local and 'biofinancial' life of the individual through the urban to the macroeconomic and the global (Langley, 2009; Randalls, 2009; Pauly, 2009; Dymski, 2009; French and Kneale, 2012). And, as the above quotation from Ewald Engelen suggests, events such as the global crisis have led critics of the performativity approach to discount it as a useful explanatory model. In opposition to this critique, the argument of this chapter is that misfire is an important category. In other words, a layered and lively conception of performativity which takes the category of misfire seriously is able to accommodate Engelen's (2009) view that performativity is about the alignment of discourse and practice. The realization in 2007 that derivative risk management practices concentrated, rather than dispersed, risk is one such example of 'misfire' that led to improvisation and a shift in money cultures at the Bank. The shift in speculative security practices was one in which speculation as taking a gamble in uncertain conditions mutated into speculation as the practice of sighting, mapping and visualizing. This analysis is born out in the following chapter through the examples of calls to adapt Value-at-Risk and to standardize and make transparent credit derivatives. Further, the chapter presents the development of stress testing as being irrevocably bound up with attempts to better understand the mobilization of risk.

Concentration not dispersal

The money culture of *speculating on risk* 'pictured risk being moved to the peripheries of the financial sector and away from the large banks' (Engelen *et al.*, 2011, p. 60). Langley (2017) provides an account of how the visual diagramming of the mobilization of risk, through 'flow diagrams – typically composed of boxes and arrows, variously coloured and arranged – representing the innovative techniques of asset-backed securitization and their associated array of capital market and derivative instruments', contributed to this money culture. This visualization of the mobilization of risk 'powerfully framed the idea' that risk was 'moving' to some 'safer zone', to investors who were most willing and able to bear it (Engelen *et al.*, 2011, p. 61).

However, Engelen *et al.* (2011, p. 58) point out that understanding securitization as a kind of chain is insincere 'because there is no natural beginning or end' to the securitization 'process … there are instead circuits between and behind the nodes'. The consequence of this is that risks were *concentrated* in the centre of circuits, rather than being *dispersed* through chains. Such circuits:

> ensured that risk was not dispersed, but rather concentrated around a small group of firms, leaving banks exposed to maturity mismatches and counterparty risk, and insurers heavily exposed to default risk … circuits like this contain many points of fragility and vulnerability.
>
> (Engelen *et al.*, 2011, p. 60)

As Langley (2017) argues, 'thinking in terms of a circuit emphasizes return loops over directional flows'. Instead, the concentration of risk proved to be a misfire for risk management discourses and practices that purported to secure by dispersing risk through a financial system.

Insecurity not security

The counter-performativity of Value-at-Risk has been long noted (de Goede, 2001). For example, this was the analysis of the volatility that arose around the Asian Financial Crisis and the collapse of Long Term Capital Management by both de Goede and MacKenzie (2005). Erin Lockwood (2015, p. 739) documents several different examples of misfire during the 1990s before pointing out that, during the Global Financial Crisis, Value-at-Risk had given financial institutions confidence, if not downright overconfidence, that future losses were under control. And, traders disregarded the 1 per cent confidence interval that was not included in the model. As such VaR posited normality and extremity occurred instead. Further than this, however, is the sense that a security technique actually led to insecurity.

Reconsidering misfire

The occurrence of a performative's opposite, in this case concentration rather than dispersal of risk, is an instance of what MacKenzie (2005) and Lockwood (2015) have both called counter-performativity and what Austin (1962) originally labelled as 'misfire'.[1] Such 'violations of the conventions necessary for a successful performative' have traditionally been seen at best as uninteresting, and at worst as failure (Loxley, 2007, p. 10). The argument I advance in this book is that misfire must be analysed with its corollary lively practice, namely improvisation.

As argued in Chapter 3, performativity as the 'simple conformity to constitutive rules can be put into question by the recognition that institutions are themselves' necessarily implicated in 'an iterability they cannot simply contain' (Loxley, 2007, p. 89). So for Butler, if it is both true that a financial 'theory tends to produce the phenomenon', but also 'that it can sometimes fail to produce what it anticipates, then it seems we have opened up the possibility of "misfire" at the basis of performativity itself' (Butler, 2010, pp. 152–153). This fundamental breaking with context is the breaking force of language (Derrida, 1988, p. 9). This then is when an 'utterance gains force through breaking with prior positions' (Butler, 1997, p. 145). And while authors such as Engelen (2009) treat the instance of a misfire as a refutation of performativity's key claims, here I want to argue that the force of this rupture was culturally significant. Misfire, rather than merely signalling the breakdown of performativity, instead has a dynamism that leads to improvisation and change.[2] Such a misfire has a 'violent' force precisely because the force is 'not derived from conformity to prior' conditions or conventions (Loxley, 2007, p. 104). In Derrida's words, such a moment calls for a new convention which it itself produces (1989, p. 119) because an:

> originary performativity that does not conform to preexisting conventions, unlike all the performatives analysed by the theoreticians of speech acts, but whose force of rupture produces the institution or the constitution, the law itself, which is to say also the meaning that appears to, that ought to, or that appears to have to guarantee it in return.
>
> (Derrida, 1994, pp. 30–33)

Moreover, I do not think it is possible to determine when a misfire will be consequential. After all, we should consider the historical instability of meaning, sensitivity to context and the way that misfire is present within every iteration (Best, 2008). On Callon's (2010, p. 165) terms perlocutionary 'performativity implies that misfires are the rules of the game. The constitution of economic markets is no exception to the rule: it is an on-going process, constantly restarted'.

As Callon reminds us, political debates are themselves opened up by the issues resulting from 'the misfires generated by their enactment' (Callon, 2010, p. 166). As such, Chapter 5 provided a close reading of the rhetorical work by Phillipe Jorion's article in a Bank of England (2002) Financial Stability Report in exonerating VaR following the LTCM misfire. Crucial here, was that the criticism VaR faced was such that the widespread use of the equation contributed to financial market volatility. Importantly, I think, volatility cannot be a fundamental problem for the speculative security techniques of VaR and financial derivatives as it is through (any) price movements that arbitrage profits are made

(Wigan, 2009; Amoore, 2013; Martin, 2015). Thus, I would argue that volatility cannot be the same existential threat to security logics that concentration and insecurity pose. Here I want to suggest that misfires that brought into question the internal logic of speculative security had a particular violence or force de rupture. The dual misfire of dispersal and insecurity required much more extensive improvisation and change.

In such a way, this dual misfire was at the heart of a cultural shift between speculating *on* risk and speculating *for* risk. To draw on Catherine Malabou's (2007) reading of Derrida, the modifiability or 'plasticity' of writing means that it can both receive and give itself new forms throughout time. The example Malabou (2007) gives is that clay receives a form – clay is plastic – and plastic surgery gives form to the body. Critical here is the shift in the use of the term 'speculation'. If, for *speculating on risk*, finance itself was thought to secure through the pervasive use of risk management tools and techniques, for *speculating for risk* regulators need to better understand the mobilization of risk. For example, while Paul Tucker (2007) argued that 'not knowing' where risk was meant that it had expediently been 'dispersed beyond the regulated centre', then, following the misfire of risk management, risk had to be understood with a greater level of precision and granularity. If the Bank argued that a particular risk had increased, then the risk has to be visible and quantified.

The widespread response to the misfire of risk management has been, in large part, driven by a wider regulatory context and an international consensus. Reforms that started at the G20 in 2008 as 'The Action Plan' in response to the Global Financial Crisis included the high order principle of 'enhancing sound regulation'. The Basel Committee responded to this by working towards the reform of the Basel Accords with reference to securitization and the pro-cyclicality[3] of the financial cycle. These reforms were completed in 2011 with the formalization of the Basel III Capital Accords. In the remainder of this chapter, I outline ways in which the Bank of England has improvised by seeking to visualize and understand risks better, through transparency, the adaptation of VaR, standardization in credit derivatives and the aggregation of risk in regulatory stress testing.

Focusing on risk

Regulatory change since the Global Financial Crisis has seen a drive to measure risk in more accurate and precise ways. Precision has been pursued through the development of stressed Value-at-Risk measures of market risk. This is a technical modification of the market risk calculation to account for market conditions that lie in a historically defined fat tail of the probability distribution. 'Stressed VaRs' were introduced by the Basel Committee in 2009 and involve including a 'historical period of elevated volatility in most or all risk factors' within a VaR estimation. The distinction between VaR and a stressed VaR (SVaR) is that while the former provides an indication of possible losses given a current portfolio and the markets as they are at present, the latter provides a window onto possible losses given much worse market conditions. A stressed VaR requires a choice of a particular 'stressed' historical period in the markets as opposed to the most recent X number of years. This then, is about drilling down into historical evidence. In a working paper Bank staff take onboard the addition of stressed VaRs within thinking about regulatory capital and volatility. For example, it is argued that:

> Projected combined (VaR and SVaR) capital components should increase to reflect increases in scenario volatility. Where projected VaR calculations are not based on a recalculation under scenarios, the Bank's expectation is that combined VaR – plus SVaR-based capital requirements increase to at least twice current SVaR when the scenario is characterised by an increase in market volatility.
>
> (Bank of England, 2016, p. 14)

A concomitant concern for accuracy has centred on steps to increase transparency.

In 2009 and alongside the injections of US Treasury money into the financial system through the TARP[4] and the SCAP[5] stress test, there was a concerted focus on the credit derivatives that were thought to lie at the heart of the financial distress. Increasingly the downside risk associated with credit derivatives seemingly reverted further and further towards a concern at the complexity of financial innovation. When the Bank of England was concerned about credit derivatives, the issue was often the perceived complexity of the CDO chains. As Andrew Haldane argued in 2009, 'financial innovation' in general and 'structured credit' in particular, was a '*complex* interlocking set of claims' (Haldane, 2009, p. 16 *emphasis added*).

Here we should note that the regulatory response was not to shut down derivatives trading or replace derivatives. Instead, the Bank of England improvised with the practices already in place. With the analysis of complexity taking prime position within regulatory thinking, the post-crisis consensus around credit derivatives is that they need to be more transparent. As Donald Kohn argued in a 2011 speech:

> The long chains of claims embodied in the securitization, re-securitization, and derivatives based on securitizations made it almost impossible for people to understand and price the risks they were taking. The complexity of the securities and their risk characteristics meant that the models used to price them were exceedingly difficult to understand.
>
> (Kohn, 2011, p. 8)

The necessary regulatory response to this was for 'transparency about these structures' in order to 'protect financial stability' and allow 'investors in the instruments and counterparties of those involved in the chains … to have the opportunity to evaluate their risk' (Kohn, 2011, p. 8).

In 2012, the Bank of England suggested that that:

> 'public disclosure of information by financial institutions can contribute to the resilience of the UK financial system' because 'transparency enables market forces to act as a disciplining mechanism on individual institutions' behaviour and enables more accurate pricing of risk within the financial system'.
>
> (FSR, 2012a, p. 57)

Further, in the second FSR of 2012, it is reiterated that 'reforms should help to mitigate systemic risk in OTC derivatives markets by improving risk management, reducing interconnectedness and improving transparency' (FSR, 2012b, p. 43).

The campaign towards greater transparency is underpinned by an entrenched belief that 'vision is the most reliable of senses'. Scientific knowledge is founded on the 'ability to observe and visualize a problem through distanciated and objective eyes' (Amoore, 2013, pp. 47, 69). Unlike the broadening of the 'space and time' in and through security visualizations, that de Goede (2012, p. *xxvi*) finds in the policing of terrorist monies, this instead is about discerning and making the ungainly acute. Rather than spreading outwards across space, this aspect of *speculating for risk* is about peering and delving down with focus and precision.

However, as admirable an ambition as it may seem, the focus on transparency has its theoretical and practical limits. As Jacqueline Best (2010, p. 41) has long pointed out, a renewed and reinvigorated drive towards 'better and more accurate measurement of financial risk' makes the understandable yet erroneous assumption that all types of uncertainty and risk are 'fully amenable to calculation'. Instead, Best (2008) entreats us to consider the ways in which modern knowledge is pushed, pulled and buffered by the indeterminacy of meaning. The shifting framework of 'language, history and self-reflexivity' means that many forms of knowledge are inherently ambiguous, to an extent that frustrates the idea that all risks are capable of being acutely visualized and calculated. More tangibly, and in practical terms, a recent speech by Bank Deputy Governor Sam Woods (2017, pp. 20–21) outlined that the Bank was aware that financial firms were innovating in ways that served to mask risks. As Woods put it:

> some innovation is pure regulatory arbitrage – that is, action taken by firms to reduce specific regulatory requirements without any commensurate reduction in their risk.... The leverage ratio requires all on-balance sheet assets to carry a minimum level of capitalization regardless of their risk. Off-balance sheet transactions are also captured in the leverage ratio, but if an on-balance sheet transaction can be restructured into an economically similar off-balance sheet transaction, it may not always attract the exact same capital charge.

In other words, risks that do not 'attract the exact same capital charge' are somewhat masked. Here Woods outlines the incentives behind financial institutions not being completely transparent about their mobilization of risk. Woods (2017, p. 21) goes on to provide the example of 'off balance sheet' derivatives where:

> Some of these structures might meet the detailed requirements for calculating a specific financial ratio whilst others may have a harmless motivation. But we have noticed that some carry material credit risk which escapes the detailed aspects of the capital framework.

Woods' (2017, p. 20) argument that such innovations adhered to 'the letter' of regulation but flouted its 'intention' implies that the spirit of the regulations was a transparency about risks being taken and mobilized by financial institutions. Woods' recent intervention illustrates the clear objective of seeing 'material credit risk' better. And, while the Bank here sets the expectation that it will clamp down on mechanisms of 'regulatory arbitrage', it is too soon to assess whether this will actually happen.

Mapping and coding risk

Alongside transparency, there has also been a regulatory movement towards the standardization of CDOs. For example, alongside tools that the newly created FPC was asking for were those that 'influence market structures (e.g. the obligation to clear certain standardised derivatives contracts through a central clearing counterparty)' (Fisher, 2012, p. 8). This, as Haldane eloquently phrased it, would seek to 're-wire the global financial web, transforming it from a dense, complex cats-cradle to a simplified hub-and spoke configuration' (Haldane, 2012, p. 15). Alongside this, Haldane argued that:

> Finance today … has no common language for communicating financial information. Most financial firms have competing in-house languages, with information systems siloed by business line. Across firms, it is even less likely that information systems have a common mother tongue. Today, the number of global financial languages very likely exceeds the number of global spoken languages. The economic costs of this linguistic diversity were brutally exposed by the financial crisis.

Here Haldane called for work to be done to develop a:

> financial product mark-up Language (FpML), which is already used in the industry for communications and processes, to provide a standardised presentation of each listed or cleared product…. These elements can be combined using a standardised syntax to describe instruments at any level of complexity. In essence, this approach is an attempt to create a '*DNA string*' for derivatives.

By drawing an analogy between the aforementioned ambitions to rewire finance and Adrian Mackenzie's (2005) work on the performativity of coding as computer language, I argue that the recoding of finance is a performative attempt to restart and structure the previously high velocity circulations of derivative instruments (Langley, 2013a). Mackenzie (2005, p. 77) writes that:

> processes of circulation themselves objectify linguistic praxis. They enact something. If we accept that information and communication constitute a central venue for the performativity of some important contemporary forms of power, then the circulation and exchange of software and code involved in the infrastructure of communication could well be analyzed there in performative terms.

In terms of coding in computer programming language, for example, 'as an operational object serving as a platform, Linux quite literally co-ordinates the circulation of specific social actions pertaining to information and communication networks' (Mackenzie, 2005, p. 77). In the case of derivatives, on the one hand many contracts will be written by taking existing products off the shelf and replicating them entirely. On the other hand, new contracts and products will be created using already existing products, bringing into being previously inscribed written forms. Coding, then, is about visibility in the sense of making new, but structured, relationships appear and the production of 'new objects for action and speculation' (Halpern, 2014). To appropriate a point by Edward LiPuma (2016), such standardization equates to inflexibility, the interlocking of 'token and type' – read ritual and citation – and securing 'the liquidity of each trade's counterparty'. In other words, the successful performance is locked into the contract or transaction.

So, in 2012 the Bank was promoting a rewiring of the structures of credit derivatives such as CDOs. By 2017 the Bank makes the case that 'a series of measures are eliminating toxic and fragile forms of shadow banking while reinforcing the best of resilient market-based finance. And more durable market infrastructure is simplifying the previously complex – and dangerous – web of exposures in derivative markets' (Carney, 2017, p. 4). The analysis that the crisis was underpinned by complexity of both financial instruments and the financial system can be considered to be an acknowledgement of 'extant limits to knowledge' (Datz, 2013). Analytical efforts have focused on the more precise visualization of derivatives. This can also be seen in a graphic published in a 2017 blogpost entitled 'Big Data jigsaws for Central Banks – the impact of the Swiss franc de-pegging' on the 'Bank Undercover' blog for Bank of England employees. The image shows 'the network of outstanding exposures in the EURCHF forward market on the day before the "depegging"' (Bank Undercover, 6 April 2017). The blog post goes onto explain the structure of the market when it states that:

> The circles or nodes are counterparties in the market which are connected by outstanding positions. The size of nodes and thickness of connections are both given by the notional amounts of aggregated positions. The colour coding is derived from the position of individual counterparties within the market.

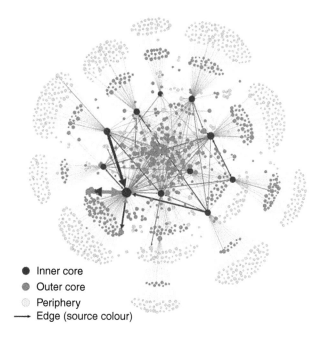

Inner core
Outer core
Periphery
→ Edge (source colour)

Figure 6.1 Illustration from Bank of England staff blog.

Source: https://bankunderground.co.uk/2017/04/06/big-data-jigsaws-for-central-banks-the-impact-of-the-swiss-franc-de-pegging/.

The Bank, then, is concerned with mapping market relationship and structures. The blog post derives two key insights from the mapping of counterparties:

> First, there is a clear segregated structure of dealer banks, serving their respective 'clouds' of clients, with large clients (mostly blue) being connected to several dealers. Second, the large size of dealer banks as depicted by the size of the red nodes, and their central position in the trading network, demonstrates the important role they play.

Such financial visualizations are important precisely because they constitute 'a set of practices central to the making of economic spaces and key to our assessments of those spaces' (Aitken, 2007, p. 22). To focus on an extended and illustrative quotation from Michael Pryke's (2010) illuminating work on 'money's eyes' (p. 435):

> Graphs, figures, even tables should not be seen as: 'primarily representational' in the sense of their ability to communicate something, but rather as primarily significatory. They always signify but need not necessarily

represent (something else). This is an important distinction. It enables us to approach visualisation (in its multifarious forms) as *constitutive of a reality rather than as a mere reflection of it* (however accurate or distorted). And this pertains to all forms of visualization.

(Thompson 1998, p. 286, *emphasis added*, cited in Pryke, 2010, p. 435)

Seen in this way, diagrams of risk are not just statements or discourses but have a visuality that contributes to bringing risk into being as a concern for financial governance. These forms of visibility are about structuring and reproducing standardized relationships of credit risk.

Understanding the functional mobilization of risk

Alongside the visualization of risk, there has been a cultural shift towards building a better understanding of the functional mobilization of risk. Haldane (2009, p. 23) made the case that new ways of analysing risk were necessary. As an example, Haldane argued that 'node-by-node diagnostics, such as VaR, have shown themselves during this crisis to offer a poor guide to institutional robustness'. Looking towards network theory, Haldane was optimistic that 'network diagnostics' such as 'degree distributions' and 'average path lengths' could 'displace atomized metrics such as VaR in the armory of financial policymakers'. These are new ways of understanding risk because, for example, degree distribution is the probability that a randomly chosen node has a certain number of connections in a network.[6] This means that a greater appreciation of causality in a network is possible.

Moreover, of perhaps greatest significance is the advent of regulatory stress testing of the financial system.[7] Stress testing involves the running of an anticipatory exercise in which the impact of a hypothetical scenario of three 'low probability/high-impact' events is measured on the balance sheets, exposures and reserve capital held across banks in a financial system (Geithner, 2014).

Regulatory stress testing emerged and was improvised as an emergency response to the Subprime Crisis in its Anglo-American heartland. Although criticized and maligned at the time (see Geithner, 2014), once the immediate dangers of this crisis had passed, the stress testing of financial institutions, and injections of capital for those failing to pass the tests, became viewed as being a turning point in the crisis. The 'precision' of the American stress tests, and the 'positive affective charge' that these generated, served to mobilize one of the emotional, psychological and affective energies at play during the crisis period, namely a feeling of confidence rising from a tumultuous emotional background of trauma (Langley, 2013b; Brassett and Clarke, 2012). The (then) US Treasury Secretary, Timothy Geithner (2014), conceived of stress testing as being 'more than a rigorous test' rather, 'it would be a mechanism to recapitalize the financial system so that banks would have the resources to promote rather than prevent growth'.

Following sections of the Basel III Capital Accords that seek to address the pro-cyclical nature of finance, stress testing has now become an annual exercise in the UK and the EU. In the Bank of England's recent stress testing exercises from 2013–2015, the Bank decided upon a scenario of macroeconomic shocks, and financial institutions had to project the impact of the shocks on their balance sheets and regulatory capital. During a stress test, the Bank of England makes a request for unstructured data relating to audits, balance sheets and methodology from participating financial institutions. This includes internal governance arrangements for approving methodologies and results, reports produced by internal audit or other review functions and 'methods related to the extrapolation of risk factor shocks'. Further, the Bank of England also requires 'an assessment of the key sensitivities of the results and details of how the stress scenarios have been translated into impacts on the income statement and balance sheet' (Bank of England, 2015). The Bank of England uses this information to assess the rigour of the financial institutions' tests and results, while also running its own stress test on the data.

The significance of stress testing following the misfire of risk dispersal technologies lies in the way that this policy tool has prompted regulators to think more systematically about the mobilization of risk. The contrast between the two separate risk cultures can be best elucidated here. *Speculating on risk* is encapsulated in Tucker's aforementioned 2007 statement that 'if we no longer know where the risk is, that implies that it has been dispersed beyond the regulated sector. One might think that was a Good Thing'. A significant cultural shift towards *speculating for risk* can be determined in a 2016 research interview with economic forecasters at the Bank who observe that:

> a financial stability report was an opportunity to say the things you are most worried about.... Once you are setting a policy tool that's numerical each quarter, you have to aggregate everything up and say is it, overall, bigger or smaller than before?
>
> (Bank of England Research Interview, 23 August 2016)

The Bank of England's stress testing programme has evolved since its private and internal implementation during and following the crisis and since its unveiling as a very public tool in 2014. 2016 was an important year for stress test improvisation. From 2016, stress testing has involved an Annual Cyclical Scenario (ACS), an important feature of which is the idea that the size of the shocks applied to different sectors are consistent with the Bank's assessment of vulnerabilities existing in the financial system. The level of risk in the test, then, should reflect the bigger picture of risks existing in the economy. For example, the following table in the Bank's 2016 stress testing guidance document set out how the Bank saw risks fitting together in the economy at this particular point in time:

In such a way, a research interview with economic forecasters at the Bank reveals that they are 'thinking about how stress testing and risk assessment would speak to each other'. As a forecaster elaborated:

Table 1 Summary of FPC and PRA Board risk assessments in the 2016 stress test

	Summary of FPC and PRA Board risk assessments
World activity	Risks to global activity associated with credit, financial and other asset markets are elevated, in large part reflecting risks in China and other EMEs. Within that assessment there are material divergences across economies.
Financial markets	Long-term interest rates remain very low, in part driven by historically compressed term premia. The risk of a sharp rise in term premia is elevated, which could have knock-on effects to other asset prices.
UK property prices	UK property prices may be vulnerable to rises in long-term interest rates. Prime CRE prices appear overvalued on some metrics. Overall risks to UK property prices are a little elevated.
UK activity	Reflecting the above risks and also that domestic debt-servicing costs are below historic averages. Risks are judged to be at a standard level.

Figure 6.2 2016 Bank of England table of their risk assessment used in Annual Cyclical Scenario.

Source: Bank of England, March 2016 Stress testing the UK banking system: key elements of the 2016 stress test, Table 1, p. 4.

I think it really helped just to think about how to aggregate risks and how to really think about the risk level. It's one thing to look around and think and worry about this thing, but thinking about how worried am I about it, quantitatively, and how should I kind of piece that together with the other risks facing the financial system. A lot of thinking had been going on in the Bank prior to this project, but I think it really helped to take that extra step for it.
(Bank of England Research Interview, 23 August 2016)

Further, a second forecaster (in the same interview) makes the case that:

the FPC publishes some core indicators and they are constantly honed and monitored over time, there were top-down ways of thinking about it, bottom-up ways of thinking about it, but one purpose of the project and the ACS is to sort of harmonize the thinking about the risk assessment and the stress tests so that the thinking for committees is sort of joined up on the two. And one way of seeing the scenario is as a quantification of the Committee's perspective on risk because they've said publicly that, each year, the scenario will change as they see the risks changing.
(Bank of England Research Interview, 23 August 2016)

The ACS, then, brings together risk assessment and the policy tool, while also translating the qualitative assessment of risk into a number. A third regulator argues that the relationship between test and risk assessment is such that:

> the risks either crystallise or kind of recede, the severity becomes less. If we see risks increasing or new risks emerging, you would have a more stressful test. And it's meant to be systematic in the way that we design it; so in part so that firms themselves can have a reasonable understanding of where we are going to be going with the scenario, so it will be easier once we have a track record of putting it out there. But the expectation ... is, you kind of want them to understand where we perceive risks, how we think about it. They can then think about how the scenario is going to evolve; do I need to do anything from a capital perspective and start work on that long before we see numbers results and engage in the end dialogue with firms. Because one of the lessons I think we have learnt from observing others' stress tests, is that you need to be able to say, here are the stress results and where firms are not as strong as you would like, here's what they are doing about it, or we have required them to take action and this is what they are doing. So, if firms are able to better understand, at least on the annual cyclical scenario.
>
> (Bank of England Research Interview, 17 October 2016)

Regulatory stress testing then has developed in such a way that much greater attention is paid to the geography of risk. Forecasters at the Bank no longer just identify risks but now seek to quantify them, aggregate them and specify inter-actions between risks in the financial system. The understandings of the mobilization of risk have an increased precision. More than this, however, is the way that the ACS operates through two distinct derivative logics. First, the way that risk is quantified, decomposed and aggregated speaks to Martin's (2012, 2015) work on the social logic of the derivative in which disparate values are recombined. Second, the ACS creates mobile networks and the fragile anchoring of commensurable risk values (Bryan and Rafferty 2006). In the case of the derivative, this works through the way that incommensurable goods can support derivatives, the price of which is determined by the value of the underlying good. In such a way, derivative prices can be compared thus constituting 'the new gold' standard by being a fragile anchor for incommensurable goods. This is a fragile and time dependent anchoring process. In the case of the ACS, this means that the scenario is derived from a time dependent snapshot of risk assessment in an economy.

Conclusions

The widely documented failures of credit derivatives and VaR models to either diversify or measure risk can be theorized as instances of counter-performativity and misfire. In this chapter I have brought the category of misfire and the 'force du rupture' to the fore. The argument is not that all misfires have this violent force that stems from breaking with prior conventions. Rather, misfires around dispersal and security posed significant breakdowns in security mechanisms. That credit derivatives concentrated rather than dispersed risk, and Value-at-Risk severely underestimated risk, served to undermine the money culture of speculating *on* risk. An extensive improvisation, from speculating *on risk* to speculating *for risk* was required.

In this chapter I have started to chart and analyse a cultural shift towards *speculating for risk*, in the sense of visualizing and understanding the mobilization of risk better. The Bank has firmly advocated the modification of VaR so that 'stressed VaRs' take into account historical data from periods of difficult economic conditions. The Bank has publicly argued that credit derivatives markets ought to be made more transparent. The Bank has also promoted efforts to recode credit derivatives by developing a process for standardizing derivative contracts. Such visualizations are important precisely because they are 'constitutive of a reality rather than as a mere reflection of it' (Pryke, 2010). And while there is some academic scepticism over the efficacy of transparency (Best, 2010) these two approaches constitute performative solutions to the misfire of derivative finance (Mackenzie, 2005).

Finally, this chapter has detailed and considered the development of regulatory stress testing at the Bank. In particular, this development has highlighted attempts to better understand the composition of and connections between different forms of risk. In particular, the advent of the ACS means that the size of the shocks applied to different sectors are consistent with the Bank's assessment of vulnerabilities existing in the financial system. The consequences of the misfire of credit derivatives has been to inject a greater emphasis on geography into risk management at the Bank. Two distinct derivative logics are here, with the recombination of values and the fragile anchoring of risk values in a scenario. This is not the only time I will consider stress testing. If in this chapter the focus has been on the geography of risk, then the following chapter will consider the role of stress testing in widening the scope of risks considered to threats and instabilities in the financial system.

Notes

1 In Austin (1962) these are violations of the conventional procedures required to achieve a successful performative utterance.
2 Malabou argues that 'this impossibility of thinking of the end of writing threatens the grammatological project' (of a science of writing) 'from the inside and from the very start of the game' (Malabou, 2007, p. 435).
3 In the sense that economic policies magnify fluctuations in financial markets. By this, I mean capital provisioning in an upturn that does not anticipate a downturn or change in the economic cycle. For example, the running down of regulatory capital reserves during a market upswing.
4 The Troubled Assets Relief Programme announced on 19 September 2008 earmarked $700 billion for the temporary purchasing of impaired or toxic assets from the capital markets. However, as Langley (2015, p. 61) documents, by October 2008 the funds

were actually used to recapitalize US banking. In such a way a way, the problem of toxicity became reconfigured as a problem of solvency.

5 The Supervisory Capital Assessment Programme of February 2009 was a stress test of 19 US institutions in which the impact of two adverse scenarios was simulated to determine what indicative losses would be to institutions and to see how much additional capital would need to be raised to meet required adequacy thresholds. The tests showed that ten of the bank holding companies needed to raise 'a cumulative total of $75 billion in equity capital' and, by November 2009, these institutions raised $77 billion (Langley, 2015, p. 106).

6 Here network scientists would be interested in the number of connections a node has to other nodes and the probability distribution of these degrees over the whole network (MIT.web, n.d.).

7 For Baker (2013a, p. 116), stress testing emerged out of the 'macroprudential' ideas which hold that (i) diversification by individual institutions using the same model could increase non-diversifiable risk and (ii) linkages between markets and market participants create externalities and unanticipated consequences.

References

Aitken, R. 2007. *Performing Capital: Towards a Cultural Economy of Popular and Global Finance*. Basingstoke: Palgrave Macmillan.

Amoore, L. 2013. *The Politics of Possibility: Risk and security beyond probability*. Durham NC: Duke University Press.

Austin, J.L. 1962. *How To Do Things With Words*. Oxford: Clarendon.

Baker, A. 2013a. 'The new political economy of the macroprudential ideational shift'. *New Political Economy 18*(1), pp. 112–139.

Baker, A. 2013b. 'The gradual transformation? The incremental dynamics of macroprudential regulation'. *Regulation and Governance 7*(4), pp. 417–434.

Bank of England. 2000. Financial Stability Review, June 2000. [pdf] Available at: www.bankofengland.co.uk/archive/Documents/historicpubs/fsr/2000/fsrfull0006.pdf (Accessed 13 May 2014).

Bank of England. 2001. Financial Stability Review, June 2001. [pdf] Available at: www.bankofengland.co.uk/archive/Documents/historicpubs/fsr/2001/fsrfull0106.pdf (Accessed 13 May 2014).

Bank of England. 2004. Financial Stability Review, December 2004. [pdf] Available at: www.bankofengland.co.uk/archive/Documents/historicpubs/fsr/2004/fsrfull0412.pdf (Accessed 13 May 2014).

Bank of England. 2005. Financial Stability Review, June 2005. [pdf] Available at: www.bankofengland.co.uk/archive/Documents/historicpubs/fsr/2005/fsrfull0506.pdf (Accessed 14 May 2014).

Bank of England. 2012a. Financial Stability Report, 29 June 2012. [pdf] Available at: www.bankofengland.co.uk/publications/Documents/fsr/2012/fsrfull1206.pdf (Accessed 14 May 2014).

Bank of England. 2012b. Financial Stability Report, 29 November 2012. [pdf] Available at: www.bankofengland.co.uk/publications/Documents/fsr/2012/fsrfull1211.pdf (Accessed 14 May 2014).

Bank of England. 2015. *Stress testing the UK banking system: guidance for participating banks and building societies*. [pdf] Available at: www.bankofengland.co.uk/financial stability/Documents/stresstesting/2015/guidance.pdf (Accessed 5 May 2015).

Bank of England. 2016. 'Stress testing the UK banking system: key elements of the 2016 stress test', March 2016. [pdf] Available at: www.bankofengland.co.uk/financial stability/Documents/stresstesting/2016/keyelements.pdf (Accessed 3 September 2017).

Bank of England Undercover Blog. 2017. 'Big Data jigsaws for Central Banks – the impact of the Swiss franc de-pegging'. [online] Available at: https://bankunderground. co.uk/2017/04/06/big-data-jigsaws-for-central-banks-the-impact-of-the-swiss-franc-de-pegging/(Accessed 1 February 2017).

Bank of England. Research Interview, 23 August 2016. London.

Bank of England. Research Interview, 17 October 2016. London.

Best, J. 2008. 'Ambiguity, Uncertainty, and risk: rethinking indeterminacy'. *International Political Sociology* 2(4), pp. 355–374.

Best, J. 2010. 'The Limits of Financial Risk Management: Or what we didn't learn from the Asian Crisis'. *New Political Economy* 15(1), pp. 29–49.

Brassett, J., and Clarke, C. 2012. 'Performing the Sub-Prime Crisis: Trauma and the Financial Event'. *International Political Sociology* 6(1), pp. 4–20.

Bryan, D., and Rafferty, M. 2006. 'Financial derivatives: The new gold?'. *Competition & Change* 10(3), pp. 265–282.

Butler, J. 1997. *Excitable Speech: A Politics of the Performative*. New York: Routledge.

Butler, J. 2010. 'Performative agency'. *Journal of Cultural Economy* 3(2), pp. 147–161.

Callon, M. 2010. 'Performativity, misfires and politics'. *Journal of Cultural Economy* 3(2): 163–169.

Carney, M. 2017. 'The high road to a responsible, open financial system', speech given at Thomson Reuters, London, 7 April 2017. [pdf] Available at: www.bankof england.co.uk/publications/Documents/speeches/2017/speech973.pdf (Accessed 15 May 2017).

Datz, G. 2013. 'The narrative of complexity in the crisis of finance: Epistemological challenge and macroprudential policy response'. *New Political Economy* 18(4), pp. 459–479.

Derrida, J. 1988. 'Signature, event context'. In *Limited Inc*, ed. Derrida, J., Evanston, IL, Northwestern University Press:1–23.

Derrida, J. 1989. *Memoires for Paul de Man: The Wellek Library Lectures at the University of California*. Irvine CA: Columbia University Press.

Derrida, J. 1994. 'Spectres of Marx'. *New Left Review* 205, p. 31.

Dymski, G. 2009. 'Financial risk and governance in the neoliberal era'. In Clark, G.L., Dixon, A.D. and Monk, A.H.B. (eds). *Managing financial risks: from global to local*. Oxford: Oxford University Press, pp. 48–68.

Engelen, E. 2009. 'Learning to cope with uncertainty: on the spatial distributions of financial innovation and its fallout'. In Clark, G.L., Dixon, A.D. and Monk, A.H.B. (eds). *Managing financial risks: from global to local*. Oxford: Oxford University Press, pp. 120–139.

Engelen, E., Erturk, Froud, J., Johal, S., Leaver, A., Moran, M., Nilsson, A., and Williams, K. 2011. *After the great complacence: Financial crisis and the politics of reform*. Oxford: Oxford University Press.

Fisher, P. 2012. 'Policy making at the Bank of England: the Financial Policy Committee', speech given at University of Warwick, London Alumni Group, 12 March 2012. [pdf] Available at: www.bankofengland.co.uk/archive/Documents/historicpubs/speeches/2012/speech550.pdf (Accessed 20 July 2017).

French, S., and Kneale, J. 2012. 'Speculating on careless lives: Annuitising the biofinancial subject'. *Journal of Cultural Economy* 5(4), pp. 391–406.

Geithner, T. 2014. *Stress Test: reflections on financial crises*. London: Random House.

de Goede, M. 2012. *Speculative Security: The politics of pursuing terrorist monies*. Minneapolis: University of Minnesota Press.

Haldane, A. 2009. 'Rethinking the Financial Network', speech given at the Financial Student Association, Amsterdam, 28 April 2009. [pdf] Available at: www.bankof england.co.uk/archive/Documents/historicpubs/speeches/2009/speech386.pdf (Accessed 10 May 2014).

Haldane, A. 2012. 'Towards a common financial language', presented at the Securities Industry and Financial Markets Association (SIFMA) 'Building a Global Legal Entity Identifier Framework' Symposium, New York, 14 March 2012. [pdf] Available at: www.bis.org/review/r120315g.pdf (Accessed 10 May 2014).

Halpern, O. 2014. *Beautiful Data – A History of Vision and Reason since 1945*. Durham NC: Duke University Press.

Jorion, P. 2002. 'Fallacies about the effects of market risk management systems', Bank of England, 2002b, Financial Stability Review, December 2002, pp. 115–128. Available at: https://merage.uci.edu/~jorion/papers/riskfall.pdf (Accessed 1 May 2014).

Kohn, D. 2011. 'Enhancing financial stability: the role of transparency', speech given at London School of Economics, 6 September 2011. [pdf] Available at: www.bankof england.co.uk/archive/Documents/historicpubs/speeches/2011/speech516.pdf (Accessed 10 March 2014).

Langley, P. 2009. 'Consumer credit, self-discipline and risk management'. In Clark, G.L., Dixon, A.D. and Monk, A.H.B. (eds). *Managing financial risks: from global to local*. Oxford: Oxford University Press, pp. 280–300.

Langley, P. 2013a. 'Toxic assets, turbulence and biopolitical security: Governing the crisis of global financial circulation'. *Security Dialogue* 44(2), pp. 111–126.

Langley, P. 2013b. 'Anticipating uncertainty, reviving risk? On the stress testing of finance in crisis'. *Economy and Society* 42(1), pp. 51–73.

Langley, P. 2015. *Liquidity Lost: The Governance of the Global Financial Crisis*, Oxford: Oxford University Press.

Langley, P. 2017. 'Financial flows: Spatial imaginaries of speculative circulations'. In Christophers, B., Leyshon, A., and Mann, G. (eds.) *Money and Finance after the Crisis: Critical Thinking for Uncertain Times*. New York: Wiley-Blackwell, pp. 69–90.

LiPuma, E. 2016. 'Ritual in Financial Life'. In Lee, B., and Martin, R. (eds.) *Derivatives and the Wealth of Societies*, Chicago Il: University of Chicago Press, pp. 37–81.

Lockwood, E. 2015. 'Predicting the unpredictable: Value-at-risk, performativity, and the politics of financial uncertainty'. *Review of International Political Economy* 22(4), pp. 719–756.

Loxley, J. 2007. *Performativity*. Abingdon: Routledge. .

Mackenzie, A. 2005. 'The performativity of code software and cultures of circulation'. *Theory, Culture & Society* 22(1), pp. 71–92.

MacKenzie, D. 2005. 'Mathematizing Risk: Models, Arbitrage and Crises', in Hutter, B., and Power, M. (eds.), *Organizational Encounters with Risk*. Cambridge: Cambridge University Press, pp. 167–189.

Malabou, C. 2007. 'The end of writing? Grammatology and plasticity'. *European Legacy* 12(4), pp. 431–441.

Martin, R. 2012. 'A precarious dance, a derivative sociality', *TDR/The Drama Review* 56(4), pp. 62–77.

Martin, R. 2015. *Knowledge LTD: Toward a Social Logic of the Derivative*. Philadelphia, Temple University Press.

MIT. Web. n.d. 'Studying Complex Networks'. In *Complex networks and collective behaviour change in nature* [online] Available at: http://web.mit.edu/8.334/www/grades/projects/projects10/Hernandez-Lopez-Rogelio/structure_2.html (Accessed 1 September 2017).

Pauly, L.W. 2009. 'The changing political geography of financial crisis management'. In Clark, G.L., Dixon, A.D. and Monk, A.H.B. (eds). *Managing financial risks: from global to local*. Oxford: Oxford University Press, pp. 27–47.

Pryke, M. 2010. 'Money's eyes: the visual preparation of financial markets'. *Economy and Society* 39(4), pp. 427–459.

Randalls, S. 2009. 'Managing financial risks in urban environments'. In Clark, G.L., Dixon, A.D. and Monk, A.H.B. (eds). *Managing financial risks: from global to local*. Oxford: Oxford University Press, pp. 209–229.

Taleb, N.N. 2008. *The Black Swan: The Impact of the Highly Improbable*. London: Penguin.

Thompson, G.F. 1998. 'Encountering economics and accounting: Some skirmishes and engagements'. *Accounting Organizations and Society* 23(3), pp. 283–323.

Tucker, P. 2007. 'A Perspective on Recent Monetary and Financial System Developments', speech given at Meryll Lynch, 26 April 2007. [pdf] Available at: www.bankofengland.co.uk/archive/Documents/historicpubs/speeches/2007/speech308.pdf (Accessed 20 May 2017).

Wigan, D. 2009. 'Financialisation and derivatives: Constructing an artifice of indifference'. *Competition & Change 13*(2), pp. 157–172.

Woods, Sam. 2017. 'Looking both ways', remarks prepared for the May 2017 Building Society Association (BSA) Annual Conference. Published 10 July 2017. [pdf] Available at: www.bankofengland.co.uk/publications/Documents/speeches/2017/speech988.pdf (Accessed 11 July 2017).

7 Widening the risk imagination

Introduction: tails of the unexpected

Prior to the Global Financial Crisis, a pragmatic and ultimately problematic support for the retention of Value-at-Risk had practical implications for the way that risk was measured in financial institutions. But, further, this was the instantiation of a particular and circumscribed risk imagination at the Bank of England. As discussed in Chapter 5, Value-at-Risk derives its projected losses from a sample size of 95 per cent of historical back data. This is an assumption of normality or normal conditions holding. When visualized as a distribution, this means that the curve is 'bell shaped' (see Figure 7.1). However, as de Goede (2001) points out, this was a normative assumption rather than a faithful description of the world

In this chapter I will discuss three key ways in which the Bank of England's risk imagination has been extended and reworked following the misfire of financial risk management in 2007 and the development of regulatory stress testing. This analysis centres on 'looking forwards', but rather than fixing onto 'the warning signs' (de Goede, 2017), this is about the production of warning signs and possible futures.

The first key extension of the risk imagination can be found in the move within stress testing towards thinking about the possibilities that lie in the 'fat tail' of the probability distribution. In other words, it is a concern for extreme or possible financial events, rather than normal or probable ones. This shift is far from straightforward, as 'possible' is an ambiguous term and at different points possibility has been invoked in subtly different ways. An analysis of the descent of the term 'possibility', which vacillates between plausibility and hypothesis, is crucial here.

Second, the development of 'Biennial Exploratory Scenarios' in regulatory stress testing is a significant development. Such scenarios are 'designed to probe the resilience of the system to risks that may not be neatly linked to the financial cycle' (Bank of England, 2016c).

The third development is a much more recent development, and, I argue, requires a radical inversion of Louise Amoore's (2013) term the 'politics of possibility' where financial possibility now encompasses political events. This can be seen in the way that the Bank of England has discussed political events in its financial stability forecasts, in the shape of climate change, cyber security and Brexit.

A possibilistic risk calculus

It must be first acknowledged that the turn to possibility was not a progeny of the Global Financial Crisis alone. Rather, the possibilistic risk calculus was embedded within the very practice of stress testing. For example, during the Basel II regime it was being used as an inward-looking device by financial institutions to stress test their own VaR models. And, during this period of stress testing as a microprudential[1] tool, the Bank of England hinted that stress testing involves, 'such an extreme combination of events' that 'we cannot assign a probability' to them (FSR, 1997, pp. 44–45). Even at this early point in our period of study, the Bank of England pointed out that even if the 'possibility' of a widespread scenario occurring seems 'remote', this 'reassuring conclusion does not rule out the possibility of an individual lender getting into difficulties' (FSR, 1997, pp. 44–45).

However, that said, it was in the aftermath of the Global Financial Crisis that Bank of England financial stability speeches evinced a noticeable increase in the language of possibility or contemplation of the 'unthinkable ... actually' happening (Fisher, 2011, p. 7). Crucially, in 2012 Andrew Haldane was critical of probabilistic risk management tools that relied on normality as a key assumption. Normal distributions of 'credit events' were thought to be problematic precisely because:

> Tails should not be unexpected, for they are the rule. As the world becomes increasingly integrated – financially, economically, and socially – interactions among the moving parts may make for potentially fatter tails.
> (Haldane, 2012b, pp. 17, 20–21)

The language of possibility recurred repeatedly in Andrew Hauser's (2013, p. 7) speech:

> The FSB identified a number of potential sources of run risk in repo markets, including:
>
> 1. The *possibility* that investors cannot meet sudden margin calls (for a given haircut[2]) if the mark-to-market value of the underlying collateral falls sharply and/or credit downgrades require collateral substitution;
> 2. The *possibility* that haircuts may be pro-cyclical, particularly for repo against lower-quality or more uncertainly-priced collateral, rising from 'too low' in benign times to 'too high' in periods of heightened risk aversion.

In this case, the language of the 'possible' enters a scenario affecting the money markets, in which liquidity could conceivably become scarce due to difficulties or uncertainty with the pricing of the underlying collateral which supports loans by acting as a security for the lender (Mehrling, 2011, p. 39). Here then, are instantiations of the 'mobile norm' whereby 'articulations of normality are no longer fixed or predictable'. Instead, we find a normalization in which there is 'no binary distinction between normal and abnormal' such that 'the differential curve of normality … is always a process of becoming' (de Goede, 2012, p. 79; Amoore, 2013, p. 65).

However, and interestingly, there also appears to be substantial evidence of the renewed significance of probabilistic risk techniques, because probabilistic language still remained central to Bank of England publications. For example, even when stress testing became a device that regulators were turning to, Haldane maintained that 'a stress scenario is just one point on a probability distribution' (Haldane, 2009, p. 5). Moving forward to a consideration of Paul Tucker's 2011 speech, he argues that 'those state-sponsored measures reduce the probability of unwarranted failure', and refers to 'likely consequences' (Tucker, 2011e, p. 5) and 'very real' risks to stability (Tucker, 2011, p. 6).

These findings can be interpreted by drawing on Amoore's (2011, 2013) recent investigations into the relationship between economy and security following the terrorist attacks on the World Trade Centre in 2001. Amoore finds a derivative logic of dispersal present in homeland security practices that separate out possible future incidents from their underlying probabilities. On such terms 'the emerging security risk calculus … distinctively coalesces more conventional forms of probabilistic risk assessment with inferred and unfolding futures' (Amoore, 2013, p. 60).

Historians of mathematics make a distinction between the objective probabilities generated through 'mathematical reasoning or statistics', and 'subjective probabilities' which are thought to be less rigorous as they are generated through 'personal estimations of probabilities' (Leclerq, 1974, p. 36). This is significant because the Bank of England statements and speeches we have considered here are suggestive that 'subjective and objective probabilities coexist together' (Gigerenzer and Swijtink, 1989, p. 237). This can be inferred from several of Andrew Haldane's speeches about shifts in financial stability governance and the idea that financial regulators ought to move closer to 'meteorologists' by 'combining empirically-motivated behavioural rules of thumb, and balance sheets constraints' (Haldane, 2012b, p. 19).

Indeed, in the same speech Haldane argued that:

> The evolution of weather forecasting may provide useful lessons on the directions finance might take – and some grounds for optimism … the processing power of computers has certainly been key to advances in weather forecasting … finance could usefully follow in these footsteps. There are already steps underway internationally to widen and deepen the array of financial data available to systemic risk regulators, filling gaps in the global network map.
>
> (Haldane, 2012b, p. 18)

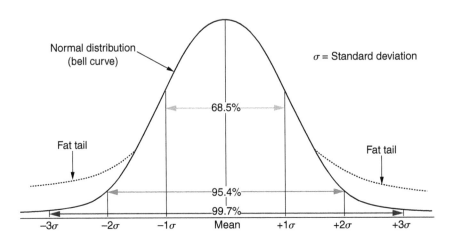

Figure 7.1 The normal distribution and fat tails.

Source: http://advisoranalyst.com/glablog/2014/10/04/fat-tails-and-hyperinflationary-fears.html.

Furthermore, elsewhere Haldane has said that 'stress-tests of the impact of extreme financial events on the functioning of the global financial web would play the role of weather warnings' (Haldane, 2012a, p. 17). What is at play here then, is the coming together of 'multiple forms of probability', in terms of 'the consideration of past frequencies and personal convictions' (Amoore, 2013, p. 45). I want to make the case that a consequence of the misfire in risk management has been a broadening of the risk imagination within the Bank of England. This has occurred through the advent of system wide stress testing.

The scenario component of the contemporary technique of stress testing meshes together the probabilistic with imaginable possibilities. In Amoore's (2013, p. 11) words, 'one must eschew probabilistic conventions of strategic prediction wherein the 1 percent possibility would be filtered out'. As such, the 'bell-shaped' curve[3] of probabilities is replaced by the imagination of the possibilities that dwell in the 'tail risk'[4] (Amoore 2013, p. 157).

The misfire of VaR reinforced for the Bank that the VaR formula suffers a 'fatal flaw' as a risk management and regulatory measure: it is essentially silent about risks in the 'fat tail' beyond the 95 per cent confidence interval (Haldane, 2012c, p. 16). This, Haldane pointed out, is problematic because:

> in real-world systems, nothing could be less normal than normality. Tails should not be unexpected, for they are the rule. As the world becomes increasingly integrated – financially, economically, socially – interactions among the moving parts may make for potentially fatter tails.
>
> (Haldane, 2012b, p. 20)

Reflecting further on the Subprime Crisis, Fisher made the case that:

A lot of the surprise seemed to come from the fact that virtually all risk management had been done within a 'local' framework, rather than genuinely extreme stress tests. If regulators, rating agencies or, for that matter, bond and equity investors had demanded analysis based on extreme stress tests, many of the repercussions in the system could have been identified.

(Fisher, 2011, pp. 6–7)

Further, in 2014 Mark Carney made the case that the Bank stress test would involve events that were not expected, but instead constituted tail-risks:

The 2015 stress test will assess the resilience of the UK banking system to deterioration in global economic conditions. The stress scenario is not a forecast of macroeconomic and financial conditions in the United Kingdom or other countries, nor is it a set of events that is expected, or likely, to materialize. Rather, it is a coherent, 'tail-risk' scenario.

(Carney, 2014)

Such scenarios are, as Wilkinson *et al.* (2013, p. 700) tell us, 'open stories' in which the 'emerging future cannot be forecasted but can be imagined and "lived in" and offers a different perspective to learning about the present than history alone provides'. It must be emphasized, however, that the shift in risk imaginations was not, and is not, paradigmatic. Possibility and inference do not fundamentally supplant and make redundant probabilistic techniques;[5] in fact quite the opposite, due to the Bank of England's agenda in which stress testing would 'inform judgement' (FSR, 2013a, p. 75). As Andrew Bailey said in 2013:

The key message here is that if the banking system is sufficiently capitalised against future losses, it can play a full role in counter-cyclical policy which seeks to respond to and lean against the conditions of the day.

(Bailey, 2013, p. 7)

The previously encountered analogy Haldane (2012b) made with the 'meteorologist' and 'weather warnings' captures the thought that there is, in this line of enquiry and analysis, a coming together of the objective with the subjective (Amoore, 2013, p. 45). More than this, the relationship between finance and security is 'instrumental' because a financial technique or logic is put at the service of security (de Goede, 2010, p. 106). I say this because, for Amoore (2013, p. 73), 'the derivative risk calculus places mobility at the service of security by trading on and through the thriving and teeming details of circulation'.

Plausibility and hypothesis

It is not enough, though, to merely introduce the category of possibility into the risk calculus. To do so would be to encounter another impenetrable 'black box' in finance (MacKenzie, 2005). Rather, it is necessary to delve further into the history of statistics and to both draw and invoke a distinction between separate and separable forms of possibility. These are 'plausibility' and 'hypothesis'. In 2012 the Bank identified it as imperative that stress testing should strive to incorporate 'severe ... yet plausible credit events and market conditions' into the calculation of a scenario (FSR, 2012b, p. 21). While 'plausibility and probability have been confused with each other for centuries', plausibility sits 'somewhere in the hinterland between objective probability and subjective probability' (Ramirez and Selin, 2014, p. 5; Leclerc, 1974, p. 40). As Ramirez and Selin document:

> probability – and the likelihood it sought to express – first started to become 'scientific' when it could start to be taken as an approximation of fact when evidence was lacking. Plausibility, and its connections with the pliable notion of what can be applauded, quite quickly became 'something which one could fashion to ends of appearing truthful when actual truth might be wanting'.

As we saw earlier, whereas objective probabilities are expressed by mathematical reasoning or statistics, subjective probabilities 'are personal estimations of probabilities' and are not obtained through a 'rigorous method' (Leclerq, 1974, p. 36). This is elaborated on by Wilkinson *et al.* (2013: p. 700) for whom plausibility is about 'intuitive logic'. In this intuitive logic approach, plausibility-based scenarios offer 'reframing devices rather than forecasting tools'. More than this, scenarios are not populated with facts but with perceptions, assumptions and expectations. Plausibility thus is an exercise of creativity which retains rigour, such as analogy. In the words of the Bank of England, the dual-demand of extreme yet plausible requires a 'necessarily subjective' inference. This is because '*stress-tests are probabilistic and state-dependent judgements ... which* point to choose – indeed, which distribution to choose – *is a matter of judgement*' (*emphasis added*, Haldane, 2009b, pp. 5–6). Stress testing therefore sees the foregrounding of subjective judgement within probabilistic techniques of governing the future through action in the present.

The Bank of England associated 'severe but plausible' stress test scenarios with being rigorous. The stress tests carried out in America are cited as a paradigm of this when FSR 2012a says that 'the assumptions used for the US tests were generally more severe than those used for the most recent stress tests for European banks published by the EBA in July 2011' (FSR, 2012a, p. 13). In the case of the 2013 Federal Reserve stress tests, scenarios included:

> a peak unemployment rate of 12.1 percent, a drop in equity prices of more than 50 percent, a decline in housing prices of more than 20 percent, and a sharp market shock for the largest trading firms-projected losses at the 18 bank holding companies would total $462 billion during the nine quarters of the hypothetical stress scenario.
>
> (Federal Reserve, 2013)

If we consider what the Federal Reserve said about stress tests being '*deliberately stringent* and conservative assessments under *hypothetical*, adverse economic conditions and ... not forecasts or expected outcomes', we can identify a tension that was present between the approaches of two major central banks (Federal Reserve, 2013). On the one hand, the Bank of England had the 'severe yet plausible', while on the other hand the Federal Reserve had 'stringent yet hypothetical'. Two concomitant questions arise here. First, did these two approaches differ in any significant way? And second, what was at stake here? The issue seems to me to be one of; if stress testing is a necessary part of the financial stability tool kit, and rigour is viewed as the most admirable methodological quality, can this economics of hypothesis be combined with a policy of forecasting scenarios of stress?

As Rene Leclerc argues, forecasting is 'intimately connected with plausible reasoning and (systematic) creativity' (Leclerc, 1974: 53). It seems however that this forecasting paradigm lies in tension with the logic employed in stress testing in America. The question raised by the alternative statements by the Federal Reserve and the Bank of England on whether stress tests could be forecasts, was a question of whether the 'deliberate' and 'hypothetical' are incommensurable within a 'plausible' forecasting paradigm. The Stanford Encyclopedia of Philosophy (2013) argues that plausibility denotes 'some level of epistemic support ... there are sufficient initial grounds for taking' a proposition 'seriously'. Plausibility is on the continuum of inductive reasoning and occurs in the space of possible events which are only partially identified, but crucially, this is more than absolute uncertainty (Brandolini and Scazzieri, 2011). So, and in opposition to the intuitive logic school encountered earlier, within stress testing the 'modal' interpretation plausibility has connotations of being based on some evidence (epistemic support), while hypothetical reasoning assumes that some statement is true and carries on until this is falsified. And further, while Mirielle Hildebrandt (2016) argues that 'predictions basically enlarge the problem space' and in doing so 'expand uncertainty and possibility', an appreciation of the distinction between hypothesis and plausibility allows one to counter that not all possibilities are weighted the same. I want to instead suggest that the criterion of plausibility serves to close down or narrow possibilistic thinking.[6] It would appear that the Bank of England was being pulled in a different direction from the Federal Reserve by virtue of its plausibility/forecast model of the stability paradigm.

Shifting from the plausible to the hypothetical at the Bank

The research presented in Chapter 3 revealed that the Bank of England understood the 2014 process of stress testing as having real economic impacts. The implication of this discussion is quite simple. If a stress test programme does have performative force, then the Bank of England must confront the distinct possibility that the 'extreme yet plausible' scenarios invoked in the stress test scenarios could themselves contribute to the extreme yet plausible scenario coming into being. This is an important scenario and one which the Bank of

England seemed to encounter during its 2014 and 2015 rounds of stress testing. Governor Carney made it clear in the June 2014 press conference that a distinction was to be made between a 'stress scenario', and a 'prediction'. Whereas in 2012, Andrew Haldane invoked forecasting with his analogy to 'meteorology', the Bank of England 2014 news release made it clear that the stress test was not designed to precipitate deterioration in global economic conditions because the stress scenario is not a forecast of macroeconomic and financial conditions in the United Kingdom or other countries, nor is it a set of events that is expected, or likely, to materialize (Bank of England, 2014).

In other words, not only was this new scenario 'not a forecast of macroeconomic financial conditions', but it was in fact defined as a 'coherent tail-risk scenario' (Carney, 2014). Here, one does not 'predetermine the form of the future'. (Anderson, 2010, p. 783). This is, as Anderson classifies it, seeing a 'performance of the future', which rather than calculation or purely imagination, 'embodies an "as if" future' (Anderson, 2010, p. 788).

To conclude this section, I want to tease out what is happening, performatively speaking. If we phrase a scenario as a prediction of the form, 'I predict that Greece will default on its sovereign debt', then what Mark Carney's (2014) clarification that 'it's a stress scenario, it's not a prediction, just to be clear' would be in effect saying, is that 'I do not predict that Greece will default on its sovereign debt, but it is a coherent tail risk'. The stress scenario is, then, what literary theorist Eve Kosofsky Sedgwick refers to as the 'peri-performative' – that is to say, an example of utterances that are 'not themselves performatives' though 'they are about performatives and, more properly, (that) they cluster around performatives' (Sedgwick 2003, p. 68). As such peri-performatives often, but not necessarily so, negate performatives by referring to them. For example, 'I will not marry you.' And, a statement refusing a marriage proposal is powerful for Sedgwick precisely because while it 'perpetuates the prestige of the performative' as a 'defining locus of rhetorical efficacy', it 'nonetheless has the property of sketching in a differential and multidirectional surround that may change and dramatize its meanings and effects' (Sedgwick, 2003, p. 79). In such a way, Carney's distinction between prediction and hypothetical scenario is dramatically forceful in its performance. This is something that the Bank of England has actively cultivated and can be considered an example of improvisation. One staff member reports in a research interview that the Bank is having some success in establishing its stress scenarios as hypothetical. They provide the example that:

> we knew that it made sense within the stress testing framework to just make an assumption about monetary policy in order to generate what we thought was a coherent stress test. And we were asked about it … and we kind of gave that explanation. Everyone seemed pretty comfortable with it, so it feels like people do, as X says, I think that people do kind of understand that we're not suggesting something about a kind of central case, likely outcome, with stress tests now.

> (Bank of England Research Interview, 23 August 2016)

So, in such a way, the globally facing stress test relies on the almost dramatic performativity of the hypothetical to prevent it from being interpreted as a prediction or forecast of instability. This is the Bank managing the performativity of financial stability statements.

Biennial exploratory scenario

A second key improvisation involving stress testing is the development of the dual stress testing programme which uses two distinct types of test. The BES was developed in 2016 to complement the aims and objectives of the ACS. Bank forecasters consider the two types of test as being:

> a package. So, relative to the previous stress tests, the ACS is more predictable and systematic. That has advantages in terms of coherent capital setting over time, systematically judging your risks over time, setting the countercyclical capital buffer. On its own, it has disadvantages in being a bit more predictable, less good at eliciting from banks whether they are good at taking a sort of new scenario and judging how it will affect them. So, having the biennial exploratory scenario as part of the package, we have a package of two, then. You think you're getting more in the systematic countercyclical capital setting space, and you are getting to be more exploratory in this space. So, by having two, you sort of beat the one you had before in a way that, if you moved to just the ACS or just the BES, you'll be getting more of something but less of something else. So again, it's consistent with this point that, looking at capital adequacy through different angles is helpful.
>
> (Bank of England Research Interview, 23 August 2016)

If, in Chapter 6, understanding the mobilization of risk involved calibrating scenarios with risk assessments across an economy, then the exploratory scenario is somewhat different. Such scenarios are not aiming to influence 'bank capital adequacy' but, rather, its purpose is to explore the impact of banks' actions on 'both the real economy and the future resilience of the system to shocks' (Bank of England, 2017a). The Bank aims to 'try and make the ACS more systematic and predictable'. And one of the aims of that 'is to help firms with their planning' (Bank of England Research Interview, 23 August 2016). The ACS is designed to generate 'significant losses for banks on their banking books and their trading books', whereas the exploratory scenario:

> is designed to probe the resilience of the system to risks that may not be neatly linked to the financial cycle. This scenario will not be used to change the Bank's risk tolerance, but will aim to explore risks that are not captured by the ACS.
>
> (Bank of England, 2016c)

In contrast, the exploratory scenario works to:

> make sure that we look up and look around and test for other new emerging risks that might not have such empirical historical precedent, but could be things that could really pose challenges to the banking sector in the future but are new things that are kind of emerging.
>
> (Bank of England Research Interview, 23 August 2016)

Retaining the emphasis outlined in the previous section, the 'macroeconomic scenario' is not a forecast. Rather than being concerned with strategic decisions designed to secure adequate levels of good quality capital as the ACS is, the exploratory scenario is investigating:

> banks' strategic reactions and the risks to their execution. Reflecting this, the Bank expects to learn more about banks' reaction functions, strategic decision-making capabilities and processes from the BES. As a result, greater focus will be placed on how the firms have arrived at their decisions.
>
> (Bank of England, 2017a)

The exploratory scenario constitutes a move closer to Amoore's (2011) conception of the 'data derivative', in which a possible scenario is acted upon without being closely causally tied to underlying assessments of risk in the financial cycle. This is analogous to the way in which the relationship between 'instrument and an assumed underlying value become fleeting, uncertain and loose' (Amoore, 2013, p. 60). In other words, the exploratory scenario is indifferent to the underlying ACS (Amoore, 2011, p. 28). When taken in conjunction with the ACS introduced in Chapter 6, there is an apparent ambiguity which the Bank is negotiating at the time this book is being written. If the BES is the clearest embracing of the hypothetical aspect of the possibilistic risk calculus, the ACS remains closer to the plausible, evidence based definition of possibility. This, as Amoore (2013) argues, means that one form of risk calculus does not supplant the other, but instead they coalesce in an unstable way.

The possibility of politics

Stress testing has one further link to Amoore's work on the possibilistic risk calculus. For Amoore (2013, p. 54) the 'politics of possibility' are 'the sovereign decisions' that appeal to 'the objective and impartial logics of mathematics and computer science but in fact involve layers of incompleteness and intuition'. And, while Amoore has much to tell us about the way that techniques from economic consultancy have traversed across to the domain of homeland security, I instead want to invert her formulation. Rather than a politics of possibility, I argue here that what is going on in money cultures is the *possibility of politics*. As such, this means that the 'stylized facts' of economics on which financial futures are premised are increasingly opened up so that political events can be folded into the risk calculus (Clark, 1998). In terms of historical record, this is nothing new. After all, one of the contributory factors to the emergence of London as a global financial centre was the displacement of financiers from Amsterdam during the Napoleonic Wars (Langley, 2002). At the same time insurers, such as Lloyd's, made significant profits from insuring during wartime (Lobo-Guerrero, 2012). However, what is significant is that during the twentieth century the Bank has generally sought to avoid 'political controversy' (Norman, 1935) and, since the separation of interest rate setting powers from the Treasury in 1997, the Bank has supposedly been insulated from politics. However, since 2011 the Bank has regained its financial supervision powers and has become concerned with contentious political issues normally thought to be beyond the Bank's remit.

As Andrew Hauser said in a speech at an international conference for risk management professionals in 2017:

> The theme of this conference has been how to understand, and respond to, ever more diverse risks: from the rise of populism and geopolitics to the opportunities and threats of new technology; from new forms of financial risk in banks, capital markets and further afield, to the latest trends in stress testing.
>
> (Hauser, 2017)

Here Hauser identifies issues that are not always tackled by central bankers when thinking about financial stability, such as 'the rise of populism and geopolitics'. I illustrate this renewed focus on contentious politics with three examples in which the Bank is concerned with the impact of politics on financial stability, namely climate change, cyber security and Britain's referendum on European Union membership. In particular, what marks these issues is that they are politically contested. We can think back to Mervyn King's statement with which the book started, that the Bank would not do (or say) 'interesting things' but instead remain in the background.

Climate change

The widening of the risk imagination has seen a problematization of what is a financial stability risk. Since he has become Bank Governor, Mark Carney has led the charge in the framing of climate change as a financial stability problem. For Carney, this is both a 'sign of the broadening of the responsibilities of central banks' to include financial as well as monetary stability and 'demonstrates the changing nature of international financial diplomacy'. Carney (2016b) elaborates that, as such:

> climate change is a tragedy of the horizon which imposes a cost on future generations that the current one has no direct incentive to fix. The catastrophic impacts of climate change will be felt beyond the traditional horizons of most actors including businesses and central banks.

As the following illustration from a Quarterly Bulletin shows, the Bank conceives of climate change as posing two distinct and significant risks to financial stability, namely physical or environmental risks to physical assets and people, and transition risks which affect profits and valuations of firms. The Bank of England (2017b, p. 100) argues that risks to UK financial stability include 'insurance claims, portfolio losses, defaults on loans and sentiment shocks'.

Perhaps more interesting is the Bank's suggestion that there could be 'a climate Minsky moment'. This development of Hyman Minsky's (1982) financial instability hypothesis borrows (from Minsky) the idea that the reassessment of financial conditions can lead to a destabilizing reassessment of previously bullish market sentiments. As Carney has it, a 'wholesale reassessment of prospects, as climate-related risks are re-evaluated, could destabilise markets, spark a pro-cyclical crystallisation of losses and lead to a persistent tightening of financial conditions'. Carney elaborates on climate change risks to financial stability as falling into one of three categories, namely physical risks, liability risks and transition risks. Physical risks are the 'impacts today on insurance liabilities and the value of financial assets that arise from climate- and weather-related events, such as floods and storms that damage property or disrupt trade' (Carney, 2016b). In an earlier speech, at the London insurance broker Lloyd's, Carney (2015) argued that:

> Insurers have to update their models constantly and adjust coverage prudently. And in time, growing swathes of our economies could become uninsurable absent public backstops ... moreover, if coverage is not maintained, the broader financial system would become increasingly exposed to large and variable physical risks ... past is not prologue and ... the catastrophic norms of the future are in the tail risks of today.

Interestingly for our present purposes, Carney implores his audience to take today's 'tail risks' seriously. Connected to such physical risks are liability impacts:

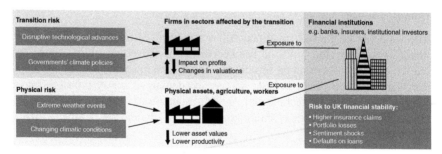

Figure 7.2 Bank of England illustration of financial stability risks connected to the climate.

Source: Bank of England, Quarterly Bulletin 2017 Q2 – Topical article The Bank of England's response to climate change, Figure 2, p. 100.

that could arise tomorrow if parties who have suffered loss or damage from the effects of climate change seek compensation from those they hold responsible. These have the potential to hit carbon extractors and emitters – and, if they have liability cover, their insurers – the hardest.

(Carney, 2015)

Carney is most concerned about the third category of risk he identifies, namely transition risk. Here the risk is one of 're-assessment of value' and repricing of 'a large range of assets' due to 'changes in policy, technology and physical risks'.

The issue of climate change represents a 'changing nature of international financial diplomacy' in which scientific controversy and environmental concern become a serious consideration for central bankers. The issue of climate change, then, demonstrates a widening of the risk imagination in a way that opens it up to risks that lie in the 'tail' of the probability distribution.

Cyber security

A second example of the possibility of politics in the risk imagination is the emerging spectre of cyber security threats to financial stability. In 2013 the FPC recommended that:

HM Treasury, working with the relevant government agencies, the PRA, the Bank's financial market infrastructure supervisors and the FCA should work with the core UK financial system and its infrastructure to put in place a programme of work to improve and test resilience to cyber attack.

(Bank of England, 2013b)

Moving forward to a 2014 speech, the Executive Director in Resolution, Andrew Gracie, identified that while:

financial stability usually conjures up questions about capital and liquidity and the network of financial exposures and interdependencies that make up the financial sector, still the sector is an operational network too. This means that risks lie in the network between market participants and end users that has to remain undisturbed on a daily basis.

(Gracie, 2014)

This 'web of settlement banks, clearing houses, settlement systems and custodians is critical for the mundane payment of salaries, for example'. This has consequences for the Bank of England's risk imagination because Gracie later argued that:

we have to contemplate the possibility that core functions in firms, the financial market infrastructure that links them together or the supply chains that support them, may be damaged in a cyber attack, either through the corruption or loss of data or outright loss of systems.

(Gracie, 2015, p. 2)

In 2014 the Bank launched a new framework to help identify areas where the financial sector could be vulnerable to sophisticated cyber attack, known as CBEST. This framework used government and commercial intelligence to 'identify potential attackers to a particular financial institution. It then replicates the techniques these potential attackers use in order to test the extent to which they may be successful in penetrating the defences of the institution' (Bank of England, 2014b).

And while it may have been tempting to class a serious cyber security breach as a major operational issue, in 2015 Gracie instead argued that 'the risks around cyber are different'. This, in part, is because 'detection of a problem may be more difficult. There is not the same symmetry of information that there might be in the event of bomb, flood or fire' (Gracie, 2015, p. 2). In 2015, the 2013 Recommendation was replaced with the following Recommendation:

> The FPC recommends that the Bank, the PRA and the FCA work with firms at the core of the UK financial system to ensure that they complete CBEST tests and adopt individual cyber resilience action plans. The Bank, the PRA and the FCA should also establish arrangements for CBEST tests to become one component of regular cyber resilience assessment within the UK financial system.
>
> (Bank of England, 2015a)

At this point the Bank was aware that:

> the mechanisms we have put in place to manage these risks may not protect against a cyber attack ... with cyber, such common systems environments between primary and secondary sites and mirroring of data between the two could, in the event of a successful attack, result in a complete loss of systems, disrupting a firm's capacity to operate and leaving the timeframe and route to recovery uncertain.
>
> (Gracie, 2015, p. 2)

The Bank acknowledged that it was facing a seemingly unsurmountable challenge. As the second *Financial Stability Report* of 2015 put it 'cyber attacks have the potential to disrupt the vital services that the financial system provides to the real economy. The impact of attacks can be amplified by interconnections in the financial system'. In the same Report the Bank acknowledges the broadening of its risk imagination:

> The risk from cyber attack has grown over time, reflecting increased use of technology in financial services. Firms need to build their resilience to cyber attacks, develop the ability to recover quickly from attacks, and ensure

effective governance – which means viewing cyber risk as a strategic priority, rather than a narrow 'technology' issue.

(FSR, 2015b)

The financial stability report of November 2016 cautioned that despite the widening of the Bank's risk imagination, 'cyber and technology-enabled attacks continue to be a serious threat to the resilience of the UK financial system' because 'high-profile incidents in 2016 have raised awareness of the importance for institutions of ensuring that they have appropriate controls and measures in place to counter fraud' (FSR, 2016b).

In 2016 the CBEST tests carried out covered 'thirty out of 35 core firms and FMIs'. Here the Bank reported that financial sector resilience against cyber attack is increasing. Alongside this positive note, the Bank still suggested caution because the Bank warned that 'many cyber vulnerabilities can be traced back to weaknesses in basic controls that all organizations should have in place to protect the confidentiality, integrity and availability of systems and information'. Further, the Bank argued that the 'mitigation of cyber risk requires both technological solutions and investment in people, business practices and ways of working' (FSR, 2016b, p. 32).

The recent near crippling of the National Health Service, and widespread allegations of cyber hackers attempting to influence general elections suggest that the risks involved in cyber security are widening. The widening of the risk imagination and an increased awareness of, and attention to, the cyber security risks to financial stability have led to the corollary of stress testing through *cyber attack testing*.

The European Union membership referendum and Brexit

A further and even more familiar example of the possibility of politics in financial stability governance is the issue of Brexit. Prime Minister David Cameron's decision to honour a 2015 manifesto pledge and hold a referendum on the UK's membership of the European Union created a highly controversial political issue, one which the Bank of England had to face head on. As Kristin Forbes (2016) of the Bank phrased it, 'the UK fishermen created the wave' through financial markets. As the election drew closer, 'the Eurozone stock market began to more closely mirror the UK market'. In March 2016, the FPC identified the risks around the referendum as 'the most significant near-term domestic risks to financial stability'. At the same time, the FPC produced a list of channels through which the referendum could increase risks to financial stability and included the 'UK commercial real estate (CRE)market', potential for buy-to-let investors to behave procyclically, amplifying movements in the housing market 'and fragilities in financial market functioning, which could be tested during a period of elevated market activity and volatility' (FSR, 2016a).

Although the Bank saw itself as acting within its financial stability mandate, supporters of the 'Leave' campaign were seemingly incensed by what they perceived to be a partisan intervention and part of the 'Remain' campaign's 'project fear' approach to scare voters into retention of the status quo. For example, within the Treasury Select Committee, out-spoken Member of Parliament Jacob Rees-Mogg asked Carney pointedly, 'in general elections you do not give a view on parties' economic policies. Why not?' Carney's response was that a general election is 'not a discrete risk' (*The Independent*, 2016). Still in May, Carney used the Inflation Report press conference to argue that:

> A vote to leave the EU could materially alter the outlook for output and inflation and therefore the appropriate setting of monetary policy. House-holds could defer consumption and firms delay investment, lowering labour demand and causing unemployment to rise.

The narrow and surprise victory for the Leave campaign on 26 June was, in the very short term, more destabilizing than could have been anticipated. As the Bank later reflected, 'the sharp increase in UK equities just before the vote … and then the sharp fall in UK equities … were both quickly reflected across the channel' (Forbes, 2016). In the immediate aftermath of the shock referendum result, Cameron resigned as Prime Minister and for three days there was a dis-cernible vacuum of leadership in the United Kingdom. Mark Carney's press con-ference on 30 June was eagerly anticipated and the press looked towards the Canadian Governor for reassurance and leadership. While his speech was not explicitly about Brexit, with the title being 'Uncertainty, the Economy and Policy', the timing and the subtext of the speech was clear. In the grandiose setting of the Court Room at the Bank, Carney (2016a) began his address by accepting the narrow result and striking a positive tone about the implications for the UK:

> The result of the referendum is clear. Its full implications for the economy are not. The UK can handle change. It has one of the most flexible eco-nomies in the world and benefits from a deep reservoir of human capital, world-class infrastructure and the rule of law. Its people are admired the world over for their strength under adversity. The question is not whether the UK will adjust but rather how quickly and how well.

The delivery of this message draws parallels with important calming interven-tions by central bankers such as Chairman of the Federal Reserve Alan Green-span after the 1987 stock market crash or Mario Draghi of the ECB during the Eurozone Crisis (Morris, 2016, p. 255). However, Carney also used this speech to temper his optimism with the warning that:

> In the coming years, the UK will redefine its openness to the movement of goods, services, people and capital … uncertainty over the pace, breadth and scale of these changes could weigh on our economic prospects for some

time. While some of the necessary adjustments may prove difficult … the transition from the initial shock to the restructuring and then building of the UK economy will be much easier because of our solid policy frameworks.

(Carney, 2016a)

Despite this seemingly negative tone, the swift appointment of new Prime Minister Theresa May in July 2016 and her statement that Article 50[7] would not be triggered immediately, thus delaying Britain's exit from the European Union, contributed to the 'Great Wave losing energy' (Vlieghe, 2017). Forbes argued that the 'Great Wave' of the 'UK referendum turn(ed) into more of a small boat wake that quickly dissipates' (Forbes, 2016). Many supporters of the Leave campaign took this to mean that institutions such as the Bank had overestimated the damaging effects of Brexit when they described financial stability prospects as 'challenging' (even though Brexit had not actually happened yet). In July, Rees-Mogg asked another provocative question in the Treasury Select Committee, 'Did the Bank of England consider whether it was in the public interest to risk its reputation for impartiality?' To date, the Bank continues to discuss the fall-out of the referendum. In 2017 Carney argued that:

The UK and EU have the potential to create the template for trade in financial services – one that leverages the tremendous progress that has been made in recent years building resilience and cooperation. But financial services are only part of a much broader negotiation. Given our responsibilities to promote financial stability, the Bank – like its counterparts on the continent – must plan, purely as a precaution, for all eventualities … Whatever is agreed, there are risks to financial stability both in the transition to the new relationship and in the new steady state.

(Carney, 2017, p. 9)

It appears, then, that the Bank of England and its Governor in particular have become embroiled in an extremely contested and contentious issue, even when giving a seemingly balanced opinion. Any mention of the downside risks is described as scaremongering by the minority Conservative Government, supporters of the Leave campaign, and prominent sections of the newspaper press. This can be brought into stark contrast with previous eras in which the Bank staunchly avoided political controversy. For example, in 1935, Governor Montagu Norman stated his philosophy on public engagement was 'not to speak in public on any aspect of the work of the Bank of England which might become the subject of political controversy'. This change has been a consequence of the widening of the risk imagination of the Bank, in a way that serves to highlight politically contentious issues that, within the broader horizon, pose risks to financial stability. The issues of climate change, cyber security and Brexit have seen the emboldenment of the Bank of England as a player in the political arena.

Conclusions

The performative misfire of Value-at-Risk and its assumption of normality had significant consequences for the risk culture of *speculating on risk*. The focus of this chapter has been how the culture of *speculating for risk* has widened the risk imagination of staff working at the Bank of England. Here I have argued that within stress testing and prior to 2016, stress testing has seen the folding together of subjective and objective possibilities into the risk calculus. As such, this chapter has highlighted three key developments in the widening of the risk imagination. The first is a move within stress testing towards thinking about the possibilities that lie in the 'fat tail' of the probability distribution. This chapter has pushed further Louise Amoore's research into possibility by opening up a distinction between plausibility and hypothesis. This initially manifested itself in the selection of 'extreme but plausible' scenarios for stress testing, before running into a disagreement with the Federal Reserve about the plausible nature of scenarios. From 2014 much rhetorical and performative work by the Bank has gone into establishing that stress test scenarios are hypothetical and 'not forecasts'.

Still within stress testing, the second key shift that this chapter identifies is one which moves closer to Amoore's (2011) idea of the data derivative, in which possibilities are eviscerated from their underlying probabilities. Something very similar is at play with the BES, which is detached from the changing depiction of the financial cycle in the ACS.

The third contribution of this chapter is to highlight the extension of risks to financial stability to include issues that cause political controversy. By using examples of climate change and cyber security we see the reformulation of two different economic formulations or devices, namely Minsky's financial instability hypothesis and stress testing, in the political formulations of climate Minsky moment and cyber attack testing. In the case of Britain's referendum on EU membership, this chapter attends to the changing and expanding nature of financial diplomacy. In the case of climate change, this could quite plausibly be a result of what Leyshon and Thrift (2007) have memorably called the 'capitalization of almost everything'. In the case of Brexit, the statement that leaving the European Union posed 'the most significant near-term domestic risks to financial stability' had two remarkable consequences. It embroiled the central bank governor in a very public spat with Members of Parliament and it somehow propelled Governor Carney into a fleeting position of quasi-leadership in the days that the United Kingdom effectively did not have a prime minster.

Notes

1 'Microprudential' refers to the atomistic managing of capital internally and by individual institutions.
2 This term refers to the losses creditors need to accept to resolve the failure of a debtor.
3 This reflects Quetelet's work on the Gaussian distribution – the observation of a clustering distribution around the mean (Amoore, 2013: 48). See Chapter 9 of Bernstein's (1996) magisterial *Against the Gods*.

4 This attention to low probabilities that lie in the fat tail can also be found in the regulatory adoption of a new measure of market risk, namely Expected Shortfall (ES). Unlike Value-at-Risk, this calculation does not include a specific threshold for recognition of a severe impairment (severe losses, such as 95 per cent in VaR). Instead, the financial institution will recognize an estimate for its expected losses on financial assets at the end of a year and this will become an allowance (McKinney and Howard, 2016). The point is that losses are expected rather than incurred. This new measure allows a greater sense of estimation of low probability events because it allows an 'average loss' for 'worst case scenarios' (Tasche, 2013). In 2013, the Basel Committee decided to implement ES as a new measure for market risk for regulatory capital requirements. While it has not been possible to determine if senior figures at the Bank of England did directly influence the move to this new measure, it is important to remember that there is dialogue between key central banks and the wider regulatory bodies. Interestingly in 2013, a PRA employee did give a seminar presentation seeking to respond to some of the criticisms of ES raised by Gneiting in 2011 (Tasche, 2013).
5 The tension between probabilistic and possibilistic methods was still present in 2015, where there was considerable debate between proponents of VaR and the 'Expected Shortfall' methodology (Acerbi and Székely, 2014). While Gneiting (2011) had demonstrated that Expected Shortfall could not be back-tested, in 2013 the Basel Committee decided to implement ES as a new measure for market risk for regulatory capital requirements. Despite this the Basel Committee has decided to adopt ES and this is estimated to occur by the end of 2019.
6 On this point, the *Stanford Encyclopedia of Philosophy* (2013) reports that there are two possible definitions of plausibility; one which is modal or categorical which means there is no assertion of degree, and the other, 'intuitive' sense, which is probabilistic or a rational subjective degree of belief. I argue that for the distinction made by central bankers between plausibility/prediction and the hypothetical to have any significance, one must take the former view of plausibility.
7 Article 50 of the Lisbon Treaty gives any EU member state the right to leave unilaterally.

References

Acerbi, C., and Szekely, B. 2014. 'Back-testing expected shortfall'. *Risk* 76.
Amoore, L. 2011. 'Data derivatives: On the emergence of a security risk calculus for our times'. *Theory, Culture & Society* 28(6), pp. 24–43.
Amoore, L. 2013. *The Politics of Possibility: Risk and security beyond probability*. Durham NC: Duke University Press.
Anderson, B. 2010. 'Preemption, precaution, preparedness: Anticipatory action and future geographies'. *Progress in Human Geography* 34(6), pp. 777–798.
Bailey, A. 2011. 'Why Prudential Regulation matters', speech given at Association of Private Client Investment Managers Conference, 11 October 2011. [pdf] Available at: www.bankofengland.co.uk/publications/Documents/speeches/2013/speech654.pdf (Accessed 10 January 2015).
Bailey, A. 2013. 'The new approach to financial regulation', speech given at the Chartered Banker Dinner 2013, Edinburgh, 1 May 2013. [pdf] Available at: www.bankofengland.co.uk/publications/Documents/speeches/2013/speech654.pdf (Accessed 10 February 2017).
Bank of England. 1997. Financial Stability Review, Autumn 1997. Available at: www.bankofengland.co.uk/archive/Documents/historicpubs/fsr/1997/fsrfull9710.pdf (Accessed 7 November 2012).

Bank of England. 2012a. Financial Stability Report, 29 June 2012. [pdf] Available at: www.bankofengland.co.uk/publications/Documents/fsr/2012/fsrfull1206.pdf (Accessed 14 May 2014).

Bank of England. 2012b. Financial Stability Report, 29 November 2012. [pdf] Available at: www.bankofengland.co.uk/publications/Documents/fsr/2012/fsrfull1211.pdf (Accessed 17 May 2014).

Bank of England. 2013a. Financial Stability Report, 26 June 2013. [pdf] Available at: www.bankofengland.co.uk/publications/Documents/fsr/2013/fsrfull1306.pdf (Accessed 24 March 2014).

Bank of England. 2013b. Record of the Financial Policy Committee, 13 June 2013. [pdf] Available at: www.bankofengland.co.uk/publications/Documents/records/fpc/pdf/2013/record1307.pdf (Accessed 10 October 2017).

Bank of England. 2014a. Financial Stability Press Conference, June 2014. [pdf] Available at www.bankofengland.co.uk/publications/Pages/fsr/2014/fsr35.aspx. Podcast: http://download.world-television.com/boe/boe_20140626.mp3 (Accessed 3 January 2015).

Bank of England. 2014b. News Release: 'Bank of England launches new framework to test for cyber vulnerabilities'. Available at: www.bankofengland.co.uk/publications/Pages/news/2014/088.aspx (Accessed 22 September 2017).

Bank of England. 2015a. Financial Stability Report, 1 July 2015. [pdf]. Available at: www.bankofengland.co.uk/publications/Documents/fsr/2015/fsrfull1507.pdf (Accessed 12 October 2017).

Bank of England. 2015b. Financial Stability Report, 1 December 2015. [pdf] Available at: www.bankofengland.co.uk/publications/Pages/fsr/2015/dec.aspx (Accessed 5 December 2015).

Bank of England. 2016a. Financial Stability Report, 5 July 2016. [pdf] Available at: www.bankofengland.co.uk/publications/Documents/fsr/2016/fsrjul16.pdf (Accessed 7 July 2016).

Bank of England. 2016b. Financial Stability Report, 30 November 2016. [online] Available at: www.bankofengland.co.uk/Pages/reader/index.aspx?pub=fsrnov16&page=1 (Accessed 5 December 2016).

Bank of England. 2016c. 'Stress testing the UK banking system: key elements of the 2016 stress test', March 2016. [pdf] Available at: www.bankofengland.co.uk/financialstability/Documents/stresstesting/2016/keyelements.pdf (Accessed 12 May 2017).

Bank of England. 2017a. 'Stress testing the UK banking system: key elements of the 2017 stress test', March 2017. [pdf] Available at: www.bankofengland.co.uk/financialstability/Documents/stresstesting/2017/keyelements.pdf (Accessed 12 May 2017).

Bank of England. 2017b. 'Topical article: The Bank of England's response to climate change'. *Quarterly Bulletin* 2017 Q2, pp. 98–109. Available at: www.bankofengland.co.uk/Pages/reader/index.aspx?pub=qb17q2article2&page=1 (Accessed 5 July 2017).

Bank of England Research Interview, 23 August 2016. London.

Bernstein, P. 1996. *Against the Gods: The Remarkable Story of Risk.* New York: John Wiley & Sons.

Brandolini, S.M.D., and Scazzieri, R. (eds.). 2011. *Fundamental Uncertainty: Rationality and Plausible Reasoning.* New York: Palgrave Macmillan.

Carney, M. 2015. 'Breaking the Tragedy of the Horizon – climate change and financial stability', speech given at Lloyd's of London, 29 September 2015. [pdf] Available at: www.bankofengland.co.uk/publications/Documents/speeches/2015/speech844.pdf (Accessed 29 May 2017).

Carney, M. 2016a. 'Uncertainty, the economy and policy', speech given in the Court Room, Bank of England, 30 June 2016. [pdf] Available at: www.bankofengland.co.uk/ publications/Documents/speeches/2016/speech915.pdf (Accessed 29 May 2017).

Carney, M. 2016b. 'Resolving the Climate Paradox', speech given at the Arthur Burns Memorial Lecture, Berlin, 22 September 2016. [pdf] Available at: www.bankof england.co.uk/publications/Documents/speeches/2016/speech923.pdf (Accessed 2 June 2017).

Carney, M. 2017. 'The high road to a responsible, open financial system', speech given at Thompson Reuters, London, 7 April 2017. Available at: www.bankofengland.co.uk/ publications/Documents/speeches/2017/speech973.pdf (Accessed 2 June 2017).

Clark, G.L. 1998. 'Stylized facts and close dialogue: methodology in economic geography'. *Annals of the association of American Geographers* 88(1), pp. 73–87.

de Goede, M. 2001. 'Discourses of Scientific Finance and the Failure of Long-Term Capital Management', *New Political Economy* 6(2), pp. 149–170.

de Goede, M. 2010. 'Financial security'. In Burgess J.P., (ed.) *The Routledge Handbook of the New Security Studies*, Abingdon: Routledge, pp. 100–109.

de Goede, M. 2012. *Speculative Security: The politics of pursuing terrorist monies.* Minneapolis: University of Minnesota Press.

de Goede, M. 2017. 'Banks in the Frontline: Assembling Space/Time in Financial Warfare'. In Christophers, B., Leyshon, A., and Mann, G. (eds.) *Money and Finance After the Crisis: Critical Thinking for Uncertain Times*, New York: Wiley-Blackwell, pp. 117–144.

Federal Reserve. 2013. 'Dodd–Frank Act Stress Test 2013: Supervisory Stress Test Methodology and Results'. [online] Available at: www.federalreserve.gov/bankin-foreg/stress-tests/severely-adverse-scenario.htm (Accessed 15 September 2015).

Fisher, P. 2011. 'Tail risks and contract design from a financial stability perspective', speech given at Clare College, Cambridge, 1 September 2011. [pdf] Available at: www.bankofengland.co.uk/archive/Documents/historicpubs/speeches/2011/speech515. pdf (Accessed 21 May 2017).

Forbes, K. 2016. 'Global economic tsunamis: Coincidence, common shocks or contagion?', speech given at Imperial College London, 22 September 2016. [pdf] Available at: www.bankofengland.co.uk/publications/Documents/speeches/2016/speech922.pdf (Accessed 20 May 2017).

Gigerenzer, G., and Swijtink, Z. 1989. *The empire of chance: How probability changed science and everyday life.* Cambridge: Cambridge University Press.

Gneiting, T. 2011. 'Making and evaluating point forecasts'. *Journal of the American Statistical Association* 106(494), pp. 746–762.

Gracie, A. 2014. 'Managing cyber risk – the global banking perspective', speech given at the British Bankers' Association Cyber Conference, London, 10 June 2014. [pdf] Available at: www.bankofengland.co.uk/publications/Documents/speeches/2014/speech 735.pdf (Accessed 20 May 2017).

Gracie, A. 2015. 'Cyber resilience: a financial stability perspective', speech given at the Cyber Defence and Network Security conference, London, 23 January 2015. [pdf] Available at: www.bankofengland.co.uk/publications/Documents/speeches/2015/ speech792.pdf (Accessed 20 May 2017).

Haldane, A. 2009. 'Small Lessons from a Big Crisis', speech given at the Federal Reserve Bank of Chicago 45th Annual Conference, 8 May 2009. [pdf] Available at: www. bankofengland.co.uk/archive/Documents/historicpubs/speeches/2009/speech397.pdf (Accessed 14 April 2015).

Haldane, A. 2012. 'Towards a common financial language', presented at the Securities Industry and Financial Markets Association (SIFMA) 'Building a Global Legal Entity Identifier Framework' Symposium, New York, 14 March 2012. [pdf] Available at: www.bis.org/review/r120315g.pdf (Accessed 10 May 2014).

Haldane, A. 2012. 'Tails of the unexpected', presentation given at 'The Credit Crisis Five Years On: Unpacking the Crisis', conference held at the University of Edinburgh Business School, 8 June 2012. [pdf] Available at: https://pdfs.semanticscholar.org/55bd/31 941afbbd1072b0b022971b3ab479db6c0d.pdf (Accessed 15 May 2014).

Hauser, A. 2013. 'The future of repo: "too much' or 'too little"?', speech given at the International Capital Market Association Conference on the Future of the Repo Market, London, 11 June 2013. Available at: www.bankofengland.co.uk/publications/Documents/speeches/2013/speech665.pdf (Accessed 17 May 2014).

Hauser, A. 2017. 'Watching the watchers: forward-looking assessment and challenge of a central bank's own financial risks', speech given at the Global Association of Risk Professionals' 18th Annual Risk Management Convention, New York, 7 March 2017. Available at: www.bis.org/review/r170310h.pdf (Accessed 5 May 2017).

Hildebrandt, M. 2016. 'The New Imbroglio. Living with Machine Algorithms'. In Janssens, L (ed.) *The Art of Ethics in the Information Society*, Amsterdam: Amsterdam University Press, pp. 55–60.

Independent. 2016. 'Jacob Rees-Mogg just Gave Mark Carney the Most Politest of Beatings', 24 May, 2016. [online] Available at: www.independent.co.uk/voices/jacob-rees-mogg-just-gave-mark-carney-the-politest-of-beatings-a7044701.html (Accessed 17 August 2017).

Langley, P. 2002. *World Financial Orders: an historical international political economy.* Abingdon: Routledge.

Leclerq, R. 1974. *The Logic of the Plausible*, London: Plenum.

Leyshon, A., and Thrift, N. 2007. 'The capitalization of almost everything: The future of finance and capitalism'. *Theory, Culture & Society* 24 (7–8), pp. 97–115.

Lobo-Guerrero, L. 2012. *Insuring war: Sovereignty, security and risk.* Abingdon: Routledge.

MacKenzie, D., 2005. Opening the black boxes of global finance. *Review of international political economy*, 12(4), pp. 555–576.

McKinney, S., and Howard, J. 2016. 'Financial Accounting Standards Board Issues Final Standard on Accounting for Credit Losses'. *Heads Up* 23(18), Deloitte.

Mehrling, P. 2011. *The New Lombard Street: How the Fed became the dealer of last resort.* Princeton NJ: Princeton University Press.

Minsky, H.P. 1982. *Can it happen again? Essay on instability and finance.* New York: M.E. Sharpe.

Morris, J.H. 2016. 'The performativity, performance and lively practices in financial stability press conferences', *Journal of Cultural Economy* 9(3), pp. 245–260.

Nahai-Williamson, P., Ota, T., Vital, M., and Wetherilt, A. 2013. 'Central counterparties and their financial resources – a numerical approach', Bank of England Financial Stability Paper No. 19. [pdf] Available at: www.bankofengland.co.uk/financialstability/Documents/fpc/fspapers/fs_paper19.pdf (Accessed 23 February 2014).

Norman, M. 1935. 'Letter', 21 February 1935, Bank of England Archives.

Ramirez, R., and Selin, C. 2014. 'Plausibility and probability in scenario planning'. *Foresight* 16(1): 54–74.

Sedgwick, E.K. 2003. *Touching feeling: Affect, pedagogy, performativity.* Durham NC: Duke University Press.

Stanford Encyclopedia of Philosophy. 2013. 'Analogy and Analogical Reasoning', n.p. [online] Available at: https://plato.stanford.edu/entries/reasoning-analogy/#Pla (Accessed 10 June 2017).

Tasche, D. 2016. 'Expected Shortfall is not elicitable – so what?', presentation given at 'Finance and Stochastics seminar', Imperial College London, 20 November 2013. [online] Slides available at: https://workspace.imperial.ac.uk/mathfin/Public/Seminars %202013-2014/Tasche_November2013_Slides.pdf (Accessed 2 September 2017).

Taylor, M. 2013. 'Remarks' given at the joint Black Country Reinvestment Society and Black Country Diners Club networking lunch, Wolverhampton Monday 21st October 2013. [pdf] Available at: https://www.bankofengland.co.uk/-/media/boe/files/speech/ 2013/remarks-given-by-martin-taylor (Accessed 9th February 2018).

Tucker, P. 2011. 'Macro and Microprudential supervision', speech given at the British Bankers' Association Annual International Banking Conference, London, 29 June 2011. [pdf] Available at: www.bis.org/review/r110704e.pdf (Accessed 1 June 2014).

Vlieghe, G. 2017. 'Good policy vs accurate forecasts', speech given at Bloomberg Headquarters, London, 5 April 2017. [pdf] Available at: www.bankofengland.co.uk/ publications/Documents/speeches/2017/speech972.pdf (Accessed 25 May 2017).

Wilkinson, A., Kupers, R., and Mangalagiu, D. 2013. 'How plausibility-based scenario practices are grappling with complexity to appreciate and address 21st century challenges'. *Technological Forecasting and Social Change* 80(4), pp. 699–710.

8 Capitalization and resilience

Introduction: the pillars of responsible finance

> The pillars of responsible financial globalisation eroded prior to the global financial crisis. Regulation became light touch and ineffective. Looming risks in the financial system were ignored. Markets were fragile and unfair, plagued by numerous instances of misconduct and limited market discipline on large firms.
>
> (Mark Carney, 7 April 2017)

In the above quotation Mark Carney is reflecting on several key aspects of 'financial globalisation' during the period I have characterised as the money culture of *speculating on risk*. Carney identifies fragile markets and a system replete with looming risks. Here Carney is reiterating Mervyn King's earlier argument that 'surely the most important lesson from the financial crisis is the importance of a resilient and robust banking system' (King, 2010 p. 2). Indeed, in 2010 Andrew Bailey argued that one of the key purposes of the stress testing regime, discussed in Chapters 6 and 7, is that it constitutes:

> an important mechanism for describing the forward-looking view though it should continue to evolve from a binary pass-fail world into one where it is a toolkit to test a range of possible future states of the world and thereby judge the wider resilience of firms.
>
> (Bailey, 2010b, p. 4)

In this chapter I argue that a central tenet of the new money culture of *speculating for risk* is the role of capitalization and resilience. And, the observant reader will point out that resilience is everywhere in contemporary social science discourse. Indeed, Ben Anderson (2015) has recently made the case that something called 'resilience' appears to have 'proliferated across multiple, at best partially connected, domains of life. Resilience, whatever it is, appears now to be everywhere ... (it is) the latest iteration of the promise of security'. Today, resilience is an intrinsic feature of speculative security. In this chapter I interrogate Bank of England thinking on capitalization and resilience, arguing that an understanding of the former provides crucial insights into the latter. I introduce two conceptions of resilience, namely a managerial systems oriented discourse, as well as a governmentality approach. I argue that both interpretations of resilience can be read into the new money culture of *speculating for risk*.

But more than this, I go on to analyse Bank of England statements about the role of capitalization within a resilient system. By doing this, I draw on Brassett and Vaughan-Williams' (2015) notion of a performative politics of resilience. In other words, this is resilience conceived as 'a series of *attempted* closures, which are nevertheless always already in excess of their own logic' and give rise to unexpected and disruptive effects. Here I provide examples where the Bank acknowledged the fragility and complexity of the way that capital absorbs losses and increased confidence. I open the politics of such misfires to argue that initially the Bank's response to this was to call for increased market discipline, but that more recently the Bank believes that resilience is promoted by the money culture of *speculating for risk*. I conclude the chapter by exploring the way the Bank has focused on the capitalization of both institutions and the system through stress testing and the SRB. Here I argue that capitalization must be considered, in Fabian Muniesa's (2017) terms, a 'cultural practice'.

What does the Bank think resilience is?

Walker and Cooper (2011) note that since the 1990s, global financial institutions such as the International Monetary Fund and the Bank for International Settlements have increasingly incorporated strategies of 'resilience' into their logistics of crisis management and financial (de)regulation. In such a way, Walker and Cooper (2011, p. 144) describe resilience as 'a pervasive idiom of global governance'. Here we need to consider what, for the Bank of England, resilience is understood as. For Louise Comfort (2010, p. 9) resilience is tied to the way a 'social system' is able to 'proactively adapt to and recover from disturbances' that 'fall outside the range of normal and expected disturbances'. Such a managerial approach appropriates the *scientific* language of early systems theories to think about resilience as the capacity that 'interconnected and interrelated ecosystems have to change and adapt in relation to shocks' (Brassett and Vaughan-Williams, 2015, p. 33).

And indeed, the Bank of England has begun to understand the financial system as a complex adaptive system or, rather, as a complex, adaptive 'system of systems' each sub-system being 'a complex web' (Haldane, 2009b). In this speech in Amsterdam, Haldane drew a memorable comparison between the Global Financial Crisis and the SARS outbreak in China. The analogy is made because:

> Both events were manifestations of the behaviour under stress of a complex, adaptive network. Complex because these networks were a cat's-cradle of interconnections, financial and non-financial. Adaptive because behaviour in these networks was driven by interactions between optimising, but confused, agents.
>
> (Haldane, 2009b)

At a point in time in which the world was watching on as the Federal Reserve, US Treasury and the Bank of England were effectively experimenting with policy responses, Haldane made the unorthodox argument that it would be fruitful to draw on distinctly un-financial disciplines, such as 'ecology, epidemiology, biology and engineering'. This network approach, reasoned Haldane, would provide 'a rather different account of the structural vulnerabilities that built-up in the financial system over the past decade and suggests ways of improving its robustness' (Haldane, 2009, p. 3).

Returning to the question of what the Bank of England thinks resilience is, Brassett and Vaughan-Williams (2015, p. 34) identify a second approach to resilience, which they label as 'neoliberal governmentality'. By this they mean a resilience in which 'neoliberal subjects', in this case banks, 'are enjoined to take entrepreneurial steps in managing their own risks in lieu of excessive state intervention' (Brassett and Vaughan-Williams, 2015, p. 34). And again, it is entirely plausible to read this into Bank of England statements. In the passage with which the chapter began, resilient and capitalized institutions are associated with 'responsible financial globalization'. This logic of resilience is clearly a security logic rather than a disciplinary logic. The latter attempts to prescribe and shut things down whereas the former system is one in which events are 'allowed to happen' (Foucault, 2007, p. 45). For example, in 2010 Andrew Bailey made it 'clear that we are not trying to design a regime in which no bank should ever fail. That's not what happens in other industries and it would not create the right incentives around risk taking' (Bailey, 2010a, p. 3).

Further, the issue of capital is central to Bank of England statements about resilience. For example, the Governor in 2010, Mervyn King, argued that:

> while banks' balance sheets have exploded, so have the risks associated with those balance sheets. Bagehot would have been used to banks with leverage ratios (total assets, or liabilities, to capital) of around six to one. But capital ratios have declined and leverage has risen. Immediately prior to the crisis, leverage in the banking system of the industrialized world had increased to astronomical levels.
>
> (King, 2010, p. 4)

Deputy Governor Andrew Bailey specified that the nature of the capital has severe consequences for systemic resilience:

> the Basel I framework ... allowed instruments to count as capital – including subordinated debt – which do not absorb losses except when a bank fails and enters an insolvency process. But this approach would only work if we could be sure that banks can enter insolvency without putting the surviving system at risk.
>
> (Bailey, 2010a, p. 6)

King went onto say that resilience and capital are inextricably linked because 'asking banks to maintain a buffer of capital above the minimum requirement allows them to run the buffer down in circumstances like the present. Rebuilding the buffer is a task for the future' (King, 2010, p. 14). Or as Andrew Bailey (2010a, p. 6) put it:

> Part of the solution lies in the quantum and form of capital issued by banks. The Bank of England's most recent Financial Stability Report emphasised that UK banks have raised their capital and liquidity buffers substantially, which has helped them to weather recent tensions.

Capital, then, is important for resilience precisely because it is thought to be 'the loss absorbing and confidence-inspiring stuff' (Jenkins, 2011, p. 2). When we go further to consider capitalization, we can find it evinces a key feature of Foucault's conception of security, namely that it is a type of governance that 'regulates at the effective level of reality'. For Foucault (2007, pp. 46–47):

> The mechanism of security works on the basis of this reality, by trying to use it as a support and make it function, make its components in relation to each other. In other words, the law prohibits and discipline prescribes and the essential function of security ... is to respond to a reality in such a way that this response cancels out the reality to which it responds – nullifies it, or limits, checks or regulates it.

Crucial to the Bank of England's understanding of capital is that it is:

> there to absorb losses from risks we understand and risks we may not understand. Evidence suggests that neither risk-takers nor their regulators fully understand the risks that banks sometimes take. That's why banks need an appropriate level of loss absorbing equity.
>
> (Jenkins, 2012, p. 3)

Jenkins was clear that losses will occur and that risks are never perfectly understood. Because of this, banks should have an appropriate level of loss absorbing equity so that when losses do occur, they can be worked through the system. Losses have to be allowed to occur within the governmental strategy of speculative security because of the need for arbitrage opportunities. As Andrew Bailey (2010b) argued, 'financial services is an industry where arbitraging rules and regulations is habitual, even addictive'. In such a way Bailey is talking about the way firms may find loopholes in regulations in order to make profits.

To return to the Bank of England's culture, Andrew Bailey went on to emphasize:

> Money is made this way. We have no desire unduly to suppress enterprise and innovation, but doing the right thing and preserving financial stability means accepting the spirit of the rules.
>
> (Bailey, 2010b, p. 3)

Taking these two analyses together does suggest both a managerial, systemic approach to resilience and a Foucauldian security perspective at the level of the individual institution. The Bank then, uses resilience in a dual sense. However, it is important to acknowledge Brassett and Vaughan-Williams' point that resilience is not reducible to a singular logic, of either adaptation nor the unwitting complement of some quasi-monolithic neoliberal governmental structure. This must mean that the two apparently different conceptions of resilience are two sides of the same financial stability coin. Seemingly, these two conceptions are the corollaries of microprudential stability of individual institutions and macroprudential stability of the system. As the Bank argues in a 2016 *Quarterly Bulletin*:

> as well as helping to measure the impact of potential future shocks on individual banks and the wider banking system, they can also be used to help set prudential policy aimed at making sure that individual banks (microprudential policy) and the banking system as a whole (macroprudential policy) are adequately resilient.
>
> (Dent *et al.* 2016, p. 131)

Further, and *pace* Brassett and Vaughan-Williams (2015, p. 34), here I seek to attend to 'the performative *politics* of resilience as a series of *attempted'*, yet imperfect and messy, 'closures'. To do this, it is necessary to examine further the role that capital plays within the Bank of England's financial resilience discourse.

The performative politics of financial resilience

So far, we have seen that the Bank of England has operated with two different conceptions of resilience. Further, the Bank believes that capital is important for resilience precisely because it is the 'loss absorbing and confidence inspiring stuff' (Jenkins, 2011, p. 2). And, if we consider an extended extract from the Global Financial Crisis, we can see a Bank of England analysis in which there is a relationship between asset losses and confidence because 'a further rise in defaults in a sub-sector of the US mortgage market prompted a general loss of confidence in asset-backed securities and other structured credit instruments, including those based on unrelated markets' (Bean, 2007, p. 6).

This shows that the Bank was aware of what Langley (2015, p. 96) has called the 'capital-confidence' relationship. Such a relationship has implications for setting the mandatory amount of capital aside as buffers against adverse economic conditions:

> Higher capital buffers would improve confidence by increasing banks' resilience to sudden changes in market sentiment and by strengthening their capacity to handle a potential downturn in the macro economy. Some banks have already begun to bolster their capital positions.
>
> (FSR, 2008a, p. 13)

Furthermore, this thought was reiterated three years later in an FSR discussing suggested changes to regulatory capital regimes during a period of concern for banks in the Eurozone:

> The regulatory capital regime is designed to require banks to fund their assets with sufficient capital to maintain confidence in their solvency. But if investors lose confidence in the design of the capital adequacy regime itself, this can pose risks to the resilience of the financial system (FSR, 2011b, p. 38) ... the methods used by banks to calculate risk weights, particularly those calculated using internal models, are opaque to investors. Market intelligence suggests that this opacity has led to a lack of confidence in risk-weighting methods and could be undermining market confidence in the capital adequacy of banks.
>
> (FSR, 2011, p. 50)

This relationship is present in many of the speeches made more recently; for example, Taylor's discussion of bank capitalization in the UK and Eurozone made the case that 'an undercapitalised bank is in no position to extend credit', while a stronger capital base gives the management of a bank more room for manoeuvre and more confidence (Taylor, 2013, pp. 4–5). New Governor Mark Carney reiterated this rationality of governance when discussing the role that capital adequacy ratios have in a sustained economic recovery. The point that Carney was making is that the rebuilding of confidence is linked here to the imposition of capital adequacy ratios of 7 per cent:

> We are building confidence in banks so they can serve the needs of the real economy by providing credit to those who can put it to work. In particular, we have required banks to repair their balance sheets so that their capital ratios at least reach a threshold of 7% by the turn of the year. Crossing these two 7% thresholds is necessary to ensure that our economy can withstand the inevitable bumps along the road to full recovery.
>
> (Carney, 2013, p. 3)

And, as the Bank of England put it when reflecting on the need to bail-out private banks during the Global Financial Crisis:

> Many banks did not build up large enough capital buffers in benign times to ensure that they could maintain market confidence when conditions eventually reversed. As a result, large-scale injections of capital – often underwritten by the authorities – have been required into banks that had previously been considered adequately or well capitalised.
>
> (FSR, 2008b, p. 41)

Considering capital as the 'loss absorbing and confidence inspiring stuff' allows a window into what Brassett and Vaughan-Williams (2015, p. 39) call the 'performative politics of resilience'. This analysis draws on generic performativity and the work of Butler (1990) to:

> examine the 'reiterative power' of the discourse of resilience 'to produce the phenomena that it regulates and constrains'. The politics of this 'reiterative power' lie in the onto-political insight that any attempted closure entailed in a given performative is always already contingent: as Butler (1993) argues, such closures depend on audience reception, uptake, phrasing, and – under certain circumstances – the potential for subversive readings.... On our reading, performativity entails fragility, complexity and radical intertextuality.

Brassett and Vaughan-Williams argue that resilience is a performative project which aims at closure, the closure here being the absorption of losses by capital buffers. However, it is precisely because of the iterative nature of language that such closure cannot be complete (Butler, 2010). What I want to establish in the chapter is that the Bank of England is well aware that the relationship between capitalization and resilience is fragile and complex. Some historical examples from Bank publications underline the speculative nature of the security provided by capitalization. Following the global economic turbulence of the Asian Financial Crisis, the Bank of England acknowledged that 'recent theoretical analysis suggests that this catalytic effect (between capital flows and confidence) is fragile and will only work in limited circumstances' (FSR, 2003, pp. 160–161 *parentheses added*). This fragility is a result of its reliance:

> on part of the financing gap being filled by spontaneous capital inflows induced by the IMF acting as a partial LOLR, but it cannot provide a cast-iron assurance to creditors that they will be repaid and hence may fail to restore confidence and prevent them running.
>
> (FSR, 2003, p. 162).

But, more than the fragility of the relationship, a performative politics of financial resilience must also attend to the complexity of resilience. In the following section I use excerpts from financial stability documents to argue that the Bank of England recognizes that a loss of confidence precipitates a decrease in capital held in financial institutions, consumer spending or investment in assets. For example, in a period in which regulatory powers were being transferred away from the Bank, the then Governor of the Bank of England stated that:

> banks remain of special importance because their balance sheets are still typically dominated by highly liquid deposits financing less liquid assets, which makes banks especially vulnerable *to a rush for the exit if there is a loss of confidence.*
>
> (George, 1997, p. 4 *emphasis added*)

What George was highlighting in the above passage is that a loss of confidence can lead to a withdrawal of more liquid assets, namely cash money in current accounts. As such, in FSR 1999 we find the analysis that:

As *confidence* in the Brazilian government's ability to service its debt fell, capital outflow increased and reserves fell sharply, despite a 20 percentage point rise in interest rates. The collapse in *confidence* was self-fulfilling, as the increase in borrowing cost and capital outflows made it harder for the Brazilian government to service its debt, which in turn reduced the willingness of investors to lend. It is hard to pin down the exact cause of the loss of *confidence.*

(FSR, 1999, p. 7 *emphasis added*)

This excerpt shows that confidence can affect capital outflows and that it is hard to specify the 'exact' cause of losses of confidence. Confidence, in some sense, seems to have a life of its own. Now I move onto the attempts by the Bank of England to mitigate the fragilities and complexities of confidence.

The politics of misfire

Key Social Studies of Finance author Michel Callon (2010, p. 165) argues that 'politics, the economy' and performativity are intimately connected precisely because of 'the misfires and overflowings inevitably produced by this formatting'. In other words, 'discourses draw boundaries, exclude and reject, and it is in these mechanisms that the political dimension lies'. Interestingly for the argument that this book develops about multiple forms of resilience, it seems apparent that the Bank of England's response to misfire is to invoke the neoliberal governmental approach to resilience. This is because the Bank forwards a strong belief in the benefits of market discipline and transparency. In 2011, and when facing concerns about the position of a variety of Eurozone banks, the Bank of England stated its analysis that for

market discipline to have a chance of enhancing financial system stability, counterparties and investors need to be able to make a reasonably accurate assessment of the financial health of an institution and how that health would be affected as economic and financial conditions change.

(Kohn, 2011, p. 5)

In such a way, transparency is thought to have a disciplining role, in which financial institutions have to post confidence inspiring regulatory capital in reserve. Moving forward to a stage where we were not yet fully into a post Eurozone Crisis era, the Bank of England was focusing on transparency and regulation as a way to augment capital adequacy measures to sustain confidence. For example:

the FPC has recommended that banks publish leverage ratios from the start of 2013, ahead of the Basel III timetables. These would act as a backstop to capital ratios, which are affected by the risk weights applied to bank assets. In making this recommendation the FPC drew on market intelligence which suggested that the opacity of the methods used to calculate risk weights has dented confidence in the published data.

(Salmon, 2012, p. 4)

Again, at this point, nearly five years after the collapse of Lehman Brothers and two years after the height of the Eurozone panic, the Bank of England argued that:

> By improving transparency and, where necessary, prompting balance sheet repair, this has the potential to improve confidence in euro-area banks. Indeed, investors drew some comfort from the fact that the ECB would be keen to begin its supervisory role with a credible process; according to surveys, investors typically thought that the assessment would require around €20 billion–€100 billion of new capital to be raised, mainly by German, Italian and Spanish banks.

(FSR, 2013, p. 13)

The Bank had by this stage already conceded that 'transparency is not a panacea' (Kohn, 2011, p. 13), and recognized that there was an inconsistency between this transparency and the Bank's own communication strategy, which can be thought of as ambiguous and as underplaying risks and threats to individual institutions and the system as a whole. As Donald Kohn said:

> To be sure, we need to protect sensitive information about individual institutions, and transparency cannot be allowed to impinge on the give and take of the deliberative process. But the FPC's reporting of its evaluation of systemic risks can play a constructive role in preserving financial stability by shaping private sector perceptions of economic and financial fundamentals.

(Kohn, 2011, p. 12)

Further, the potential benefits of transparency were said to be contingent precisely because 'although better market discipline may not be sufficient for financial stability, it is essential, and better transparency is a necessary condition for better market discipline' (Kohn, 2011, p. 4).

In such a way, transparency is thought to have a disciplining role, in which financial institutions have to post confidence inspiring regulatory capital in reserve. This, as Jacqueline Best (2007, p. 95) reminds us in the context of 'global governmentality' initiatives following the Asian Financial Crisis, 'combines a certain economic faith in markets' efficient use of information with a liberal political belief in the positive power of publicity'. Elsewhere, and as mentioned in Chapter 6, Best (2005, 2008) argues that a neoliberal governmental approach to the systems of writing that constitute finance will always be undermined and frustrated by the ambiguities of linguistic understanding and the historicity of knowledge. It is, then, not clear that the Bank of England has a response to the performative politics of financial resilience.

Measures to build capital

More recent debates about the resilience of the financial system are closely related to the stress testing procedure, which, as I have detailed in the previous two chapters, have contributed to both the Bank of England understanding the mobilization of risk better and the broadening of the risk imagination to include exploratory scenarios. When the Bank of England produced a news release to announce the first of its public stress tests in 2014, the Bank framed the test as being:

> built on the EU-wide stress test, announced in January 2014 by the European Banking Authority (EBA), which will assess the resilience of EU banks under a common adverse scenario and which provides for national variants. The UK stress test will be run alongside the EBA's EU-wide exercise. The Bank of England will add a number of additional UK layers to the EBA stress test (UK variant) which explore particular vulnerabilities facing the UK banking system.
>
> (Bank of England, 2014)

Even at this initial stage of the Bank's deployment of stress tests, the Bank framed the stress test in terms of assessing 'resilience' of institutions and exposing 'vulnerabilities' of the system. This framing was again present when the results of the 2015 stress tests were announced, with the Bank revealing that:

> The resilience of the UK banking sector to deterioration in global financial market conditions and the macroeconomic environment, including in emerging market economies, has been assessed in the 2015 annual stress test. The stress-test results and banks' capital plans, taken together, indicate that the banking system would have the capacity to maintain its core functions, notably lending capacity. Beyond the core banking sector, the resilience of important intermediaries of market-based finance continues to improve but underlying market liquidity in some core financial markets could be fragile, as underlined by recent episodes.
>
> (FSR, 2015, p. 39)

The role of stress testing in raising capital was built into the technique due to its role in the governance of the Global Financial Crisis. As a member of Bank staff who worked on stress testing for the FSA during its crisis mobilization said:

> The stress testing obviously began in earnest from a Micro Prudential perspective back in 2009, as I said primarily with a view to having a good understanding of the capital needs of the firms at that time and the extent to which they would need a capital injection, either through public or private means and [in] 2009 I would say the FSA worked very hard and stress tested all the major institutions at least once and the majority of the building societies as well at that time … once the banks had been recapitalized, the

purpose of the stress test became to look at the extent of any buffer that they might need above regulatory minima, in order to meet those regulatory minima in a period of stress, for a micro-prudential purpose. And I don't think that purpose has changed over time for a micro-prudential purpose.

(Bank of England Research Interview, 17 October 2016)

It is also clear that capitalization is still a key consideration of stress testing in its split scenario ACS/BES form. As the same capital manager said in an interview:

So the annual cyclical scenario is meant to be counter cyclical in terms of the way it operates from a capital perspective. So we don't want banks to be over capitalised and we do want buffers to be usable and the way in which it works it to say, as the risks in the environment increase, severity of the test increases, but as those risks either crystallise or dissipate, they are not tested for any more. And the severity is not as strong, it's a much weaker scenario, relative to baseline, I would say.

(Bank of England Research Interview, 17 October 2016)

A research interview with forecasters involved with stress testing clarifies that the Bank sees one of the things it can do to increase capitalization is:

to try and make the (stress testing) scenario more systematic and predictable. And one of the aims of that is to help firms with their planning. We know that it takes time for firms to build capital. So to the extent that we can make one of the scenarios more systematic and predictable, it can help the firms with that.

(Bank of England Research Interview, 23 August 2016)

What has changed since the use of stress testing as a crisis management tool is, according to capital management staff at the Bank, that:

the interaction between macro-prudential policy and micro-prudential policy because back in 2010, the CRD 4 buffers were still being dreamt up and had not come in yet so we were front running aspects of that buffer regime with our stress testing internally. And so because we were operating a regime that delivered capital buffers, there was a need to work much more closely with macro-prudential colleagues as the policy framework emerged and it was clear that we were moving towards a joint institution on prudential regulation with the Bank, so that encapsulates what I think has changed ... this coming year will be a test of that and the other benefit of the ACS is it provides a framework for integrating capital setting, for both macro and micro-prudential purposes. So we are operating off the same set of results, the same data sets, the same views of risks, when thinking about macro-prudential tools and micro-prudential tools.

(Bank of England Research Interview, 17 October 2016)

In relation to the Annual Cyclical Scenario, another Bank staff member reiterated the thought that there remains a clear link between the ACS and the drive to improve capitalization regardless of the immediate pressure this could put on financial institutions:

> if that scenario (ACS) suggested that a number of banks wouldn't have sufficient capital in it, then there might be areas of the Bank that would immediately try and start work on nudging those banks into raising more capital. But it wouldn't put you off doing it because it's sort of your job.
>
> (Bank of England Research Interview, 23 August 2016)

However, this forecaster went onto qualify that statement by saying that:

> The one exception to that that I would raise is, when we designed the annual cyclical scenario for the first time, we were designing it at the same time as other areas of the Bank had just done a lot of work on what the optimal capital level for the system was. And they were looking at the history of different financial crises and banks' losses in those crises and how much capital reduced the probability of them falling over. And there's clearly – they are not the same but there is an interaction between that optimal capital level for the system and the severity of stress tests. And so one of the metrics in designing the ACS was, in a time where all risks were normal and in a time when banks' balance sheets were normal, how much – how severe would that stress test be and would that level of capital coming out look consistent with this average level of optimal capital that's coming out of this other work? Because if they are not, you know, there are different – they are sort of different ways of looking at the same thing, so they should be consistent. So that was one metric.
>
> (Bank of England Research Interview, 23 August 2016)

The point here then is that the first iteration of the ACS worked with a level of capital that historically had significance for distressed institutions. This ACS then, was less of a possibilistic *as if* scenario and much closer to a probabilistic *like when* scenario of historical back testing. There are different types of modality at play in the two scenarios. Moving further forward and towards public documents, the tone of the second financial stability report in 2016 was somewhat triumphant when it proclaimed that:

> The 2016 stress test, which is the first conducted under the Bank's new approach to stress testing, examined the resilience of the system to a more severe stress than in 2014 and 2015. It also judged banks against the Bank's new hurdle-rate framework, which held systemic firms to a higher standard reflecting the phasing-in of capital buffers for global systemically important banks.
>
> (FSR, 2016b, p. 31)

The more severe scenario involved a synchronized UK and global recession with associated shocks to financial market prices, and an independent stress of misconduct costs. The Bank argued that this testing regime contributed to the 'resilience of the UK banking sector', because of its role in securing 'substantial capital and liquidity positions'. For the Bank then, an improved and more rigorous series of stress testing techniques and practices meant that the UK banking sector is 'in aggregate, capitalized to support the real economy in a severe global and domestic stress'. This is not to say that the financial stability report was completely panglossian because at the same time it reports that the PRA Board judged that some capital inadequacies were revealed for three banks. The FSR also reported that these banks now had plans in place to build further resilience (FSR, 2016b, p. 31).

The Bank retained a considerably more measured tone in this financial stability report, where it drew attention to the way that 'some major UK banks continue to face the challenge of weak profitability'. The Bank was concerned that 'a prolonged period of low returns could harm banks' ability to absorb the impact of future shocks through retained earnings and threaten the resilience of the provision of financial services to the real economy'. Moving to tackle this risk head on, the Bank confirmed that this is 'a risk that will be assessed in the 2017 exploratory scenario' (FSR, 2016b, p. 25).

A second significant development which is still similarly geared towards fostering resilience through capitalization has been the implementation of the Vickers Report, as set out by the ICB in 2011 and the responses to procyclicality set out in Basel III. The Bank is clear 'that financial firms need to be able to absorb losses. The failure or near-failure ("distress") of an institution, or institutions, can have consequences well beyond the institution itself'. The Bank (2016a) is explicit in spelling out the role of capitalization here as it makes the case that 'the Global Financial Crisis demonstrated how insufficiently capitalized institutions resulted in severe restrictions to credit supply, which in turn deepened the recession and hampered recovery'. The vision that both the Bank and the Basel Committee have for capitalization is visualized in Figure 8.1.

As Langley (2015, pp. 134–135) reports, regulators are embarking on a concerted effort to combat having systemically important but chronically undercapitalized institutions in a financial system, so-called 'too big to fail' banks. 'Ring fencing' is the practice of a company creating a legal entity separate from itself in order to protect certain assets. The Bank argued that:

> the main channel by which these firms falling into distress could cause damage to the financial system and the real economy is through contraction of their household and corporate lending. Because ring-fencing limits their activities, household and corporate lending is likely to comprise the bulk of their total assets.
>
> (Bank of England, 2016a, p. 5)

As set out in Chapter 1 of this book, legislation required the FPC 'to establish a framework for a Systemic Risk Buffer (SRB) that applies to ring-fenced banks

Box 1

Summary of FPC proposals

- Systemic importance is measured and scored using the total assets of ring-fenced bank sub-groups and building societies in scope of the SRB, with higher SRB rates applicable as total assets increase through defined buckets (see Table A).

- Those with total assets of less than £175 billion are subject to a 0% SRB. The FPC expects the largest SRB institutions, on current plans, to have a 2.5% SRB initially. Thresholds for the amounts of total assets corresponding to different SRB rates could be adjusted in the future (for example in line with nominal GDP or inflation) as part of the FPC's mandated two-yearly reviews of the framework.

- The FPC leverage ratio framework is applied to UK G-SIBs and other major banks and building societies at the level of the ring-fenced bank sub-group (where applicable) as well as at a consolidated level.

Table A SRB rates corresponding to firms' total assets

Risk-weighted SRB rate	Total assets (£ billions)	
	Lower threshold	Upper threshold
0%	–	<175
1%	175	<320
1.5%	320	<465
2%	465	<610
2.5%	610	<755
3%	≥755	

Figure 8.1 Bank of England summary of risk weighting for systemic risk buffer.

Source, January 2016 The Financial Policy Committee's framework for the systemic risk buffer A Consultation Paper, Chart A, p. 8.

and large building societies that hold more than £25 billion of household and small/medium enterprise deposits' (Bank of England, 2016a, p. 5). SRBs are designed to address long-term, non-cyclical risk that are not covered under the legal capital requirements. Implementation of the systemic buffer system is an emerging and ongoing development. The Bank is developing metrics for assessing systemic importance and to calibrate the SRB for firms that are deemed too systemically important. This can be considered another example of the money culture of quantifying and understanding risk better. Below, in Figure 8.2, is an example of *speculating for risk* through the identification and measurement of sub-groups of ring-fenced banks.

Further, key firms 'would also be subject to an additional leverage ratio buffer rate, calculated at 35% of the SRB rate'. At the time of writing (in June 2017), Bank Governor Mark Carney (2017, p. 4) has publicly argued that the financial system and its banks are 'now much more resilient, with capital requirements for the largest global banks that are ten times higher than before the crisis and a new leverage ratio that guards against risks that may seem low but prove not'. Here it is clear that the Bank is connecting capital to resilience. This speaks to the discussion in both this and the previous chapter. It is, of course, important to note that the Bank's position on this is not without its critics. Journalist Martin Wolf (2017) argues in *The Financial Times* that:

> Senior officials argue that capital requirements have increased 10-fold. Yet this is true only if one relies on the alchemy of risk-weighting. In the UK, actual leverage has merely halved, to around 25 to one. In brief, it has gone from the insane to the merely ridiculous.

This can be thought of as pushback against the cognitive authority of regulators (Coombs and Morris, *under review*). However, it could be argued that a security

Chart A 2019 Tier 1 capital requirements[a]

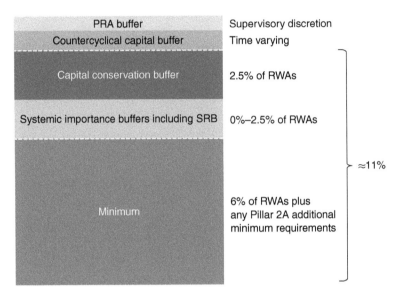

(a) This chart outlines minimum capital requirements, structural and time-varying
     system-wide capital buffers, and additional firm-specific requirements.

Figure 8.2 Bank of England illustration of 2019 tier 1 capital requirements.

Source: Bank of England, January 2016 The Financial Policy Committee's framework for the
systemic risk buffer A Consultation Paper, Box 1, p. 6.

mode of governance that does not seek to entirely eliminate the risky and does
allow banks to fail would require a level of paradigm shift that is politically
unfeasible (Foucault, 2007). This would require a logic of enclosure rather than
circulation and a shift from security to disciplinary governance (Langley, 2015).

Finally, and directly connected to the discussion of chapter, Carney tries to
make the case that 'the financial system is simpler', due in no small part to 'the
more durable market infrastructure … simplifying the previously complex – and
dangerous – web of exposures in derivative markets' (Carney, 2017, p.3).

By *speculating for risk*, the Bank believes that the resilience of the financial
system is significantly stronger than during the money culture of *speculating on
risk*. To take a step back from this, and to draw on Muniesa *et al's* (2017, p. 17)
'cultural' reading of capitalization, then our object of enquiry can be seen as an
event or process. The new cultural practices, of understanding the mobilization
of risk, and considering a wider range of risks, are processes which drive the
renewed capitalization in banks. Stress testing and the SRBs are 'the scenarios in
which value is created', while the practices of *speculating for risk* constitute the
'gaze that stimulates this value-creation' (Gilbert, 2017, p. 2).

Conclusions

This is the final substantive and empirical chapter of the book and brings Part III of the book to a close. This chapter has taken as its focus the Bank of England's ideas around the resilience of the financial system. The analysis offered here is that the Bank has had a somewhat confused conceptualization of resilience. At some points, and particularly through Andrew Haldane, Bank speeches and publications have forwarded a managerial and natural science understanding of resilience as that of a complex adaptive system. At other points, however, the Bank has evinced a narrative around resilience that invokes concepts of responsibility, prudence, the aleatory and of capital absorbing shock once that shock has occurred. In such a way then, the Bank provides a neoliberal governmental conception of resilience. This suggests that the Bank is torn between a focus on resilient systems and an attention to the resilience of individual financial institutions.

The chapter went onto borrow a performative conception of resilience from James Brassett and Nick Vaughan-Williams (2015) to argue that the way that the Bank of England connects capitalization, confidence and resilience is an attempt to close down instability through loss absorption and capital inspiring qualities of good quality capital. The analysis of Bank statements on this suggests that the Bank is aware of the fragility and complexity surrounding successful performance. In other words, Bank staff are well aware of misfire and the performative politics of financial resilience. The chapter investigates the Bank's responses to these misfires and identifies transparency as a key trope. This, it is suggested, is a recapitulation of a neoliberal and governmental approach to resilience. Finally, this chapter draws to a conclusion by documenting the role of stress testing – and therein both the better understanding of risk mobilization and the widening of the risk imagination – in promoting an improved yet tentative level of resilience as a by-product of the money culture of *speculating for risk*. Contributing to this money culture is the ongoing project of developing a systemic risk buffer of capital. In doing so, this book presents the case that capitalization and resilience are cultural processes (Muneisa *et al.*, 2017).

References

Anderson, B. 2015. 'What kind of thing is resilience?'. *Politics* 35(1), pp. 60–66.

Bailey, A. 2010a. 'The Financial Crisis Reform Agenda', speech given at the Annual International Banking Conference Merchant Taylor's Hall London, 13 July 2010. [pdf] www.bankofengland.co.uk/archive/Documents/historicpubs/speeches/2010/speech441. pdf (Accessed 5 January 2015).

Bailey, A. 2010b. 'Remarks on Financial Reform', remarks made at the Lord Mayor's City Banquet London, 21 September 2010. [pdf] Available at: www.bankofengland.co. uk/archive/Documents/historicpubs/speeches/2010/speech447.pdf (Accessed 5 January 2015).

Bank of England.1999. Financial Stability Review, June 1999. [pdf] Available at: www. bankofengland.co.uk/archive/Documents/historicpubs/fsr/1999/fsrfull9906.pdf (Accessed 20 September 2013).

Bank of England. 2003. Financial Stability Review, December 2003. [pdf] Available at: www.bankofengland.co.uk/archive/Documents/historicpubs/fsr/2003/fsrfull0312.pdf (Accessed 20 September 2013).

Bank of England. 2008a. Financial Stability Report, 1 May 2008. [pdf] Available at: www.bankofengland.co.uk/publications/Documents/fsr/2008/fsrfull0804.pdf (Accessed 14 January 2016).

Bank of England. 2008b. Financial Stability Report, 28 October 2008. [pdf] Available at: www.bankofengland.co.uk/publications/Documents/fsr/2008/fsrfull0810.pdf (Accessed 14 January 2016).

Bank of England. 2011. Financial Stability Report, 1 December 2011. [pdf] Available at: www.bankofengland.co.uk/publications/Documents/fsr/2011/fsrfull1112.pdf (Accessed 7 December 2013).

Bank of England. 2013. Financial Stability Report, 28 November 2013. [pdf] Available at: www.bankofengland.co.uk/publications/Documents/fsr/2013/fsrfull1311.pdf (Accessed 26 March 2014).

Bank of England. 2014. 'News Release – Bank of England publishes details of UK stress test for major UK banks and building societies'. [online] Available at: www. bankofengland.co.uk/publications/Pages/news/2014/071.aspx (Assessed 29 October 2014).

Bank of England. 2015. Financial Stability Report, 1 December 2015. [pdf] Available at: www.bankofengland.co.uk/publications/Pages/fsr/2015/dec.aspx (Accessed 5 December 2015).

Bank of England. 2016a. *The Financial Policy Committee's framework for the systemic risk buffer – A Consultation Paper.* [pdf] Available at: www.bankofengland.co.uk/ financialstability/Documents/fpc/srbf_cp.pdf (Accessed 20 September 2016).

Bank of England. 2016b. Financial Stability Report, 30 November 2016. [online] Available at: www.bankofengland.co.uk/Pages/reader/index.aspx?pub=fsrnov16&page=1 (Accessed 5 December 2016).

Bank of England. Research Interview, 23 August 2016.

Bank of England. Research Interview, 17 October 2016.

Bean, C. 2007. 'Risk, Uncertainty and Monetary Policy', speech given to Dow Jones, at City Club, Old Broad Street, 31 October 2007. [pdf] Available at: www.bank ofengland.co.uk/archive/Documents/historicpubs/speeches/2007/speech327.pdf (Accessed 9 February 2015).

Best, J. 2005. *The Limits of Transparency: ambiguity and the history of international finance.* Ithaca: Cornell University Press.

Best, J. 2007. 'Why the economy is often the exception to politics as usual'. *Theory, Culture & Society* 24(4), pp. 87–109.

Best, J. 2008. 'Ambiguity, uncertainty, and risk: rethinking indeterminacy'. *International Political Sociology* 2(4), pp. 355–374.

Brassett, J., and Vaughan-Williams, N. 2015. 'Security and the performative politics of resilience: Critical infrastructure protection and humanitarian emergency preparedness'. *Security Dialogue* 46(1), pp. 32–50.

Butler, J. 1990. *Gender trouble and the subversion of identity.* Abingdon: Routledge.

Butler, J. 1993. *Bodies That Matter: On the Discursive Limits of Sex.* Abingdon: Routledge.

Callon, M. 2010. 'Performativity, misfires and politics'. *Journal of Cultural Economy* 3(2), pp. 163–169.

Carney, M. 2013. 'Crossing the threshold to recovery', speech given at a business lunch hosted by the CBI East Midlands, Derbyshire and Nottinghamshire Chamber of Commerce and the Institute of Directors at the East Midlands Conference Centre, 28 August 2013. [pdf] Available at: www.bankofengland.co.uk/publications/Documents/speeches/2013/speech675.pdf (Accessed 2 April 2015).

Carney, M. 2017. 'The high road to a responsible, open financial system', speech given at Thomson Reuters, London on 7 April 2017. [pdf] Available at: www.bankofengland.co.uk/publications/Documents/speeches/2017/speech973.pdf

Comfort, L.K., Boin, A., and Demchak, C. (eds.) 2010. *Designing resilience: Preparing for extreme events*. Pittsburgh PA: University of Pittsburgh Press.

Coombs, N., and Morris, J.H. *Under review*.

Dent, K, Westwood, B., and Segoviano, M. 2016. 'Topical articles: Stress testing of banks: an introduction'. Bank of England *Quarterly Bulletin* Q3, pp. 130–143. [pdf] Available at: www.bankofengland.co.uk/publications/Documents/quarterlybulletin/2016/q3/a1.pdf (Accessed 19 October 2017).

Foucault, M. 2007. *Security, Territory, Population*. Basingstoke: Palgrave Macmillan.

George, E. 1997. 'Speech', given at Lord Mayor's Banquet in the Guildhall London, 12 June 1997.

Gilbert, P. 2017. 'The anthropology of financial intent'. *Finance and Society*, Early View, pp. 1–8.

Haldane, A. 2009. 'Rethinking the Financial Network', presentation given at the Financial Student Association, Amsterdam, 28 April 2009. [pdf] Available at: www.bankofengland.co.uk/archive/Documents/historicpubs/speeches/2009/speech386.pdf (Accessed 10 May 2014).

Jenkins, R. 2011. 'Why banks must think carefully before they shrink their assets', article published in *The Times*, 14 December 2011. [pdf] Available at: www.bankofengland.co.uk/archive/Documents/historicpubs/speeches/2011/speech538.pdf (Accessed 10 June 2017).

Jenkins, R. 2012. 'Basel II proved to be inadequate so are the new rules really so severe?', article published in *The Independent*, 26 April 2012. [online] Available at: www.independent.co.uk/news/business/comment/robert-jenkins-basel-ii-proved-to-be-inadequate-so-are-the-new-rules-really-too-severe-7682512.html (Accessed 10 June 2017).

King, M. 2010. 'Banking: From Bagehot to Basel, and Back Again', lecture given as The Second Bagehot Lecture at the Buttonwood Gathering, New York City on 25 October 2010. [pdf]. Available at: www.bankofengland.co.uk/archive/Documents/historicpubs/speeches/2010/speech455.pdf. (Accessed 26 February 2015).

Kohn, D. 2011. 'Enhancing financial stability: the role of transparency', speech given at London School of Economics, 6 September 2011. [pdf] Available at: www.bankofengland.co.uk/archive/Documents/historicpubs/speeches/2011/speech516.pdf. (Accessed 10 March 2014).

Langley, P. 2015. *Liquidity Lost: The Governance of the Global Financial Crisis*. Oxford: Oxford University Press.

Muniesa, F., Doganova, L., Ortiz, H., Pina-Stranger, A., Paterson, F., Bourgoin, A., and Ehrenstein, V. 2017. *Capitalization: A Cultural Guide*. Paris: Presses des Mines.

Salmon, C. 2012. 'Three principles for successful financial sector reform'.

Speech given at 'City Week 2012: The International Financial Services Forum', The Queen Elizabeth Conference Centre, London, 7 February 2012. [pdf] Available at:

www.bankofengland.co.uk/archive/Documents/historicpubs/speeches/2012/speech545.
pdf (Accessed 2 February 2015).

Walker, J., and Cooper, M. 2011. 'Genealogies of resilience: From systems ecology to
the political economy of crisis adaptation'. *Security Dialogue* 42(2): 143–160.

Wolf, M. 2017. 'Why banking remains far too undercapitalised for comfort'. *The Financial Times*, 21 September 2017. [online] Available at: www.ft.com/content/9dd43a1a-
9d49-11e7-8cd4-932067fbf946 (Accessed 22 September 2017).

Conclusion
Financial stability in the twenty-first century

This book began with Mervyn King's statement from 2004 that while, on the one hand, financial professionals 'will be interesting', on the other hand central banks 'will not be … and will be faceless'. It was tentatively suggested that such a self-ascription can go some way to explaining the lacuna of empirical research into the financial stability roles of central banks when compared to the plethora of interdisciplinary work on central bank monetary operations. This book has sought to provide a renewed empirical focus on financial stability by analysing some 1,000 financial stability publications from the Bank of England as well as drawing on interview research and participant observation at Bank of England public events. It is argued that this contributes a 'method assemblage' of materials that can be parsed together to form a detailed account of the very public functions of a central bank (Law, 2004).

In addition to this, four years after King's statement, central banks became headline grabbing and gained a suite of new responsibilities and policy levers over the financial system. Academically speaking, the reception of these developments is mixed. On the one hand, some authors were quick to identify the Global Financial Crisis as a catalyst for a 'paradigm shift' in financial governance (Mackintosh, 2015). On the other hand, political economists have argued that these new responsibilities and tools are extremely superficial (Helleiner, 2014).

Instead, this book has argued that while there has not been paradigmatic change, there have been important cultural changes in financial regulation. Further, even before the collapse of Lehman Brothers, webs of meaning and related practices at the Bank of England were beginning to change. But, even so, this change was not paradigmatic. The financial system is better capitalized, and this has a cultural dimension as well as a political economy of accumulation. Here the book introduces the analytical tool of money cultures to shine a light on the change observed at the Bank of England. It is argued that both before, during and after, the Bank of England's culture towards and around financial stability can be called, using Marieke de Geode's (2012) phrase, 'speculative security'. This argument hinges on the polysemy of the term 'speculation'. Before the crisis, the dominant meanings about the new financial risk management were to do with the profit seeking trading activities of financial institutions and the way that the derivative instruments traded would contemporaneously contribute positively to financial stability. As such the Bank was taking a gamble on the propensity and efficacy of risk management techniques in the financial sector. In discussion, the Bank was often wont to list upside and downside risks that could be attributed to a particular development in the financial markets with a broad brush. For example, publicly available sources appear to quantify, compare or contrast different risks in less precise ways when compared with work after the crisis. I have characterized this money or regulatory culture as *speculating on risk.*

Following the concentration of risks at important hubs such as insurance giant AIG, it became clear that the new financial risk management had not dispersed risk but instead had pooled it, thus creating specific breaking points in the system. Similarly, the assumption within the risk measuring calculation, Value-at-Risk, that financial events fell into the 95 per cent confidence interval – normal conditions – proved to be erroneous. The presence of extreme events meant that a device that promised security actually delivered insecurity. This is analysed using the conception of finance as a lively, layered and performed domain. Such dynamic instances of counter-performativity, or misfire, served to provoke improvisation and a cultural change in financial regulation.

The functional mobilization of risk in a way that increased systemic instability led to practical changes in the meaning of 'speculative' security. This was still a security governance that allowed events to happen, recirculated the risky alongside the safe and dealt with an infinite series of events, but the terms of speculation changed. Instead, greater efforts were turned towards the visualization, sighting and understanding of financial risk. I characterize this money culture, then, as *speculating for risk.* The book has argued that an increasing number of statements by regulators calling for increased transparency and standardization of derivatives are themselves concerned with seeing, understanding, coding and mapping risk better. Further, it is argued that attempts to quantify, aggregate and connect various risks are aiming to better understand how risk is being mobilized in the global financial system. Similarly, the advent of stress testing has led to a widening of the risk imagination at the Bank. In particular, this has operated through the increased inclusion of possibilities rather than probabilities, the development of the BES and inclusion of contested political issues within the remit of financial stability.

In the final concrete chapter of the book, the argument was that cultural processes of understanding/mapping risk better and widening the risk imagination have, for the Bank, improved resilience in both financial institutions and the financial system by increasing the capitalization within institutions. This, it is reasoned, increases stability because capital is thought to absorb losses and thereby inspire confidence. And while the Bank does not believe that there will not be another crisis at some point in the future, the Bank is relatively pleased with the change in resilience in the ten years after the Global Financial Crisis. This has been a result of money cultures, stress testing and the development of the SRB.

Having reiterated the core argument of the book, and touched upon the two key theoretical planks utilized, in the concluding part of this chapter I want to explore four key themes that emerge across both the theoretical and empirical chapters of the book. This is not intended to merely repeat points that we already made but instead to gather together strands that cut across the book. In doing this, I explore why these insights around the performative politics of central banking and understanding the mobilization of risk are relevant to financial stability discussions today.

Multiple derivative logics

This book has situated itself within an interdisciplinary literature preoccupied with the interstices of finance and security. In particular, the security logic of the derivative is an avenue through which finance and security have a close level of conceptual congruence (de Goede, 2010). This is primarily because both domains can fix onto the indifference between underlying asset and reward characteristic through which the derivative operates (Martin, 2007; Wigan, 2009). Within this theoretical context, London and the Bank of England were identified as being of interest to finance/security precisely because of London's position within global derivatives practices. The analysis that I have developed, of Bank of England culture, has invoked multiple and different definitions of derivative logics. In Chapter 4, I have argued that in 1998 the Bank of England identified that the credit derivative has the potential to disperse risk throughout a financial system, making the default risk indifferent to the underlying credit relationship. This logic is also present in Louise Amoore's (2013) work on the way that the possibilities of scenarios are eviscerated from the underlying probabilities of those scenarios actually occurring. And, in Chapter 7 and my discussion of widening the risk imagination, I argue that this logic of the 'data derivative' (Amoore, 2011) is evident in the development of the BES in stress testing. This results from the scenario presented in this test process being indifferent to the underlying financial stability cycle captured in the ACS and the Bank's assessment of underlying risks in the UK economic picture.

But, this is not the only interpretation of the derivative logic that I make use of in this book. In Chapter 6, I argued that the ACS, which reflects the Bank of England's ongoing and developing assessment of risks in an economy, at any one time provides a snapshot, or fragile anchoring of interconnected risks. This, I argued, invokes Bryan and Rafferty's (2006) conception of the financial derivative as potentially being a 'new gold' or anchoring for exchange. For Bryan and Rafferty, derivatives are a fragile and dynamic system of anchoring prices of incommensurable good or even corporations (Martin *et al.*, 2007).

Third and finally, in Chapter 2 the book drew on Randy Martin's (2015) work on the social logic of the derivative as being one of kinesthetics or movement. This was applied to the mobilization of risk and elucidated in Chapter 6 where the post-misfire bank was concerned with mapping, coding and better understanding the mobilization of risk, drawing on Martin's reading of multiple types of, and relations to, movement in the form of arbitrage, hedging and speculation. The argument gathered together across these chapters, then, is that there are multiple derivative logics, precisely because there are different forms of derivative contracts and different strategies of trading derivatives. To summarize the point, financial stability and financial security in the twenty-first century operate through multiple derivative logics. The most prescient issue for the Bank here is how to continually balance the performativity of stress testing through split scenarios, and in doing so face the challenge of maintaining a distinction between the first derivative logic of indifference between probability and possibility and the second of fragile anchoring of scenario in underlying analysis of financial risk.

Performative politics and misfire

In Chapter 6 and Chapter 8 the study has outlined attempts by the Bank of England to engender greater transparency in the financial system, particularly in relation to credit derivatives and bank capital ratios. However, my discussion was sceptical about the effectiveness of this. Perhaps both the more interesting and prescient theme cutting across this book has been the performative politics of financial stability. And, although I think there is much merit to Lockwood's claim that 'reliance on VaR ... undergirds banks' authoritative claim to responsibly manage risk, a claim which limited the regulation of banks by the Basel Committee on Banking Supervision, I want to forward a much more dynamic conception of misfire or counter-performativity.

In some cases, such as the attempt to rewire and standardize derivative contracts from Chapter 6, this is about governing through performativity. By creating a common set of derivative forms, which can then be used off the shelf, the Bank is effectively arguing for a discursive formulation which will shape future transactions. More often however, rather than seeing financial governance as harnessing performativity, what we in fact see is the mitigation of performative effects. The crux of the cultural economy of financial stability is that public fear about instability can lead to instability. The central bank has to manage this performativity in its public discourse.

This, as I have drawn out, is a delicate task. This can be seen most clearly in Chapters 7 and 8, with the advent of stress testing, and the development of adverse scenarios against which the health of financial institutions and the resilience of the system itself is assessed. Between 2014 and 2017 much representational or rhetorical labour went into managing the performative force of the scenario. As I have documented in the first financial stability press conference of 2014, Mark Carney drew on the layered performativity and peri-performativity of the Bank Governor, both the reiteration of institutional authority and the drama that clusters around performativity, to establish that the stress scenario is not a prediction or a forecast. Instead, and through the Governor, the Bank of England aligned itself with the Federal Reserve by emphasizing the hypothetical nature of the scenario. Unlike plausibility, which proceeds through building upon evidence, hypothesis operates through proceeding as if there is a particular underlying evidence. Hypothesis, then, is much more firmly rooted in assumption. By 2016, Bank of England staff were satisfied that repetition of the term 'hypothetical' had led to the widespread view that the instability built into stress scenarios was at the level of assumption. However, the ongoing development of stress testing has seen the Bank vacillate between the two interpretations. The split scenarios, where the Bank developed the ACS and the BES, demonstrate the way that the Bank plays with the meaning of possibility. The ACS is underpinned by the Bank of England's assessment of the financial risk cycle currently operating at any given time. Conversely, the BES is designed to operate detached from the Bank's view of underlying risk levels in the financial system. There is then a distinction between evidence and assumption between the two types of scenario. The performative politics of stress testing is fragile and finely balanced, with the Bank needing to skillfully manage this performativity.

The finely balanced nature of financial performativity can be seen in the politics of misfire. This is mostly clearly evident in Chapter 5, which discusses two key flaws in risk management through Value-at-Risk. The outcome of these two flaws were starkly dissimilar, which is reflected in the extent to which the Bank is able to improvise. The collapse of hedge fund Long Term Capital Management allowed some room to improvise by shifting the burden of accuracy to precision. In the case of the build up of risk in the mid-2000s and the advent of extreme conditions, the Bank had to go to much more radical lengths.

At the end of the 1990s, misfire of Value-at-Risk was widely thought by the financial media to have played a contributory role in the volatility that emerged in the global financial markets. In a 2002 financial stability report, the Bank of England took a remarkably political step by publishing a chapter penned by the leading academic proponent of VaR, namely Professor Phillipe Jorion. In this chapter, Jorion argued that the VaR charge was not primarily concerned with being accurate but, instead, had an inbuilt stability in the market risk charge (Jorion, 2002, pp. 116,125). Jorion proceeded to improvise by arguing that the market risk charge meant that Value-at-Risk did not lead to mass position cutting in the global financial markets. While it is impossible to say when a misfire will gain traction or 'force de rupture', I have suggested that VaR was still considered to be useful and that volatility was consistent with the internal logic of *speculating on risk* through derivatives, and so did not have a *discursive violence* that undermined the use of Value-at-Risk. In other words, dropping VaR techniques would have required a wider series of shifts and improvizations. This then, was not a critical problem for Value-at-Risk and *speculating on risk*, although we should note that the Bank did intervene in the debate. Jorion and the Bank were able to improvise to prolong the practice of financial risk management through VaR. Later, and following a series of extreme events and conditions in financial markets during 2006 and 2007, the misfire of the normality assumption with Value-at-Risk became apparent and the charge against *speculating on risk* was led by influential figures at the Bank such as Andrew Haldane. This, it is argued in Chapters 6 and 7, stimulated a cultural shift within speculative security towards a culture of *speculating for risk*. In Chapters 6 and 7 efforts by the Bank of England to quantify, understand and imagine risk better have been prompted in no small part by this second misfire of *speculating on risk*.

The third example of the performative politics of misfire that I will attend to here is one that arises most clearly in Chapter 8 and the discussion of the finely balanced ambiguity of conceptions of resilience. While the chapter argued that the Bank of England did vacillate between systemic and governmentality conceptions of resilience, throughout this period the Bank realized and reiterated that the relationship between capitalization and resilience was fragile and complex. The Bank's improvised response to this was to argue that the remedy for misfire was transparency and increased market discipline. What this case serves to illustrate is the delicate and nimble balancing act between different definitions of contested and ambiguous terms. That at times ambiguity is the Bank's ally, while at others it is not.

And, while most of the existing literature on power in central banking can be characterized as falling into at least one of three camps, namely functional, structural and social constructivist, this book instead situates itself in a disparate literature concerned with performativity. The argument I forward, then, is that when we take the performativity of financial stability seriously, we must attend to the way that central banks knit together narratives and discourses about money and finance. The Bank has at its disposal overlapping and interlocking layers of performativity with which it must foster a 'background of stability'. The intrinsic nature of misfire within iteration needs to be finely balanced and negotiated by central banks. More concretely, this can be seen in Chapter 5 where the Bank helped to improvise and consolidate the position of normal and probabilistic interpretations of financial futures in the early 2000s, before taking a much more drastic position later in that decade. When the Bank is stretched by the situation it faces, much more extensive and drastic cultural change occurs. This can be seen in moves to understand the mobilization of risk better and to widen the risk imagination.

Risk imaginations and the politics of the Central Bank

In Chapter 7, I argued that a key shift in the culture of *speculating for risk* has been the widening of the Bank's risk imagination. While this included the inclusion of subjective probabilities, hypothesis and exploratory scenarios, I have also charted the inclusion of contentious political issues within the financial stability conversation. Such an expansion of the risk imagination has been important from the perspective of financial resilience. The Bank has reformulated primarily economic theory or techniques, such as Minsky's instability hypothesis or the practice of stress testing, in ways that address political security questions such as climate change or cyber security. The most pressing issue facing the Bank today is the pushback from politicians as the purportedly independent central bank takes controversial political events such as Brexit in its cross-hairs. This has predominantly been pursued through the high-level figure of the Governor, Mark Carney, rather than more ancillary staff who try to avoid speaking about political issues at public events. And indeed, Carney has experienced significant push-back on Brexit from members of Treasury Select Committees, such as Jacob Rees-Mogg. The open question is, whether the renewed focus of financial stability means that the Bank's relationship with politics must also change. In raising this pertinent question, an attention to money cultures at the Bank of England retains a firm focus on the interconnection between culture, politics and economics. It is an open question whether the necessary component of the new financial resilience can withstand political pushback as it creeps more squarely into the political realm.

Money cultures, security and capitalization

The money culture of *speculating on risk* worked through the imaginary of finance as being an enterprise through which risk was thought to be distributed through chains in a relatively linear process, up to the point where it is not exactly clear where the risk was. And while this was a security logic of circulating the risky alongside the safe, this was an undercapitalized system which could not actually allow extreme events to happen. This led to a misfire in terms of risk dispersal and security. The shift towards a money culture of *speculating for risk* is important for speculative security in two key ways. The first case is that practices of speculation such as visualizing and understanding contribute to the process of capitalization – certain levels of capital are valued over others and *speculating for risk* helps to determine this level. In such a way, *speculating for risk* is the gaze that stimulates the value creation of assets as capital (Muniesa *et al.*, 2017). Second, to demand a resilient and capitalized system means that the vision for a financial system is an aleatory space of circulation in which events such as losses are allowed to happen, because capital absorbs losses and inspires confidence. The improvizations that followed the violent misfires – in Muniesa *et al's* (2017) terms the 'scenarios in which value is created' – shifted the terms of speculation. This has contributed to a renewal of the imperatives of financial security and a money culture of speculative security as financial stability.

References

Amoore, L. 2011. 'Data derivatives on the emergence of a security risk calculus for our times'. *Theory, Culture & Society* 28(6), pp. 24–43.

Amoore, L. 2013. *The Politics of Possibility: Risk and security beyond probability.* Durham NC: Duke University Press.

Bryan, D., and Rafferty, M. 2006. 'Financial derivatives: The new gold?'. *Competition & Change* 10(3): pp. 265–282.

de Goede, M. 2010. 'Financial security'. In Burgess, J.P., (ed.) *The Routledge Handbook of the New Security Studies.* Abingdon: Routledge, pp. 100–109.

de Goede, M. 2012. *Speculative Security: The politics of pursuing terrorist monies.* Minneapolis: University of Minnesota Press.

Helleiner, E. 2014. *The status quo crisis: Global financial governance after the 2008 meltdown.* Oxford: Oxford University Press.

Jorion, P. 2002. 'Fallacies about the effects of market risk management systems'. Bank of England (2002b) Financial Stability Review, December 2002, pp. 115–128. Available at: https://merage.uci.edu/~jorion/papers/riskfall.pdf (Accessed 1 May 2014).

Law, J. 2004. *After method: Mess in social science research*. Abingdon: Routledge.

Lockwood, E. 2015. 'Predicting the unpredictable: Value-at-risk, performativity, and the politics of financial uncertainty'. *Review of International Political Economy* 22(4), pp. 719–756.

Mackintosh, S. 2015. *The Redesign of the Global Financial Architecture: The Return of State Authority*. Abingdon: Routledge.

Martin, R. 2007. *An Empire of Indifference: American War and the Financial Logic of Risk Management*. Durham, NC: Duke University Press.

Martin, R. 2015. *Knowledge LTD: Toward a Social Logic of the Derivative*. Philadelphia: Temple University Press.

Martin, R., Rafferty, M., and Bryan, D. 2008. 'Financialization, risk and labour'. *Competition & Change* 12(2), pp. 120–132.

Muniesa, F., Doganova, L., Ortiz, H., Pina-Stranger, A., Paterson, F., Bourgoin, A., Ehrenstein, V. 2017. *Capitalization: A Cultural Guide*. Paris: Presses des Mines.

Wigan, D. 2009. 'Financialisation and derivatives: Constructing an artifice of indifference'. *Competition & Change* 13(2), pp. 157–172.

Index

Page numbers in *italics* denote figures.